"Mead's book makes me feel hopeful and inspired about the future, and my own role in helping to shape it. His grounded, practical wisdom reminds us that stories have always been the way forward for humanity, and it is time for us to take more concerted action to counter the dominating master narrative of our most recent history. You will find his words a balm for the soul, evoking a meaningful walk in the woods with a wise elder."

Doug Paxton, Faculty and Co-Director of the Leadership Center,
Saint Mary's College of California

"We have often forgotten to listen to patients and staff with devastating effect on the standard of healthcare and organizational health. Listening to their stories connects the organization and its leaders back to what really matters. If you have ever doubted how stories can be a powerful force for good this thought-provoking and practical book will encourage you to consider your leadership practice from a whole new perspective."

Dr Liz Redfern CBE, formerly Chief Nurse, NHS South of England

"The title of this book says it all, this is a heartfelt and soulful book taking us on a journey where we can discover ourselves and achieve leadership success. It is only by finding and acknowledging our authentic truth that we can inspire others to follow. If you want to find out what it takes to be an inspiring and successful leader, step into this world of storytelling."

Jacob Tas, Executive Director of Operations, Action for Children

"In many spheres of my life, I have learnt that getting the basics right is the platform on which success is built. Geoff's book turns the spotlight on one of the basic activities of leaders and leadership teams – that of storytelling. The book comprehensively covers the theoretical and practical aspects of storytelling. The case studies and associated experiences of other leaders provide rich detail and inspiration. The book is a catalyst for self-improvement which in turn produces better organizational outcomes and a more successful future."

Sir David Varney, formerly Chairman O2, CEO BG, Commissioner HMRC

"Geoff Mead is a master of both the theory and practice of narrative leadership. *Telling the Story* is refreshing in its frankness and insight. It left me feeling challenged, energized and inspired to think about the stories I want to live and tell through my own leadership. Wonderful reading for anyone who wants to enhance their positive impact on the world."

Lindsay Levin, Founder and Managing Partner, Leaders' Quest

"This is surely a 'must-read' for anyone in a leadership role (which is pretty much everybody!). Geoff's ability to explain narrative leadership is unsurpassed and his passion for storytelling comes through loud and clear in his writing. Understanding and using narrative has completely transformed my approach to leading an organization and influencing others with great success. *Telling the Story* will inspire you and equip you to use your inherent storytelling ability to influence those around you in a powerful and memorable way. I could not recommend this book more highly!"

Libby Hackett, Chief Executive, University Alliance

"In my work with scenario planning I've experienced the transformational power that arises when a group of people decides to imagine and tell new stories about the future. In this book, Geoff Mead explains with clarity, humor and precision, how we can all collectively create and tell the stories we need in order to bring a better world into existence."

Marcelo Michelsohn MSc, Associate Consultant and Scenarios Editor, Reos Partners

"I especially appreciate how clearly Geoff Mead sets the power of storytelling within an appreciation of current global challenges and fractures including climate change. The book's blend of ideas, stories, advice and invitations is evocative, encouraging, instructive, supportive and also deliberately provocative. This combined form exemplifies well its messages about the communicative power of storytelling – a thoroughly animating read."

Judi Marshall, Professor of Leadership and Learning,
Lancaster University Management School

"As we change our story we change the world. Effective leaders tell authentic stories that address the needs of their time. The needs of our time are great indeed. Geoff Mead's clear and concise wisdom will transform current and aspiring leaders into 'Chief Storytellers' and 'Meaning Makers' in their organizations and communities."

Richard Olivier, Artistic Director, Olivier Mythodrama Associates

"Geoff Mead has written what will become the classic text on narrative leadership. With heart, humor and deep insight, he draws on his many years of organizational experience to show how, through the skillful use of stories and storytelling, business leaders can provide a more meaningful, purposeful and rewarding environment for us all. A practical guide to the major cultural shift awaiting organizations today."

Sue Hollingsworth MBA, Director, International School of Storytelling

"As a leader I know that the stories I tell matter. *Telling the Story* is a vital resource for leaders, full of great tips and thought-provoking advice. It reminds us that narrative leadership is as much about sharing our own personal stories as it is about telling the big stories of our time. It encourages us to stand tall in our stories, to rediscover our authentic selves, and to reflect on the implications of the stories we choose to tell: for whom and for what do we lead?"

Alan Woods, Group Chief Executive, Skills for Justice

"*Telling the Story* invites the reader to connect again with the potential of storytelling in our adult work lives. Any leader who wishes to be released from PowerPoints and corporate jargon will experience the book as liberating. Trust me it works! Introducing stories into my work life has given me a verbal toolkit to navigate the most challenging situations."

Sonia Crozier, Deputy Chief Executive, London Probation Trust

"Organizational theorists talk about the 'narrative turn' in their attempts to understand the dynamics of change. Geoff Mead helpfully makes a bridge between this literature and practice, weaving in allegory, metaphor, narrative and simile that deepen leaders' practical insights into the art of story in the context of change. This book is easy to read, packed with great examples and is also a helpful guide to complementary resources. Practitioners will find it invaluable, as they craft their own identities and their organization's through story."

Dr Marc Thompson, Fellow in Strategy and Organization,
Said Business School, University of Oxford

Telling the Story

Telling the Story

The Heart and Soul of
Successful Leadership

Geoff Mead

JB JOSSEY-BASS™
A Wiley Brand

This edition first published 2014
© 2014 John Wiley & Sons Ltd

Under the Jossey-Bass imprint, Jossey-Bass, 989 Market Street, San Francisco, CA
94103-1741, USA
www.josseybass.com

Registered office
John Wiley & Sons Ltd, The Atrium, Southern Gate, Chichester, West Sussex, PO19 8SQ,
United Kingdom

For details of our global editorial offices, for customer services and for information about
how to apply for permission to reuse the copyright material in this book please see our
website at www.wiley.com.

Wiley publishes in a variety of print and electronic formats and by print-on-demand.
Some material included with standard print versions of this book may not be included in
e-books or in print-on-demand. If this book refers to media such as a CD or DVD that is
not included in the version you purchased, you may download this material at http://
booksupport.wiley.com. For more information about Wiley products, visit www.wiley.com.

Library of Congress Cataloging-in-Publication Data

Mead, Geoff, 1949-
  Telling the story : the heart and soul of successful leadership / Geoff Mead.
    pages cm
  Includes bibliographical references and index.
  ISBN 978-1-118-61716-8 (hbk)
  1. Leadership. 2. Small business–Management. I. Title.
  HD57.7.M4293 2014
  658.4'092–dc23

                    2014002214

A catalogue record for this book is available from the British Library.

ISBN 978-1-118-61716-8 (pbk) ISBN 978-1-118-61709-0 (ebk)
ISBN 978-1-118-61701-4 (ebk)

Cover design by Rawshock Design

Set in 10/14 pt ITCGaramondStd-Bk by Toppan Best-set Premedia Limited
Printed in Great Britain by TJ International, TJ International Ltd, Padstow, Cornwall, UK

To those in all walks of life (whether or not you call yourselves leaders) who are striving to tell and live the stories needed in our time. Your courage and imagination are vital for our future. This is narrative leadership and Telling the Story *is for you.*

Contents

Acknowledgments

Few books are the product of a single mind. Wise authors recruit friends, colleagues, and clients to test their ideas and to help them shape the text to make it more relevant to its audience and more readable. In this regard at least, I showed some wisdom and I am grateful to a number of people whose comments and suggestions have been enormously helpful.

In the early stages of writing, the following people all suggested practical questions they thought the book should answer, to make it as useful as possible: Libby Hackett, Chief Executive of University Alliance; Jacob Tas, Executive Director of Operations at Action for Children; Sonia Crozier, Service Director and Deputy Chief Executive of the London Probation Trust; Jane Cotton, HR Director at Oxfam; Tony Russell, Director for Senior Executive Development at L'Oréal; Liz Redfern, Deputy Chief Nursing Officer for the NHS; and David Wright, Director of the Top Management Programme at the National School of Government. Many of their thoughtful suggestions have been incorporated and I hope they feel that the final result justifies their interest.

My friend and colleague at Narrative Leadership Associates, David Green, critically read every word of the final manuscript – challenging conclusions, adding examples, and saving me from many potential errors and at least one embarrassing, unintended double entendre. His generous and knowledgeable contribution, though it will not be immediately obvious to the reader, was invaluable.

Much of what I know about the art of storytelling I have learned from Ashley Ramsden, Sue Hollingsworth, and Roi Gal-Or at the International School of Storytelling in Forest Row, Sussex. They are generous and inspiring teachers and Sue, in particular, has consistently encouraged me to write about the power of stories and storytelling in organizations and the practice of narrative leadership.

In recent years, the breadth and depth of experience of my colleagues at Narrative Leadership Associates and of the members of the Centre for Narrative Leadership have deepened and extended my understanding of the whole field. Each time we meet, I learn something new from them and get the chance to hone my own ideas and practice. In truth, though, as a narrative leadership consultant, my most significant learning has occurred in the service (and at the expense) of clients who were open to new conceptions of leadership and invited me to develop corresponding, new ways of working with story and storytelling. They are too numerous to mention individually here, though many of them are listed on the Narrative Leadership Associates website www.narrativeleadership.com.

Rosemary Nixon and Jonathan Shipley, commissioning editors at John Wiley & Sons, Ltd, have championed *Telling the Story* from conception to completion. They encouraged me to write boldly and helped to make the publication of the book an enjoyable and satisfying experience. Assistant Editor Ashton Bainbridge painlessly managed the sometimes tricky business of obtaining permissions and beavered away behind the scenes to ensure the quality and timeliness of its production.

Finally, I am hugely grateful to my partner Chris Seeley – who never let me make excuses for not writing and held my feet to the fire in many a long conversation about the scope and purpose of narrative leadership. Her contribution to this book and to my life is immeasurable and I am very relieved that my writerly angst did not seem to put her off when I recently asked her to marry me.

But that's another story.

Foreword

Since the earliest times, story has been an implicit part of our journey as humans. We see its traces throughout history, from the story of Gilgamesh, inscribed on clay tablets in 1700 BC, through the epic poetry of Homer and Beowulf, to the tragedies and comedies of Sophocles and Shakespeare. Today we tell our stories differently but our fascination with them has not diminished in the slightest: from Mumbai to Hollywood, our film, theatre, book, television and computer game industries generate billions in revenues each year.

But there's much more to storytelling than entertainment. In many ways story defines us. It allows us to feel part of something greater than ourselves; that we are not alone. It describes that which we are conscious of, and that which sits in our subconscious (through different lenses and experiences) and gives us insights into cultures very different to our own.

As this book shows, individuals, groups and organizations use story – explicitly or tacitly – to express their purpose, to choose what part of their history they will bring into the present, and to describe what they value. Stories also shape our concept of leadership (whether of the heroic Chief Executive, the whistle-blower or the social activist). They are used – ethically and sometimes cynically – to promote the brands and lifestyles to which we are encouraged to aspire and to define what it means to be an ideal citizen or employee.

But much of this use of story is done without a real understanding of its power and thus of its potential for good or ill. In today's world of climate change, economic and social challenges, organizations with unprecedented levels of power and a low level of trust in leaders, the need for new stories that connect us with the positive aspects of our past and a more sustainable future, has never been greater. As the author says: "The stories we tell are fateful: our ability to change ourselves, our organizations and our world depends on our capacity to re-imagine them."

Telling the Story offers not just an insight into the power and uses of story, but more importantly for those given the responsibility of leading, the approaches and tools to use story to better lead their organizations. If you take it seriously and follow the journey laid out before you – I have no doubt that your capacity to lead your organization and ensure its positive legacy will be transformed.

Dr. Andrew White
Associate Dean for Executive Education,
Said Business School, University of Oxford

Introduction: Turning the Page

If there is a book that you want to read, but it hasn't been written yet, you must be the one to write it.

TONI MORRISON[1]

Do you read leadership books from cover to cover? Me neither – well, not many of them anyway. They often seem to run out of steam: ideas pushed beyond their limits; themes that are difficult to apply in practice; extravagant claims for gimmicky techniques; a catchy title that doesn't live up to its promise.

Personally, I like to have my thinking and my practice challenged in ways that invite me to build on what I already know and do. I like leadership books that marry big ideas to everyday situations and leave me both better resourced and asking myself tough questions. So, how can you decide whether this leadership book – catchy title and all – is one that you really want to read? Perhaps the next few paragraphs will help you decide.

> *A few years ago I was sitting in a plush seat at the back of a seminar room in a leading business school, when the managing partner of a very large and financially successful professional services firm stood up to share his vision for the future of the company with the 30 or so senior partners in the room. He used a catchphrase which I will not repeat for fear of identifying the company concerned, but it boiled down to this: "We will increase our revenue by 30% in the next 2 years."*

> *He then went on to explain how he expected everyone in*
> *the room to pull their weight – it was in their interests too,*
> *wasn't it? And that was it. Nothing about the contribution*
> *their work made to their clients; nothing about its wider*
> *impact in the world; nothing beyond "We're big and let's*
> *get bigger. We're rich and let's get richer."*

I was in the room because I had agreed to work with the senior part-ners on the benefits of storytelling. If you are expecting me to tell you how I taught the managing partner to deliver his message in a more inspiring way, or how I helped the senior partners to make more money through the instrumental use of storytelling, then you will be disappointed (as they were when I suggested that they might have to think about what the vision was actually about, not just how to communicate it more dynamically).

If, on the other hand, you were a bit shocked by the vision's unreflec-tive appeal to an outdated business orthodoxy and naked greed; if you think that being a leader requires you to examine the purposes for which you lead; if you are curious about the power of story and storytelling to contribute to a more humane and generative society – then this could be just the book you've been waiting for.

The challenging story of our times demands more than "telling a good tale." To play our part in making sense of the world around us it is necessary for us to look at the assumptions underlying the stories that unconsciously shape our behaviors and choose carefully which stories we really want to tell. If you want to find your own authentic leadership stories and to make a difference by telling them well enough to stir the hearts and engage the imagination of your audience – read on.

Narrative leadership

> *The ultimate impact of the leader depends most signifi-*
> *cantly on the particular story that he or she relates or*
> *embodies, and the receptions to that story on the part of*
> *audiences (or collaborators or followers).*
>
> HOWARD GARDNER[2]

This was the conclusion that Howard Gardner reached in his brilliant analysis of twentieth-century world leaders, *Leading Minds: An Anatomy of Leadership*. It is also the understanding I have come to after working for 30 years in the field of leadership development. Successful leadership depends on the stories we tell and the stories we live and how well they speak to the needs of our time.

Gardner reveals something about what makes the difference between leaders who have real impact and those who don't. My interest has been *how* to make the difference, especially – as Gregory Bateson put it – the difference that makes a difference. Isn't that what all leaders strive to do: make a significant difference with the limited personal resources at their disposal? Let me use a well-known metaphor to show you what I mean.

> *The world's largest oil tankers carry 500,000 tonnes of cargo. It's a cliché that once in motion they take a long time and a lot of effort to change direction. Everything about them is enormous, including the rudders that turn them, so the large rudders themselves have small rudders to move them through the water. Turning the small rudder creates the kind of difference that makes a big difference.*

What is the large rudder that turns an organization or even a society around? For the sake of argument, let's say that it is the beliefs and values that guide people's actions and behaviors. And what is the small rudder that moves the large one? The stories that mould our identities, give meaning and significance to our experience, and shape our understanding of the world. If you want to influence where we are heading then you need to understand how stories work and how to tell them. The name I give to understanding and using stories in this way is "narrative leadership" and it is what this book is designed to help you do.

For over a decade, my colleagues and I at Narrative Leadership Associates have been taking our work into businesses, government departments, universities, business schools, NGOs, social enterprises, and charities. We have worked with chairmen, chief executives, directors, permanent secretaries, managers, front-line staff, consumers, customers, and patients. During that time, what began as a hunch that stories were important has been honed into a rigorous body of knowledge and a wide range of tried-and-tested methods. When we began, few people had identified the contribution that storytelling can make to leadership. Now the urgent need to find new stories for our changing times is widely recognized and leaders – inside and outside organizations – are asking for help.

Once upon a time

> *Three apples fell from heaven: one for the storyteller, one for the listener and one for the one who took it to heart.*
> ARMENIAN PROVERB[3]

Let me begin at the beginning, as every good storyteller should. I first got an inkling of how stories work and of the power of storytelling to make a difference in 1996, when I found myself unexpectedly (and rather against my better judgment at the time) in the audience for a performance by two professional storytellers: Ashley Ramsden and Bernard Kelly. They had been invited to give a performance by the organizer of the conference on complexity theory that I was attending. But my field of practice was and remains that of leadership development and I was highly sceptical about the whole thing: what on Earth had this to do with organizations or grown-up people – storytelling was for kids, wasn't it?

The first story of the evening was *The Banyan Deer*[4] (from the Buddhist Jataka tradition) and within minutes I was hooked. The storyteller's words conjured up images and feelings so powerful it was as though I was in the story. Soon, said the storyteller, the world of the Banyan deer was disturbed by a new power in the land, Brahmadatta, the young King of Benares who loved nothing more than hunting:

> *The king and his retinue rampaged through the country-side trapping and shooting every creature that came into their view. Each evening they returned to court followed by wagons piled high with the spoils of the hunt; carcasses of bear, leopard, tiger, monkey, boar, buffalo and deer.*

Something extraordinary seemed to be happening to me because, in my imagination, I could see, hear, touch (even smell and taste) the hunt and everything in the story. My heart was moved too, so that 10 minutes later when the story ended I found myself weeping at the fate of the deer and of the man who had hunted them. As I glanced round the room, I could see the rapt expressions on the faces of my colleagues and the glistening of tears in their eyes. Whatever was happening to me was happening to them too: we had all been swept up by the story and while it was being told, we had drawn closer to each other. Even now, more than 15 years later, I can recall the story, the images it evoked, and the feelings it stirred.

I fell in love with stories and storytelling that evening and committed myself to mastering the craft of the storyteller. Since that time I have trained, practiced, and performed as a storyteller all over the United Kingdom and as far afield as Canada and Japan. I have learned how to hold an audience in the palm of my hand: how to make them laugh, wonder, and shed a tear. I have learned a lot about how storytellers weave their magic, whether they're telling a traditional tale, a personal story, or a strategic vision for an organization (or a whole society).

It's an everyday magic that's available to each of us once we know how to put a good story together and tell it competently. You don't have to be a natural performer, hugely extrovert, or a creative genius. But you do need to know what really matters to you so can choose stories you can tell with authentic passion; you do need to allow yourself to be vulnerable (as you inevitably are when you stand up in front of people and let them see who you are and what you care about); you do need to get your ego out of the way so you can serve the story and those for whom you are telling it. Telling stories well, whether for instruction, entertainment, or inspiration, is as much about how you show up as it is about technical mastery. As the title of this book implies, good storytelling is both heartfelt and soulful – as is good leadership.

Why we need new stories

It's all a question of story. We are in trouble just now because we do not have a good story. We are in between stories. The old story, the account of how we fit into the

world, is no longer effective. Yet we have not learned the
new story.

THOMAS BERRY[5]

You will have gathered by now that narrative leadership is about more than increasing profits, market share, and shareholder value. It neither takes our consumerist society for granted nor does it advocate the adoption of simplistic utopian alternatives. But leadership that does not take account of its context is unlikely to offer much beyond pious hopes and platitudes. So a key issue for any leader to consider is the scope of the context within which they operate. Where do we set the boundaries of our responsibility? How broadly and over what time frame do we consider the consequences of our decisions? What is the purpose and intention behind our leadership? For whom and for what do we lead?

There are some who would deny it (I doubt if they will still be reading this book) but the plain fact is that we are in trouble. We have been living beyond our planetary means for some time as the Club of Rome's report *The Limits to Growth*[6] pointed out in 1972. But so strong was the tacit belief that we lived in a world of infinite resources and inevitable progress that we did not take the actions that might have spared us from the worst consequences of our way of life. Now, 40 years later, in the second decade of the twenty-first century, in the light of climate change, massive environmental degradation, multiple species extinction, and a global economic crisis, it would be perverse to pretend that we are not in trouble.

What makes this particularly difficult to grasp, as John Michael Greer points out in *The Long Descent,*[7] is that it is no longer a problem that can be solved (if it ever was) but a predicament to be lived through. It is an important distinction to make and a challenging premise to accept. If it is not a problem that can be solved, what then is the leader's task? If the old story is broken and there is not a new story to be found, what does narrative leadership have to offer?

Both the leader's task and how narrative leadership might help are counter-intuitive to our problem-solving minds (our desire to find the one true story). We need to end our attachment to the old story and learn how to live well in the predicament – in the "multi-storied" space between the apocalyptic story of catastrophic collapse and the utopian story of socio-technical solutions. In whatever domain leaders operate, their most important task is to help us face the truth of our situation and to act accordingly.

We would rather not be in this predicament, but that is where we are. I am reminded of a moment in J.R.R. Tolkien's *Lord of the Rings*, written in another time of trouble during World War II. The hobbit Frodo Baggins tells the wizard Gandalf that he wishes that the great evil resulting from the finding of the ring and the rise of Sauron had not happened during his lifetime. Gandalf replies in words that might speak to us all:

> *So do I and so do all who live to see such times. But that is not for them to decide. All we have to decide is what to do with the time that is given us.*[8]

As leaders, what shall we do with the time that is given us? It is easy to become dispirited and overwhelmed by the difficulties that surround us; it is so much easier to pretend that the difficulties do not exist or to believe that it is not worth doing anything because nothing we can do will make any difference. Yet we need not lose heart; it is surely better to make a modest contribution even if we cannot measure its effect. We might not be able to change *the* story in one fell swoop, but narrative leadership tells us that the stories we tell and the stories we live do matter.

We might, for example, decide to use our talents and energy to help meet our finite human needs (as Manfred Max-Neef defined them in *Human Scale Development*)[9] for subsistence, leisure, affection, participation, protection, understanding, freedom, creativity, and identity, rather than use them actively to encourage and feed our infinite and insatiable desire for material goods and services. Of course this is easier said than done; most of us are still caught by the consumerist fantasy to some extent – at the time of writing I am agonizing over whether to give up a much-loved but preposterously impractical and quite unnecessary sports car.

At the very least, we can all ask ourselves what stories are called for at this time and what our children and grandchildren would make of the stories we are living and telling now. That is quite a challenge for us as leaders but slight in comparison to the stricture placed upon tribal chiefs by the Great Law of the Iroquois:

> *Look and listen for the welfare of the whole people and have always in view not only the present but also the*

coming generations, even those whose faces are yet beneath the surface of the ground—the unborn of the future Nation.[10]

Such concern for the coming generations might help explain why the Iroquois revere their ancestors. One way we could learn how to care for our planet better might be to ask ourselves what stories our grandchildren (and their grandchildren) will tell about us and what we decided to do with the time that was given us.

About this book

The book is intended for thoughtful leaders inside and outside organizations who can feel the winds of change blowing; who have the courage to face into the wind and contribute to the changing story of our times. The art of narrative leadership is vital for senior executives, managers, practitioners, and concerned citizens. It is vital for anyone who is interested in the state of the world and wants to know how to make a difference through stories and storytelling.

Telling the Story opens a door into the world of narrative leadership: what stories are and how they work; when to tell a story and how to tell one well; how the stories we tell (and the language and metaphors we use) influence our actions and shape the way we think about the world. The book also offers a challenge to consider the purposes behind our stories: What are we leading for? What are the big stories of our time and how can our own stories help to create the kind of future we want for ourselves and our children?

Telling the Story is both practical (with tips, exercises, and examples) and thought provoking. It argues for a re-enchantment of our disenchanted world and for the recognition of more human and humane values in our organizational lives. Above all, I hope this book will help us be the kind of leaders we want to become by encouraging us to stand up for what really matters and enabling us to take more responsibility for the world we bring into being through the stories we tell and the stories we live.

The book can be read as a whole, taking the chapters in sequence or – having first read Sections One and Two to set the scene – you can choose the order in which you read the other sections according to interest and need.

Section One – Foundations: Chapters 1 and 2 explore why stories matter (in terms of identity, community, and possibility) and consider leadership from the perspective of meaning-making and storytelling.

Section Two – On Stories: Chapters 3, 4, and 5 look at our innate human propensity to tell stories, offer a whistle-stop tour through fact, fiction, and fantasy, and show how stories engage our imaginations and feelings.

Section Three – Narrative Leadership: Chapters 6, 7, 8, and 9 delve more deeply into the practice of narrative leadership to help leaders understand their own stories better, use storytelling to create a stronger sense of community, and stand up for what they believe in.

Section Four – Storytelling: Chapters 10, 11, and 12 offer practical guidance – drawn from the art of the traditional storyteller – for choosing, shaping, and telling the stories that we need to tell as leaders.

Section Five – Time and Change: Chapters 13 and 14 look at how stories and storytelling can be used to learn from the past, make sense of the present, and imagine the future. Chapter 15 looks at storytelling in our hypermodern age, briefly considers the impact of social media and globalization on the kind of stories we tell, and explores the shadow side of storytelling in business and government.

Section Six – Between Stories: Chapter 16 ends the book by reflecting on the scope and ambition of our leadership in response to the narrative wreckage caused by the environmental and social challenges of our time. Finally, it invites us to reflect on previous chapters and on how narrative leadership can help us lead successfully with heart and soul.

The Appendix includes additional storytelling resources and a comprehensive set of notes and references are included at the end of each chapter.

Many of the chapters include reflective questions and exercises designed to help you draw on your own experience and to engage with the material on your own terms. This is a book about the praxis of narrative leadership, praxis being the place where ideas and practice meet. I invite you to read it in the spirit of inquiry, testing it against what you already know about storytelling and leadership, and seeing what works for you. I hope that reading it will be both engaging and challenging, that you will be interested in what it has to say and moved to do things differently. Please do let me know how you get on.

Water on the rock

The act of storytelling and the stories we tell matter for all of the reasons given in this introduction. But there is one more reason – maybe the most important of all – to tell stories: they can be hugely enjoyable and life-affirming. Bringing storytelling into the realm of leadership and organizations recognizes our essential humanity, makes our lives brighter, and helps to heal the split between the life-world and the system-world that has so damaged our relationship with the planet. This small story from South Africa (which was first told to me by Sue Hollingsworth of the International School of Storytelling, and which colleagues and I used to introduce the inaugural meeting of the Centre for Narrative Leadership in 2007) makes the point.

> *Some years ago, a group of Bushmen agreed to lead a party of anthropologists into the Kalahari to see some ancient rock paintings that were rumoured to be found deep in the desert. After two weeks, travelling through the sandy wastes, they came to an escarpment and the Bushmen announced that they had arrived.*
>
> *The anthropologists took out their equipment and scoured the sacred site. They peeked and peered, they brushed and scraped but found nothing, not a single painting. After a while they gave up, complaining that they had been brought to the wrong place.*
>
> *The Bushmen laughed and went up to the same spot that the anthropologists had so closely examined; they unstoppered the gourds of water they had with them and splashed the contents over the sun-bleached surface of the*

rock. Dozens of dazzling colored images – women, children, hunters, eland, kudu, wildebeest, and lions – sprang from the rock and burst into life.

See what I mean?

Notes and References

1 Attributed to writer Toni Morrison.
2 Gardner, H. (1996). *Leading Minds: An Anatomy of Leadership* (HarperCollins: London, p14).
3 Traditional Armenian proverb.
4 The whole story of the *Banyan Deer* can be found in my book, Mead, G. (2011). *Coming Home to Story: Storytelling Beyond Happily Ever After* (Vala Publishing: Bristol).
5 Berry, T. (1978). "The New Story: Comments on the Origin, Identification and Transmission of Values," *Teilhard Studies*, No. 1: 1.
6 Meadows, D.H., Meadows, D.L., Randers, J., and Behrens, W.W. III (1972). *The Limits to Growth: A Report to the Club of Rome*, available at http://www.askforce.org/web/Global-Warming/Meadows-Limits-to-Growth-Short-1972.pdf. The findings of this influential report were confirmed and updated in a revised edition published by Routledge in 2004.
7 Greer, J.M. (2008). *The Long Descent: A User's Guide to the End of the Industrial Age* (New Society Publishers: Gabriola Island, BC).
8 Tolkien, J.R.R. (1996 [1954]). *The Lord of the Rings* (illus. ed. in 3 vols.), (HarperCollins: London, p64).
9 Max-Neef, M.A. (1991). *Human Scale Development: Conception. Application and Further Reflections* (Zed Books: London).
10 Article 28, "The Constitution of the Iroquois Nations: The Great Binding Law *GAYANASHAGOWA*," http://www.indigenouspeople.net/iroqcon.htm.

Section One
Foundations

Chapter 1

Why Stories Matter

Anthropologist Dr Frances Harwood – a student of Margaret Mead's – once asked a Sioux elder why people tell stories. He answered: "In order to become human beings." She asked, "Aren't we human beings already?" He smiled. "Not everyone makes it."

LAURA SIMMS[1]

Swimming in a Sea of Stories

The world is full of stories. But not everything is a story; we communicate in other ways as well: we analyze data, exchange information, proffer opinions, make arguments, and plead our case, to name but a few. So, what exactly is a story? My favorite definition comes from organizational storyteller Annette Simmons who says that a story is:

> *an imagined (or re-imagined) experience narrated with enough detail and feeling to cause your listener's imagination to experience it as real.*[2]

A story happens somewhere in the space between the teller's imagination and the listener's imagination. "Ah. But I don't deal in imagination," you might say. "I deal in facts. I only want to know what's really happening." Actually, imagination is how we *create* reality. We rely on our capacity to make images in the mind to interpret immediate sensory information (sight, sound, touch, smell, taste): we smell baking and imagine the pie; we hear a bang and imagine a gunshot; the hairs on the back of our neck stand up and we imagine an intruder. In this way, imagination is closely related to our basic survival instinct.

But with our highly evolved monkey brains, we humans have learned to combine imagination with language to convey to others things that are not actually happening here and now in front of us. We use our imaginations to "make things up" even when we are doing our best to recall an event accurately and tell it as truthfully as possible. We use our imaginations every time we listen to someone speak and try to make sense of what they are saying.

When we tell (narrate) a story – as Annette Simmons says – we use words and gestures to convey enough detail and feeling to stimulate our own and our listener's imaginations to create an experience that is real in the mind. Paradoxically, therefore, the essence of storytelling is its tangibility: the storyteller seeks to convey an experience (something that actually happened or might have happened or might yet happen) in such a way that it seems real. It might be a story remembered – and perhaps embroidered – from life; it might be a conscious fiction made up about ourselves or others; it might even go beyond what is humanly possible into the realms of folklore, fairytale, and fantasy. But in whichever of these spheres a story has its center of gravity, something has to happen and it has to happen to somebody (human or otherwise).

Stories necessarily involve particular events happening to particular characters. Narratives that veer toward generalities, explanations, and abstractions, or which insist on telling us their moral or meaning, have abandoned storytelling in favor of propositional knowing and advocacy, and thereby lose their extraordinary ability to stimulate both the feelings and imagination of teller and audience.

Wise leaders know this. Martin Luther King, standing on the steps of the Lincoln Memorial, in front of 200,000 civil rights supporters, in Washington on August 28, 1963, probably knew it. His friend, the gospel singer Mahalia Jackson, who urged him from the crowd "Tell them about the dream, Martin," certainly knew it. Responding to her encouragement, King broke off from his prepared speech and told the story of a future nation in which there would be racial justice and equality. Over 50 years later

we still remember that story – barely 300 words – though we might be
hard put to recall the rest of his 1,600-word speech. It was a story so
powerful that even the story of telling the story has become iconic. A
short extract reveals its power to move us:

> *I have a dream that one day on the red hills of Georgia*
> *the sons of former slaves and the sons of former slave*
> *owners will be able to sit down together at the table of*
> *brotherhood. I have a dream that one day even the state*
> *of Mississippi, a state sweltering with the heat of injustice,*
> *sweltering with the heat of oppression, will be transformed*
> *into an oasis of freedom and justice. I have a dream [that]*
> *my four little children will one day live in a nation where*
> *they will not be judged by the color of their skin but by*
> *the content of their character.*[3]

Stories touch us in ways that other forms of communication do not. A
good story, well told, can slip past the defenses of the rational mind,
pluck at our hearts, and stir our souls. Martin Luther King was an exceptional orator but we too can draw on the power of stories to make (and
remake) our worlds.

Stories and storytelling are ubiquitous. There have been human societies and civilizations that have flourished without benefit of the wheel but
none has existed without stories. As recent studies in anthropology, philosophy, cognitive psychology, and neuroscience consistently tell us, we
are storytelling animals; to be human *is* to tell stories. We are, so to speak,
swimming in a sea of stories and as Buddhist scholar David Loy says:

> *Like the proverbial fish that cannot see the water they*
> *swim in, we do not notice the medium we dwell within.*
> *Unaware that our stories are stories, we experience them*
> *as the world. But we can change the water. When our*
> *accounts of the world become different, the world becomes*
> *different.*[4]

Therein lies the essence of why storytelling matters: to tell a story is
not simply to give an account of something but to change our relationship
with it; to listen to a story is to allow the possibility of being changed by

it. Stories shape who we are, how we relate to others, and how we make sense of the world. They are so fundamental to how we think, feel, and act that it is not possible to reach our full potential as leaders (or indeed as human beings) without understanding how stories work and using them effectively.

That is a big claim to make. It is the basis on which the whole field of narrative leadership has been developed and the main reason for writing (and perhaps for reading) this book. So let me be absolutely clear; I am asserting that stories are:

1. the primary way we make sense of our experience, giving meaning and significance to our lives and creating (and re-creating) our sense of self;
2. a vital means of building relationships, bringing groups and communities together (discounting others' stories can cause conflict and divisions);
3. a powerful force in the world, acting on our imaginations to shape, extend, and constrain our sense of what is desirable and possible.

Let's look briefly at each of these propositions in turn (we'll explore them in more detail in subsequent chapters) and test their value from your own knowledge and experience.

Imagining ourselves

> *What kind of story are we in? Is it the story of an adventure, a journey, a voyage of discovery? Or is it something simpler like the story of a child playing by the sea.*
>
> JOHN S. DUNNE[5]

---

1. Ask yourself "Who am I?" or – even better – get someone else to ask "Who are you?" Notice what you say and answer the same question again. And again. And again. When you've had enough, do it again. Keep on going for a few minutes. Notice what you say each time you respond to the question.

If you're anything like me, this will drive you crazy. It's a variation of an old Zen koan that novice monks once spent hours, days, or even weeks contemplating. The point is that behind whatever responses we give lie the constitutive stories of the experiences that lead us to identify ourselves in particular ways. Here for example are a few of my straightforward – factual – responses to the question, each followed by a reference to the kinds of story from which the "facts" arise:

I'm Geoff Mead . . .	stories of ancestry and naming
I'm a storyteller . . .	stories of learning about storytelling
I'm a father . . .	stories of my four (grown-up) children
I'm a divorcee . . .	stories of love, sadness, and recovery
I'm a British citizen . . .	stories of history and nationhood

It's virtually impossible to reflect on that apparently simple question (who am I?) without touching the stories of what made us who we are. Our identity – our sense of self – comprises a more or less coherent collection of stories encoding who we think we are and what matters to us. Becoming aware of the storied nature of our being is the first step in developing a more responsible and authoritative relationship with our own histories. We cannot choose our parents or the kind of childhood we experienced, we cannot change what we have done or left undone in our adult lives. But we can learn to recognize how the stories we tell ourselves about our experiences shape the way they influence us; we can give ourselves greater freedom and choice by unhooking ourselves from dysfunctional and limiting stories; we can tap into and draw upon those stories that nourish and sustain us, that enable us to realize more of our potential, to live bigger and more generative lives.

Imagining each other

The shortest distance between two people is a story.
ANON.

An enemy is one whose story we have not heard.

ANON.

Human relationships necessitate the sharing of stories – it is how we come to know (or more accurately, imagine) the other. In healthy relationships there is room for each of us to share our stories: we are curious about and accepting of each other's stories. At first we may be quite selective in what we say about ourselves; we may choose our stories carefully to present ourselves in a particular light. Soon, though, if the relationship is to deepen, we must open up and let ourselves be seen "warts and all." It is another of the paradoxes of storytelling that we get closer to each other by sharing our differences and thereby discovering what we have in common.

2. Recall a time in your life when you made a new friend or fell in love with someone; remember how hungry you were to find out about each other, how you shared your life stories and were eager to hear theirs. Think about how, as your relationship developed, it became defined by the shared stories of your life together.

This phenomenon is equally true for organizations, groups, and whole societies. As with so many basic human needs, our understanding and way of talking about relationships tend to become abstracted and jargonized in organizations. "Inclusion" and "engagement" are currently fashionable terms (and matters of concern) for organizational leaders trying to make sense of the disenchantment and alienation of co-workers and colleagues – particularly those working at the front line. Organizations spend vast amounts of time and money administering and analyzing staff surveys looking for ways to increase employee loyalty and satisfaction. But unless they are also asking "Whose stories are most valued? Whose stories don't get heard? How can we create opportunities to share and listen to each other's stories?" they are largely wasting their time because few things exclude and disengage people quicker than ignoring or discounting their stories.

We can see how this works by looking at some major social and political divisions in recent history. For example, we have only to think of the "troubles" in Northern Ireland in the late twentieth century to see what happens when groups within a community (in this case Protestant and Catholic extremists) no longer give credence or legitimacy to the stories of other groups. It was not so much that the stories of each group were disagreed with, it was that they fell completely outside the discourse of the other group: they literally held no meaning or significance for each other. Conversely, the Truth and Reconciliation Commission in post-apartheid South Africa was – for all its difficulties – a conscious exercise in storytelling across boundaries. Healing divisions requires that we can once again tell our stories to each other and be heard.

Imagining the world

Stories are the secret reservoir of values: change the stories that individuals or nations live by and tell themselves and you change the individuals and nations.

BEN OKRI[6]

The third and most audacious proposition claims that our perception of the wider world (and hence the ways we think and act) is unconsciously shaped and constrained by the limits of our imagination. The "big stories" are so pervasive that it can be difficult to see them as stories at all; the truth of them may be so widely accepted that just to question them is seen as subversive. Philosopher Michel Foucault called such stories "regimes of truth" because they become institutionalized to the point where, instead of being understood as just one among many constructions of reality, they become the standards by which reality may be judged. Author Philip Shepherd graphically describes how this process occurs:

The story upheld by each culture defines a landscape of behavior and thinking as "normal" and then, like a chameleon, disappears within it. When this happens, the definition is mistaken for the world itself, and passes itself off as the one true reality.[7]

Even so, such stories may be challenged and their dominant influence resisted and overcome. Who now believes that the Earth rather than the

Sun sits at the center of our planetary system? Yet in 1633, the Catholic Inquisition found Galileo Galilei "vehemently suspect of heresy" for circulating his heliocentric astronomical theories, placed his *Dialogue Concerning the Two Chief World Systems* on the Index of Forbidden Books (a prohibition that was not lifted until 1835), and sentenced him to life imprisonment. At the time, his views were seen by those in power as dangerously subversive. Why? Perhaps because if his theory – placing humankind on one of several planets orbiting the Sun rather than at the center of the Universe – were to be accepted, it would be more difficult also to believe that all things had been created by God solely for our benefit.

Nearly 400 years after the event, we cannot really know what drove the Catholic Church to react so strongly but we can see how these iconic events undermined a "regime of truth" such that the "big story" of our Universe expanded to allow other imaginative possibilities. It is much harder to see this process at work in contemporary times when we ourselves are so deeply implicated in the stories.

> 3.   Consider some of the "big stories" that have affected the way you perceive the world and how these may be changing in your lifetime. How have these changing stories influenced the way you think and act?

When I considered the "big stories" that have changed or might be changing in my lifetime, some were obvious to me in hindsight while others are still being contested, their futures in doubt. Here – hugely simplified – are a few of the "big stories" that I have encountered.

Limitless Earth: Like so many postcolonial baby-boomers, I was brought up believing that the resources of the Earth were, for all practical purposes, limitless. It was the view of Earth from space taken by the crew of Apollo 17 in December 1972 – a small and inconceivably beautiful blue marble – that revealed the interconnectedness and fragility of our planet and caused me to question for the first time the modernist orthodoxy of unlimited industrial exploitation and economic growth. For me, that iconic image – Spaceship Earth – created the necessity for a different story of the future. It seems obvious now, but it suddenly became clear to me then that we are all in this together: there is no other spaceship, no other resources to use, and no one to save us if we mess it up.

Right on cue came the 1973 oil crisis when the Organization of Arab Petroleum Exporting Countries (OAPEC) declared a 70% rise in price and an embargo limiting oil exports. Our reliance on cheap oil and other fossil fuels to maintain our standard of living was immediately apparent as prices rose and share markets tumbled; rationing and restrictions on the use of fuel were imposed; currencies inflated and economies stagnated. I was lucky to be able to walk to work and fortunate that my job as a police officer was not threatened by redundancy.

It seemed then that the "big story" of a limitless planet might have changed for good as measures were taken to reduce energy consumption. But it is a seductive story for those of us who are able to sequester more than our fair share of the world's resources and it was quickly resurrected in the 1980s and 1990s. Instead of finding a sustainable way of living, our energy consumption continued to rise until now the effects of our wastrel lifestyle can be seen in climate change, environmental degradation, and multiple species extinction. Our awareness of the need to change this story has never been greater, though in practice we cling to it like a limpet to a rock as the tide goes out.

Idea of Progress: One of the most powerful and pervasive "big stories" of the past 300 years, born in the Enlightenment movement of the eighteenth century, is that the human condition will continuously improve through the application of more effective technology and better social organization (capitalism and communism tell different versions of the same story). But it is dangerous to assume that progress is a one-way track; improvements in both quality of life and material living standards are not inevitable and, in much of the world, in recent decades they have been produced by squandering limited and decreasing supplies of fossil fuels and purchased on a wave of consumer credit that neither individuals nor nations can afford to repay.

Many of us who have enjoyed the fruits of post-World War II prosperity currently see our children and grandchildren struggling to find work, unable to afford decent housing, and accumulating debt to pay for their education. Some regard this as a temporary disruption to our fortunes, for others it constitutes grounds to reconsider our whole way of life.

The Information Business: What is the first place you would look to find out about the history of the *Encyclopedia Britannica*? Wikipedia. In the very recent past, information – even general knowledge – was expensive. Parents went without luxuries to buy a decent encyclopedia for their children to use for homework. A bookshelf groaning with 24 leather-bound volumes from aardvark to zygote was a matter of great pride. From 1768 when the first edition of *Encyclopedia Britannica* was published until the advent of the Internet, it was a highly profitable business. In March 2012, Encyclopedia Britannica Inc. announced that it would no longer publish a printed edition.

What has changed? It is not just the comparative cost of print and digital media but the whole philosophy of how knowledge is produced. Instead of teams of editors and writers producing exclusive, authoritative articles for our consumption, knowledge can be crowd-sourced and freely shared: anyone can write, challenge, or correct an entry for Wikipedia. Instead of waiting 25 years for a new edition of a printed encyclopedia, online reference material is subject to constant revision and instant free access. Information has become a new commons owned and managed by everyone.

The World Wide Web is reshaping many of our "big stories" about the availability of knowledge and goods. I recently bought a vintage silver brooch from Denmark, bidding online on my iPhone while queuing for ice-cream in a cinema foyer in England. While the auction was in progress, I also checked my emails and looked up the train times for my journey to London the next day. Apart from buying the ice-cream I could not have done any of those things 10 years ago. Now, we expect to have everything everywhere: ubiquity is the watchword for our age.

Unearned Privilege: Another largely unquestioned "big story" in my youth, deriving perhaps from a national history of empire and colonial exploitation, concerned the tacit (and sometimes explicit) assumption of entitlement associated with gender, race, class, and religion: specifically male, white, Anglo-Saxon, middle class, and Protestant. By birth and upbringing, I fell into all these categories, although I soon left behind the one I could change by declaring myself agnostic and then atheist. Throughout my public school education and early working life, everything around me mirrored back and reinforced the assumed superiority of the archetype that I represented and my sense of entitlement to the privileges I claimed.

It is as uncomfortable for me to describe myself in these terms as it may be for you to read such a description, but this very discomfort is a reflection of the extent to which this story has changed and is still changing. The Britain of which I am a part today is proudly multicultural and multiracial; my sons and daughters were brought up to consider themselves different but equal; in a former career as a senior police officer I did what I could to redress inequality and exclusion on the grounds of race, gender, or sexual orientation. Now I am learning about a different order of systemic privilege that comes from the direct and indirect exploitation of some of the poorest people in the world.

Careers for Life: Lastly, though I could cite other stories, there was the prospect of a secure career for life promised by the post-Great Depression, post-World War II governments of Europe and the United States. In Britain this coincided with the establishment of the welfare state, the National Health Service, and the growth of professionalized public sector organizations such as the police service, which I joined after graduating from university in 1972. This "big story" had a moral dimension: the social contract between state and citizen shifted toward greater mutuality and care. The generation that had fought for its country demanded and was seen to deserve greater social and economic opportunities and protections than hitherto.

As a child of that generation, I was able to take advantage of those opportunities and protections: free university education, wide choice of career, promotion on merit, final salary pension. But this new "big story" has itself been largely overturned for it depended on a level of economic prosperity that we have not been able to sustain. What happens next is a matter for conjecture but politicians of all stripes seem to recognize that the gravy train has run out of steam (and out of gravy).

What "big stories" did you come up with in response to the exercise, I wonder? What stories do you tell yourself about the way the world works? Which stories do you question and which leave unquestioned? These are vital concerns for anyone in a leadership role, for anyone who wants to shape the future as well as make the most of the present. Visionary leaders are both far-seeing and far-shaping: their grasp of imaginative possibilities is more clearly aligned than most with the unfolding future and therefore enables them to influence it more strongly. They are able, at least to some extent, to change the story.

Changing the story

> *A story that can't change is as useful as a parachute that can't open.*
>
> ANON.

The stories we tell are fateful: our ability to change ourselves, our organizations, and our world depends on our capacity to re-imagine them. In a profound sense, nothing changes unless the stories change. This book is about the stories we tell and the stories we live; the stories that shape us, our organizations and communities, and our worlds. It is about differentiating between those stories that serve our human needs and those that do not; about knowing when to hold on to a story and when to let it go.

Changing our stories is not easy and often the hardest thing is letting go of stories that have served us well enough in the past but have become outmoded and dysfunctional. Even high stakes may not be enough to make us release our grip on such stories – especially when we are unwilling to bear the short-term consequences of facing long-term issues.

> *In parts of India where people still catch monkeys to eat, they put a morsel of food inside a hollowed-out gourd which is staked to the ground. There is a small hole in the gourd, just large enough for the monkey to reach through and grab the bait inside. The monkey clenches its fist round the food and, overcome by greed, cannot remove its hand. If it refuses to release its prize, the monkey is caught, captured and eaten.*[8]

Nevertheless, as leaders, we need to understand how and when to let go of old stories – as well as developing the skills to tell a good, new story – because, going back to the three propositions that framed this chapter:

1. our sense of identity – who we are – only changes when we change the stories we tell ourselves about ourselves;
2. organizations, groups, and communities only change when the stories, and storytelling dynamics (i.e., the processes by which stories are told and made sense of) between people, change;
3. our view and experience of the world only change as we question the prevailing "big stories" and imagine new possibilities.

The notion of narrative leadership which we will explore in depth in later chapters means taking responsibility for consciously using story to make meaning with and for other people in all of these domains. Often it is about changing the stories that we tell and to which we listen. But storytelling always occurs in a context, so narrative leadership is not about dreaming up some ungrounded fantasy. Nor is the practice of narrative leadership about claiming the exclusive truth of any single story, or about imposing a story on others – those ways lead to fundamentalism and oppression.

This is an important reminder that stories can be used for malign as well benign purposes (Hitler was a practiced and skillful storyteller) and their very power demands that we pay careful attention to what stories we have earned the right to tell, our intentions in telling them, and how we tell them. Narrative leadership is the antithesis of spin-doctoring: it demands courage, integrity, and authenticity.

Bonus: *Life of Pi*

At the end of each chapter, I'll give you a bonus: a movie or a story that illustrates one of its main themes. You won't have to watch or read them to make sense of the chapter but they will offer another perspective and a different way of engaging with the material. I've chosen the 2012 movie *Life of Pi* for this chapter; it's a film (and Booker Prize-winning novel) about why stories matter. The protagonist Pi Patel tells the story of how he survived for 227 days adrift in a lifeboat with a Bengal tiger for company. His story is disbelieved by representatives of the company investigating the shipwreck and he tells another equally dramatic but more believable version. The film puts me in mind of Joan Didion's famous remark that:

> We tell ourselves stories in order to live . . . We look for the sermon in the suicide, for the social or moral lesson in the murder of five. We interpret what we see, select the most workable of the multiple choices. We live entirely . . . by the imposition of a narrative line upon disparate images, by the "ideas" with which we have learned to freeze the shifting phantasmagoria which is our actual experience.[9]

In an interview on the DVD, the author Yann Martell shares his view that a life made up of bare facts is meaningless and that it is the stories we weave around the events of our lives that make them meaningful. *Life of Pi* invites us to think about how we choose the stories that give our lives meaning. It is readily available on DVD and well worth watching.

Summary

- We use our imagination to create and understand our reality. Storytelling uses voice, words, and gestures to convey enough detail and feeling to stimulate the imagination to create an experience that is real in the mind.
- Stories are always about particular events happening to particular characters (human or non-human) in a certain time and place. They may be about the past, present, or future; they can be based on fact, fiction, or fantasy.
- Stories and storytelling are everywhere: story is our primary way of making sense of our experience, giving meaning and significance to our lives. To be human is to tell stories – we are the storytelling animal.
- We create (and re-create) our sense of self through the stories we tell ourselves; groups and communities are built upon the stories they

share; our view of the world and what is possible and desirable are shaped by the "big stories" of our times.

- Nothing changes unless the story changes because our inner world of feeling and imagination governs how we think and act. Changing our stories requires that we learn to let go of old stories as well as telling new ones.

- Narrative leadership recognizes the importance of storytelling and consciously uses stories to make meaning with and for other people. It is an essential leadership practice which demands courage, integrity, and authenticity as well as skill.

Notes and References

1 Simms, L. (2011). *Our Secret Territory: The Essence of Storytelling* (Sentient Publications: Boulder, CO, p52).
2 Simmons, A. (2007). *Whoever Tells the Best Story Wins* (AMACOM: New York, p19).
3 Find the complete text at http://news.bbc.co.uk/1/hi/world/americas/3170 387.stm.
4 Loy, D.R. (2010). *The World is Made of Stories* (Wisdom Publications: Boston, MA, p5).
5 Dunne, J.S. (1975). *Time and Myth: A Meditation on Storytelling as an Exploration of Life and Death* (University of Notre Dame Press: Notre Dame, IN, p1).
6 Okri, B. (1998). *A Way of Being Free* (Phoenix: London, p112).
7 Shepherd, P. (2010). *New Self, New World: Recovering Our Senses in the 21st Century* (North Atlantic Books: Berkeley, CA, p2).
8 A version of this traditional Indian story can be found in Kornfield, J. and Feldman, C. (1996). *Soul Food* (HarperSanFrancisco: San Francisco, p323).
9 Didion, J. (1979). *The White Album* (Simon & Schuster: New York).

Chapter 2

Rethinking Leadership

There are almost as many different definitions of leadership as there are persons who have attempted to define the concept.

RICHARD STOGDILL[1]

Management "guru" Warren Bennis once famously said that leadership is one of the most studied yet least understood of all social phenomena. He spoke as a pre-eminent practitioner of leadership development for more than 50 years and as the author of many books on the subject. I can vouch for the truth of his claim from my own 30 years of work in the same field.

Despite there being no generally agreed definition of what leadership is, research studies and theories abound. Fashions come and go: trait theory (either you've got it or you haven't got it), participative leadership, leader–member exchange theory (you scratch my back and I'll scratch yours), situational leadership, contingency theory, path–goal theory, servant leadership, transformational leadership, authentic leadership, charismatic leadership, functional leadership, relational leadership, systemic leadership, even (and I hold my hand up to this one) narrative leadership.

Faced with such a welter of models (both complementary and competing) we can be forgiven for feeling a bit confused about what we actually mean by the term *leadership*. Nevertheless, we can identify a dominant discourse – a set of underlying tacit assumptions – running through most of the extensive literature produced by the academic and professional "leadership industry" in the twentieth and twenty-first centuries. Professor Amanda Sinclair of Melbourne Business School brilliantly exposes these tacit assumptions in her iconoclastic book *Leadership for the Disillusioned*:

> *We have been so surrounded by this view of leadership that it has become difficult to think of leadership outside this framework of meanings. In this view, leadership is:*
>
> - *a weighty responsibility that is usually borne by men in high places;*
> - *an individual performance (despite claims that followers are part of leadership);*
> - *an activity developed and played out in interlocking elites of the military, business and politics, centered around the interests of large-scale global capital;*
> - *generally concerned with expanding an organization's growth, "reach" or material success through normative influence, and without mention of power;*
> - *of such importance as to generate a leadership development industry, involving many people in teaching and training others to be leaders;*
> - *of such importance that it is among the most researched of all subjects, demanding large-scale surveys and a proliferation of instruments to measure leadership or its potential;*
> - *a task requiring disembodied, cerebral command and tending to assume physical manifestations of leading and following to be irrelevant; and*
> - *assumed to be of inherent moral value, neglecting frailties, vulnerabilities or the darker side of the leader psyche.*[2]

Sinclair's book – which I thoroughly recommend – goes on to develop a critical view of leadership exemplified by stories and case studies of a much more inclusive range of leaders. Of course, individuals can and do make a difference but I too wish to open up the idea of leadership beyond the heroic ideal of a handful of supremely able and charismatic (usually male) leaders. How we think and talk about leadership matters because the language we use to conceptualize a phenomenon tends to frame our relationship with it and hence our behaviors.

The heroic discourse, which Sinclair so eloquently describes, is long past its sell-by date. These ideas, which are still widely promoted by the business education and leadership development industries, have become what Michel Foucault called a "regime of truth": a way of thinking and talking about something that is unconsciously held in place because it serves to maintain existing power structures. Over time, Foucault says, such discourses get so embedded in our thinking that they become almost impossible to question either from within the dominant group or from outside. Challenging dominant discourses whether in business, government, academia, or society at large is not for the faint-hearted. Unsurprisingly, most of us are reluctant to change our minds when the privileges accruing from our way of life rather depend on our holding a certain point of view: turkeys rarely vote for Christmas.

Nevertheless, if there was ever a time to rethink what we mean by leadership this is it. Whatever our local context, we all face the prospect of significant climate change, massive environmental degradation, and a global economic crisis. These systemic failures arose from complex inter-locking patterns of behavior in which we are all to some extent implicated. Whatever the causes of our predicament, our ability to respond adequately will require not just different leaders but new ways of thinking about and enacting leadership capable of engaging whole populations in collective action, preferably without resorting either to utopian fantasy or despotic tyranny. As Einstein is alleged to have said: "No problem can be solved from within the level of consciousness that created it."

Making common sense

Making sense is the process of arranging our understanding of experience so that we can know what has happened and what is happening, and so that we can predict what

*will happen; it is constructing knowledge of ourself and
the world.*

DRATH AND PALUS[3]

I have always found the question of what leaders actually do when they
are leading much more interesting and useful than attempting yet another
conceptual definition of leadership. So let's begin this section by putting
the term "leadership" in its place. Why does this need doing? Because
leadership is an abstract noun (and a somewhat overinflated one at that):
leadership as a phenomenon; an attribute; a quality; a trait. So it tends to
take us down blind alleys like the argument between nature and nurture:
are we born leaders or are we made?

> *I once put that question to a class of MBA students in
> Athens, inviting them to stand in a line, choosing their
> position according to their answer. They spread themselves
> along the entire continuum from "born" to "made" includ-
> ing several students who declared without any trace of
> irony or self-doubt that they themselves were born leaders
> (although I'd seen no sign of it in their conduct in the
> workshop and nor apparently – judging by the raucous
> response to their declaration – had their colleagues).*
>
>   *It provoked a lively (and as it turned out largely gen-
> dered) disagreement between the opposing camps. "Hold
> on a minute," I said. "Wherever you are standing in the
> line, I want you to consider this: whatever you believe
> about leadership, do you think you could learn how to
> lead better if – instead of continuing this polarized debate
> – we look instead at the process of leading?" Rather to my
> surprise, they all agreed that it might indeed be a more
> productive line of inquiry to follow. They sat down and I
> reached for my well-thumbed copy of* Making Common
> Sense *by Wilfred Drath and Charles Palus of the Centre
> for Creative Leadership to help me explain what I had
> meant by the process of leading.*

   I have the same copy by my side as I write this chapter (it's another
book I unreservedly recommend). What happens, Drath and Palus ask, if

we think of leading less in terms of taking charge and making things happen and more in terms of participating in a social process of making sense of things? There is a lot in that last sentence, so let's unpack it a bit. It implies that although some people may have nominal positions of leadership (supervisor, manager, director, CEO, for example) they exercise their responsibilities by engaging in an ongoing process of sense-making with other people who in turn, by virtue of their participation in the process, are also engaged in the process of leading.

It also implies a more inclusive notion of leadership (it is hard to get away from the word) and a more dynamic sense of how systems and organizations actually work: leaders emerge from or step into a set of relationships between people already engaged in multiple processes of sense-making from which shared (and contested) understandings materialize and from which shared (and contested) commitments to goals and actions flow. Thus, as Drath and Palus say:

> *The process of making meaning in certain kinds of social settings [actually] constitutes leadership. In other words, we can regard leadership as meaning-making in a community of practice.*[4]

Thinking of leadership as a process of meaning-making that permeates a group promotes a more fluid and realistic view of human relations and a less lofty and exclusive idea of what it means to be a leader. Leadership becomes the life blood of a living system and not just the perquisite of those in high places. This does not deny that some people have more power and influence than others in the process of meaning-making because of formal hierarchy, acknowledged experience, intelligence, political alliances, personal charisma, etc. But it does offer the possibility of engaging a wider range of people in taking responsibility for their contribution to meaning-making and it does suggest that an important shift in attitude is required from those in nominal leadership roles. Drath and Palus, again, say:

> *Because leadership is seen as a process residing in the community of practice, the person with authority and power will not so much see his or her role as taking charge as participating. The key movement is from I need to make*

things happen to we need to make things happen and I
need to figure out how best to participate in the process of
us making things happen.[5]

This is quite heady theoretical stuff, so let's bring it down to Earth by
relating it to your own leadership practice in a short reflection on how
you operate.

1. Take a few minutes to think about what you actually do when you are
    leading. List some of the things you do that are intended to make sense
    of things either with or for other people.

Your list will probably include many of the activities that are commonplace in any hierarchical organization (even if you do not work in one)
such as articulating a vision, defining the mission, identifying goals, debat-
ing policy, agreeing contracts and performance targets, solving problems,
influencing stakeholders, arguing your point of view, listening to others,
and telling stories. More significant than the list of activities of *what* you
do is *how* you go about doing them.

2. Look at the activities on your list and rate each one according to the
    balance between, on the one hand, taking charge and making things
    happen and, on the other hand, helping to create the conditions and/
    or participating in a social process through which things happen.

How did you get on? Were your scores weighted toward taking charge
and making things happen or toward creating the conditions and/or
participating in social processes? Some kind of blend is inevitable and
probably desirable. What matters is that we are able to make conscious
choices about what is most appropriate and effective in the circumstances.
For example, there were situations when I was a senior police officer that
called for decisive unilateral command: when in charge of policing a live
public order operation such as a football match or an armed incident,
there was little time for debate. But those occasions were few and far

between; most of the time running a police force requires the active engagement of its staff in sense-making and decision-making, not merely obedience to orders.

The idea of leadership as participation in a social process, as I've been describing it, is not value-neutral. Shared participation in meaning-making inevitably points toward wider distribution of power and influence. This may sit comfortably with you personally or it may not; you might think that it fits well with the type of organization or system within which you exercise leadership or you might not. Having spent many years as a member of a large police organization, these days I'm a member of several small organizations in each of which this issue is dealt with differently: Vala Publishing Co-operative (where maximizing participation in all aspects of its work is a core value); The Centre for Narrative Leadership, a not-for-profit network which I co-founded to raise awareness of story-telling in organizations (in which member participation is welcomed and encouraged but not a core value); Narrative Leadership Associates, a company that I established and through which I earn a living as a con-sultant (over which I keep quite close control and in which the extent of participation in sense-making and decision-making is under constant review and renegotiation). Each of these organizations has its own way of doing things and although, in principle, I espouse the same value of participation, in practice the nature of my participation in each of them is different.

I invite you now in the third and final part of this reflection to cast your eyes over the various organizations of which you are a member (or with which you are involved) and consider how participatively leadership is exercised in them.

3. List the three most significant organizations/systems/groups of which you are a member or with which you are involved. Write a phrase or sentence about each (as I have done above) describing the extent of participation in sense-making and decision-making. Take a few moments to consider how appropriate you consider that to be in each case. What would you change about the degree of participation with which you and/or others exercise leadership if you could?

An important question that arises from reflecting on the way we lead is how far we feel constrained to lead in a particular way by the prevailing culture of the group, organization, or system we are a member of or involved with. It is all very well to theorize about leaders participating in an ongoing social process of sense-making, you might be thinking, but it cannot be done in the real world. I disagree and, to prove my point, let me give you a real-life example of taking a radically participative approach to meaning-making and decision-making in a very hierarchical and conservative organization. I reckon that if it could happen here then it could happen just about anywhere.

Case Study: The Force Review

Some years ago, the Senior Management Group (SMG) of a certain police force was doing its best to run the organization as it had done for the past couple of decades. I won't identify which particular force it was for reasons which will become obvious. There was no doubting the integrity or commitment of the SMG whose members were mostly long-serving Superintendents who had risen through the ranks to take charge of territorial divisions, specialist functions (such as Criminal Investigation), and administrative departments (such as Human Resources). Performance was quite good: detection rates at about the national average; incidence of serious crimes acceptably low; fatal road incidents on a par with other comparably sized forces. There was a strong leadership ethos of command and control by expert managers; tricky issues got pushed up the line for decisions; mistakes were not much tolerated; and risk-taking of any kind discouraged. In short, it was a tight ship and well regarded by many within the wider police service.

But when a new Chief Officer was appointed he saw an organization poised on the brink of decline: operational commanders unable to innovate because they didn't have control of their resources and budgets; substandard aging police buildings; inadequate IT and no professional IT expertise; a consequent lack of management information; no long-term planning or strategy; back-covering management by standing order and reliance on precedent. He was surprised that SMG seemed not to have noticed any of these things and disturbed when his attempts at reform through existing channels ran into the sand. SMG always seemed to find good reasons to delay, divert, or deny novel ideas. Those who in the Chief Officer's mind should have been driving change appeared to be blocking it.

I've painted a rather black and white picture which doesn't fully do justice to the people involved or to the complexity of the situation, but you get the idea. The Chief Officer's response to this impasse was – for it's time and context – breathtakingly radical. Using a small group of expert facilitators from outside SMG to support the process, he ordered (nothing participative here) a root and branch bottom-up review of structure, process, and strategy. Dozens of working groups were established with clear terms of reference and tight time-scales. Any member of the force (police or civilian) could apply to chair a group but were disqualified from groups reviewing their own areas of work. SMG was reassured that all working group recommendations would be brought to it for final decision and the process began. Working groups took expert evidence, researched best practice elsewhere, and produced their results in a common format giving a list of options, with the pros and cons of each and their opinion as to which was the best. Six months later all the working groups had reported and it was decision time.

Already you can see how the Chief Officer was making the move from "I need to make things happen" to "We need to make things happen." In doing so he released a flood of energy and talent across the organization that had hitherto been damped down by years of restrictive management practices – the genie was out of the bottle. But that still left him with the crucial issue of how to engage SMG in the process of meaning-making that he had instigated; in other words, he had still to "figure out how best to participate in the process of us making things happen." What he actually did was quite inspired.

With an external facilitator to manage the process, he took the SMG away for three days to finalize the review process. He began with words to this effect: "It is our job to make these decisions. I'd prefer that we decide by consensus but if we can't all agree then we'll go with the majority. I expect our decisions to be based on the evidence presented in the working papers and I will abide by whatever decisions we reach. We will record the grounds for each decision and report back to the working groups."

By opening up the sense-making and decision-making process, the Chief Officer held SMG's feet to the fire; there could be no ducking and diving. In the three days that followed, SMG made the decisions that laid the foundations for modernizing the force. Although some of the changes SMG agreed were anathema to certain individuals, the process of meaning-making that the Chief Officer had introduced obliged them to take responsibility for their own participation. Subsequent implementation of the decisions was not painless but it was relatively straightforward. Members of SMG were charged with implementing specific proposals with a timetable, clear accountability, and support from the review project office. Given such unambiguous tasks, it became a matter of pride for SMG to be seen to deliver. And deliver it did.

Conclusions

Leadership as participation in a social process of meaning-making is not a soft option. In fact, it can be much more demanding than "taking charge and making things happen" but it can also result in the genuine engagement of a wide range of people in the business of the organization. The review process described above involved the entire organization (anyone was entitled to submit views and evidence and between a third and a half of all staff did so). It demonstrates that engagement comes, not from formulating a plan and then "getting people on board," but by enabling their participation in the real business of the organization, including its transformation.

When this happens, people are in a sense co-creating the stories of which they are a part – which brings us rather neatly back to the place of storytelling in leadership. We might speculate that if the Chief Officer had told a more convincing story about the future of the organization then he might have encountered less resistance from the SMG in the first place. Be that as it may, the stories that flowed out of the process of the review to make their way round the organization were legion: stories of people finding their voice; stories of thinking the unthinkable and doing the undoable.

Leadership as meaning-making is a powerful meta-concept that side-steps the definitional quagmire that has plagued the whole field of leadership studies since its inception. Whether leaders are born or made, heroic or non-heroic, insiders or outsiders, may affect their institutional power and influence but does not alter the business of leading: participating in an ongoing process of meaning-making with other people. It invites people occupying nominal positions of authority to think differently about their role than simply "taking charge and making things happen" and it opens up the possibility of participating in acts of leadership to anyone who initiates or contributes to the process of meaning-making.

Drath and Palus talk about leadership as meaning-making in a community of practice which usefully reminds us that leadership has a context and that the context is not necessarily an organizational one. I want to reinforce that point, because to restrict it to the domain of organizations is unwittingly to fall back into the dominant discourse of leadership as being "an activity developed and played out in interlocking elites of the military, business and politics" as opposed to being a universal facet of human interaction in which we all participate from time to time. I'm very interested in the nature and quality of leadership in organizations, having spent most of my professional life trying to understand how people lead and helping them get better at it, but leadership as meaning-making has as much to offer to activists and community leaders as it does to business leaders and senior civil servants (indeed, who is to say that these are not sometimes the selfsame people?).

We can think of narrative leadership (the conscious use of stories and storytelling in leadership) as a special case within the broader concept of leadership as meaning-making. If leading is about meaning-making and telling stories is the primary way in which we give significance to and make sense of our experience, then storytelling really is close to the heart and soul of leadership.

Narrative leadership challenges the framework of meanings embedded in the dominant discourse of leadership because it offers ways of thinking about and practicing leadership that are open to anyone trying to make a difference, whether on the world stage, in organizations, in communities, or at home. It is about how we use stories and storytelling to make sense of ourselves, our communities, and our worlds. It does not ignore the realities of power and vested interest nor does it pander to them; its purpose may be to transform, preserve, or disrupt the status quo. It is a social process rather than a solitary pursuit and it speaks to the needs of our time. We need new stories to live and to tell.

Bonus: *Erin Brockovich*

In this book, we will explore how narrative leadership works in many different contexts. As a token of which, I want to end this chapter by introducing someone who galvanized a community in pursuit of justice, someone who didn't fit the corporate mould at all.

In 1992, Erin Brockovich, an ex-beauty pageant queen and unqualified single mother of three young children, was working as a filing clerk in the offices of lawyers Masry & Vititoe in Thousand Oaks, California. She noticed that files for a property case involving residents of a small desert town called Hinckley also contained their medical details; her curiosity was aroused and she delved deeper. She eventually gathered damning evidence against Pacific Gas & Electric proving that over a period of 30 years the corporation had discharged dangerous levels of a highly toxic chemical into the water supplying the community of Hinckley. Brockovich engaged directly with local residents, a relatively high proportion of whom had suffered cancers and other debilitating diseases. Patiently, she formed relationships and shared the information she had discovered. She helped the residents realize that they had been deceived and encouraged them to believe that they were not powerless in the face of an enormous corporation. By 1996, thanks largely to her efforts, 648 Hinckley plaintiffs shared in a $333 million payout from PG&E.

We could say that Brockovich instigated and participated in a collaborative process of meaning-making, out of which a new story gradually emerged. Julia Roberts won an Oscar for her portrayal of Erin Brockovich (in the 2000 film of the same name). It is a convincing story, although the film naturally uses some dramatic license in telling the tale. Try to get the DVD version that includes an interview with the real Erin Brockovich in the extras. She does not think of herself as a leader (and in the conventional terms of the dominant leadership discourse, she was not) but her words paint a vivid picture of leading by "making common sense."

Summary

- Despite much research and study, there is no generally agreed definition of leadership. As an abstract concept it takes our attention away from the process of leading, toward unproductive debates about qualities and traits.
- The professional and academic "leadership industry" is embedded within an uncritical dominant discourse of charismatic individuals (usually men) in high places, exercising disembodied, cerebral command over their followers.
- The meta-concept of leadership as participation in an ongoing social process of meaning-making extends the notion of leading beyond the limitations of the dominant discourse and invites new behaviors.
- The key movement (say Drath and Palus) is from *I* need to make things happen to *we* need to make things happen and *I* need to figure out how best to participate in the process of *our* making things happen.
- As The Force Review case study shows, leadership as meaning-making is not a soft option for anyone involved but it can lead to genuine engagement: participation by a wide range of people in the real business of the organization.
- Erin Brockovich's campaigning work among the residents of Hinckley in the 1990s illustrates how leadership as meaning-making can operate outside the box, building relationships, sharing information, and "making common sense."
- Telling stories is the primary way we give significance to and make sense of our experience; Narrative leadership (the conscious use of stories and storytelling in leadership) is a powerful form of leading as meaning-making.

Notes and References

1 Stogdill, R.M. (1974). *Handbook of Leadership: A Survey of Theory and Research* (Free Press: New York, p7).
2 Sinclair, A. (2007). *Leadership for the Disillusioned: Moving beyond Myths and Heroes to Leading that Liberates* (Allen & Unwin: Crows Nest, NSW).
3 Drath, W.H. and Palus, C.J. (1994). *Making Common Sense: Leadership as Meaning-making in a Community of Practice* (Center for Creative Leadership: Greenboro, NC, p2).
4 Ibid., p4.
5 Ibid., p19.

Section Two
On Stories

Chapter 3

Stories in Our Bones

Stories are as ubiquitous as water or air. There is not a single person who is not touched by the silent presence of stories.

BEN OKRI[1]

I once heard that, somewhere in the world, there are indigenous people whose name for human being, when literally translated, is "featherless storytelling creature." I love the image this apocryphal tale conjures up so much that I have often shared it with audiences and workshop participants, sometimes adding that though I *presume* on the available evidence that we are all featherless, I *know* that we are all storytellers.

Since I first started storytelling I have been curious about our fascination with stories. Story seems to be a universal human phenomenon: from our dreams and daydreams to the entries in our journals; from the anecdotes we tell about ourselves and our families to literary masterpieces; from traditional wonder tales to Hollywood epics. The narrative form is so deeply embedded in our lives and in our culture that I have often wondered how this evolution in our consciousness came about. Where did this uniquely human mode of expression come from? Why do we humans tell stories at all?

If we can answer these two questions then we will be better able to understand stories and potentially tell them more effectively. To do so, we will have to make two journeys: one inside our brains to explore how they work with story; the other back through time to the emergence of story in human history. *How* we make these journeys is also important to consider because they each imply different ways of engaging with the world – different forms of sense-making that bear directly on stories and storytelling.

Distinguished cognitive psychologist Jerome Bruner summarized the fruits of his 30 years of research into developmental psychology this way:

> *There are two modes of cognitive functioning, two modes of experience, two modes of thought, each providing distinctive ways of ordering experience, of constructing reality. The two (though complementary) are irreducible to one another. Efforts to reduce one mode to the other or to ignore one at the expense of the other inevitably fail to capture the rich diversity of thought.*[2]

Bruner calls these the logico-rational (or paradigmatic) mode and the narrative mode. The former uses our ability to think in abstract concepts to search for universal truth conditions as in the scientific method; the latter uses our ability to imagine particular circumstances to explore what he calls the "vicissitudes of human intentions." The former deals in data and logical argument; the latter deals in stories. Problems arise when we ignore the potential of each mode or confuse them. The issue is not that either mode is somehow better than the other, but that they serve different purposes:

> *The imaginative application of the paradigmatic mode leads to good theory, tight analysis, logical proof, sound argument, and empirical discovery guided by reasoned hypothesis . . . The imaginative application of the narrative mode leads instead to good stories, gripping drama, believable (though not necessarily "true") historical accounts.*[3]

Bruner's thesis encapsulates an age-old puzzle about how our minds work. The ancient Greeks described these two modes in terms of *logos* (reasoned discourse) and *mythos* (report, tale, or story). These days, we commonly – though inaccurately – speak about the logical left brain and the intuitive right brain. Whatever we call them, we can probably agree that we need to draw upon both modes to manifest the full range of our human potential. Yet, the educational systems of western societies have increasingly driven a wedge between them, and the conventions of organizational life undoubtedly privilege the paradigmatic mode at the expense of the narrative mode.

Narrative leadership recognizes the importance of paradigmatic thinking but is more concerned with narrative practice. The aim of this book is primarily to help you develop the know-how needed to use stories and storytelling effectively as a leader. To achieve this, it helps to know about the subject as well, but since our main focus is practical (and because I am assuming that most readers will already feel quite comfortable and confident operating in the paradigmatic mode) the book places more emphasis on the less familiar narrative mode to redress the imbalance.

With that in mind, it is now time to undertake our two journeys: one inside our brains to explore how they work with story; the other back through time to the emergence of story in human history.

Logos: The science of storytelling

How can a three-pound mass of jelly that you can hold in your palm imagine angels, contemplate the meaning of infinity, and even question its own place in the cosmos?
V.S. RAMACHANDRAN[4]

I will confess now (it will quickly become apparent in any case) that I am not a scientist. That is to say, I do not have expert knowledge of any of the natural sciences. Even so, I find myself fascinated by scientific studies of our storytelling minds.[5] For the purposes of narrative leadership, three key scientific discoveries have proved important for people to know and understand, at least in principle. One comes from studies of the psychology of perception and the other two are drawn from the field of neuroscience (the anatomy, physiology, and biochemistry of the brain and nervous system).

We seem to have an in-built need to make sense of ourselves, our relationships with each other, and our environment. It is not hard to intuit the survival value in knowing what is going on around us (indeed the form of our sense organs and the need to process the data they generate may explain the evolutionary development of self-awareness and intelligence). But for our purposes, *how* we came to have the need to make sense of our world does not really matter; what matters is that we humans have it and we have it in spades. We are constantly sifting data, trying to distinguish patterns from random events and attributing possible meanings to what we perceive as patterns.

Psychologists Fritz Heider and Mary-Ann Simmel conducted a landmark experiment in the 1940s that powerfully demonstrated how we attribute causality to perceived behavioral patterns. They showed a short animated film (from which the still image below is taken) of lines and geometric shapes in motion and asked the audience what they saw. When the research subjects who were shown the film were asked to "write down what happened," only one responded literally by reporting the movement of abstract shapes. All the other subjects attributed human personalities to the shapes and created some kind of story to explain their behavior.

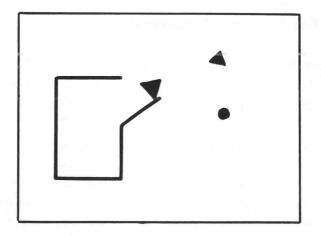

You can see a reconstruction of the film for yourself on the Internet. It lasts less than two minutes and is well worth watching to experience your own reactions. If you can see it without attempting to make meaning of it then you are a very unusual person (and narrative leadership is probably not for you)!

1. Experiment: Look up Heider Simmel Film on your Internet browser, or enter the URL http://vimeo.com/48908599 which was active at the time of writing. Watch the 90-second film and afterward write down what you saw happening.

The results of the original experiment can be found at www.all-about-psychology.com/fritz-heider/html. I won't spoil your enjoyment or try to influence your responses by giving mine. When you've finished, see how your comments compare to those of Heider and Simmel's research subjects. It's said that "man is a being in search of meaning" and this experiment proves the point. Our intrinsic search for meaning helps to explain why storytelling – our most potent way to make sense of the human condition – is so important.

Few people have traveled further inside the human brain than Professor Vilayanur Ramachandran, Director of the Neurosciences Graduate Program at the University of California, San Diego. Fortunately for us, as well as being a respected researcher, he is also a great communicator. His book *The Tell-Tale Brain*[6] explains some of the recent advances in brain research. He describes how the synapses in our brains can be observed responding to vicarious experiences (through the action of "mirror neurons") in much the same way as they do to similar real-life experiences.

In the 1990s, Ramachandran tells us, Giacomo Rizzolatti and his colleagues at the University of Parma were monitoring neuron activity in the brains of Macaque monkeys during a range of actions such as reaching for a banana. What surprised the researchers was that another monkey watching the one reaching for the banana displayed virtually identical patterns of neuronal activity (the firing of "mirror neurons"). It was as if the monkey's brain was rehearsing what it had observed. Rizzolatti and his team had discovered a mechanism to explain imitative learning in primates.

Ramachandran and his co-workers have since found evidence that human brains use mirror neurons in similar though more complex ways, responding to vicarious stimuli as if actually responding directly to a sensory experience. He suggests that mirror neuron activity enables us to do some remarkable things. For example, as our brains rehearse what we observe, we are able to work out others' intentions. We can see the world from their conceptual vantage point (we literally "see what they mean"). Mirror neurons thus provide a mechanism for empathic and sympathetic connection (in a certain sense we *can* feel another's pain, joy, fear). In a rather complex way which Ramachandran calls cross-modal (e.g., linking sight and sound), it seems that we might even use this mechanism for abstract and metaphorical thinking.

Research in this area is in its infancy and Ramachandran's conclusions have attracted some controversy. Nevertheless, they suggest that we are, in effect, "hard-wired" for story. When we see and hear a storyteller, our brains respond to the images they create through language and gesture. We pick up on particular sensory details and descriptions that activate our imaginations, allowing us to have a vicarious experience of the story. The better the storyteller, the livelier and more engaging that experience will be and the more we can learn from the story as a potential reality that we might or might not choose to enact.

The ability to learn from such vicarious experiences is thought to have provided potential evolutionary advantage to our ancestors in terms of survival, the spread of innovation, and the development of culture. While the pleasure to be derived from hearing a good tale might have contributed to social bonding and even to the selection of a mate, no one has yet gone so far as to suggest the existence of a storytelling gene!

Another neuroscientific concept reinforces the significance of the emotional charge of stories and of our finely honed ability to sense emotion in others. It is the notion of the *triune brain*, originally formulated in the 1960s by Dr Paul MacLean.[7]

"How many brains do you have?" I sometimes ask people in order to make the point. Responses vary: "One"; "Several"; "No idea"; "One but we only use 10% of it"; "Two"; "Three."

"The answer," I say, "is three brains that work together as one. And by the way the 10% thing is a complete fallacy."

MacLean popularized the idea that the long process of evolution resulted in our inheriting a reptilian brain responsible for processing instinctual functions, which was supplemented as we evolved by the mammalian limbic system responsible for processing the emotional requirements of reproduction and nurturing, and completed by the cerebral neocortex dealing with language, abstraction, and planning.

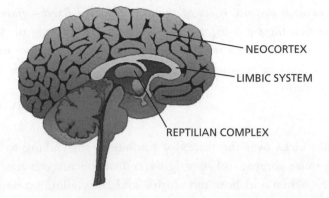

Although more recent research has revealed both greater integration of these elements of the human brain and a more complex evolutionary journey than MacLean suggested, his theory usefully highlights the extent to which our very survival depends on our capacity to read and project emotions. Mammalian offspring, humans in particular, are the most vulnerable and dependent in the natural world; to enable the parental and family bonding without which we would not survive infancy, our species has developed a unique capacity for what Daniel Goleman calls *emotional intelligence*.[8]

Leaders who neglect the importance of appealing to the feeling limbic system, as well as to the cerebral neocortex, will discover that although their audiences may nod in agreement, not much happens. Facts and figures might convince us but leave us unmoved. But a story told with "enough detail and feeling for the listener's imagination to experience it as real" can move hearts as well as minds. The science of storytelling tells us why this is the case; the story of storytelling will show us how.

Mythos: The story of storytelling

> *Great oral traditions produce great stories. Great storytellers keep these stories alive, make them real. And into the*

heart of such stories – the ones that survive through gen-erations – are worked the steps each of its tellers will follow. The details, the riches of the narration, vary. But a central drama, a set of themes, becomes fixed – fixed, because these are themes at the heart of being human. So the story becomes mythic, and the footsteps become the trail leading to and from the wonders and mysteries of the world.

HUGH BRODY[9]

This section kicks over the traces of traditional storytelling to see if we can catch some glimpses of its origins and of the place it has occupied in our lives. When and how did stories and storytelling come into your life? The chances are that you were first told or read stories as a child. I've often done the following short reflection in groups to bring these early experiences of storytelling to mind; sometimes, the stories we encounter in our early years shape our imaginations for the rest of our lives. It's good to do this exercise with a partner but you can also find a few quiet moments to do it on your own.

2. Reflection: Think back to your early childhood, to when you first became aware that there were stories. See if you can imaginatively connect with that time. Were stories told when you were a child? Or was there an absence of stories? What was your favorite story in your childhood? Who was your favorite character? How did the story come to you? Who told it to you?

Here are a few of the responses that this reflection has elicited over the years. Each quotation is from a different person. I wonder how they compare with your experience.

"I thought about going to stay with my great-aunt – who was like my granny because she brought my mum up – and she'd do things with me that she did with my mum like tie my hair in rags to make ringlets. And as she was doing that she'd tell me about my mum . . . stories about my mum when she was a child like me."

"My grandfather used to tell stories, like story-history. At first I thought it was real history and then I realized that they were lots of his stories. I remember him sitting down without his teeth in the middle of the night and wearing this great big nightshirt and launching into a story."

"The first stories that I remember were Marvel Comics. I think it was themes about saving the world and something about being heroic and good triumphing over evil. It was a lot about that stuff that really captured me. It took quite a long time for me to realize that the world isn't actually like that."

"I immediately thought of Enid Blyton's books, which I read avidly for years and years and years. The Secret Garden *by Francis Hodgson Burnett was probably my favourite story. And I loved Arthur Ransome's stories, especially* Swallows and Amazons *because I lived near where they are set in the Lake District. I used to absolutely lose myself in these books."*

I've done the exercise myself and here are my own recollections and reflections.

I spent a lot of my childhood on my own, away from my mother and sister, and I dived into books. I've got a book called Stuart Little *by E.B. White; it's the one thing I still have from my childhood. It's about a strange child, a mouse who is born to human parents. He falls in love with*

a bird, a beautiful bird called Margalo who flies away.
Most of the book is about his search for her. I love the last
few lines, "Stuart . . . climbed into his car and started up
the road that led towards the north . . . As he peered ahead
into the great land that stretched before him, the way
seemed long. But the sky was bright, and he somehow felt
he was headed in the right direction."

Looking back, I can see how the image of Stuart Little, heading north in his car, traveling with hope, searching for his love, sustained me as a child and continues to hold a certain truth for me now: life is still a journey and on the whole I feel that I'm traveling in the right direction. As Ben Okri says in the quotation at the head of this chapter: "There is not a single person who is not touched by the silent presence of stories."

These days there are many ways to narrate (or tell) a story: theater, dance, music, puppetry, mime, film, books, articles, blogs, emails, etc. The list is almost endless, but at the core of narrative leadership is face-to-face storytelling. Why? Because the more distant the act of narration, the less its impact. Think of the most engaging TED[10] talk you have ever watched on the Internet and imagine what it would have been like to have been in the audience when it was recorded. Sharing our stories on Facebook, Vimeo, or WordPress is a step up from the monthly newsletter, but there really is no substitute for direct oral communication.

In literate societies, the spoken word has largely been displaced by the written word. Few of us come from an unbroken tradition of oral storytelling but that is – incontrovertibly – where the roots of storytelling are to be found. Walter J. Ong in his classic study of the development of language and literacy explains the psychodynamics of the spoken word for our pre-literate ancestors (and indeed for us when we experience it):

> *Oral peoples commonly, and probably universally, con-*
> *sider words to have great power. Sound cannot be*
> *sounding without the use of power. A hunter can see*
> *a buffalo, smell, taste and touch a buffalo when the*
> *buffalo is completely inert, even dead, but if he hears a*
> *buffalo, he had better watch out: something is going on.*

In this sense, all sound, and especially oral utterance, which comes from inside living organisms, is "dynamic."[11]

Although similar in many ways, the experience of writing (and reading) a story differs from the experience of speaking (and listening to) a story because, in the former, the relationship between teller and audience is less immediate than in the latter. There can be no eye contact with the writer and no sense of his or her physical presence as one reads; the writer's words do not fall upon the ear but linger before the eye so they can be read and reread at will, whereas the words of the oral storyteller are ephemeral and must command our attention moment by moment.

Listening to someone speaking creates the possibility of a unique form of collective experience: we find ourselves coming into a relationship, not just with the speaker and what the speaker is saying, but also with each other. This is vitally important when as leaders we want to bring people together through our words. Oratorical skills and a good story help, of course, but simple words spoken authentically can also create tremendous impact. Ong explains how:

> *Because in its physical constitution as sound, the spoken word proceeds from the human interior and manifests human beings to one another as conscious interiors, as persons, the spoken word forms human beings into close-knit groups. When a speaker is addressing an audience, the members of the audience normally become a unity, with themselves and with the speaker.*[12]

Do not underestimate this power, which has been used and abused throughout history. Examples of both abound: Christ's Sermon on the Mount; Alexander the Great rallying his Macedonians before the decisive Battle of Gaugemela in 331 BCE; Martin Luther King telling an audience of 200,000 in front of the Lincoln Memorial that he had a dream; Adolf Hitler whipping up massed rallies to an anti-Semitic frenzy at Nuremberg. Public speaking, of which storytelling is an essential part, is intrinsically neither benign nor malign; it can be put to an almost infinite variety of uses. *Telling the Story* argues that no one seeking to exercise leadership can afford to ignore its capacity to move and inspire people.

Since most of us now derive our knowledge of oral storytelling from written sources, we must turn to them to learn more about its origins. The literature is vast but if we pick our way through it selectively, there are some key landmarks to be found on the trail back through time. The existence of a vibrant oral culture in Northern Europe as late as the mid-nineteenth century is revealed by collections of folktales such as those published by the Brothers Grimm in Germany, Asbjørnsen and Moe in Norway, and Alexander Afanasev in Russia. These stories were collected either directly or at one remove from oral sources – from country folk and servants of the well-to-do – though where and when the stories originated remains a mystery.

Although it would be naive of us to think of the stories collected during this golden age of European folkloric studies as somehow pure and unadulterated, we can still rely on their cumulative effect to get a strong sense of the folk cultures from which they were drawn. They reflect the ancient forested landscape of Northern Europe in which it was still easy to believe that the human and the more-than-human worlds conversed with each other; they are stories of common people and stories of kings, queens, and nobles seen through the eyes of the common people; they are stories of wee folk and giants, wizards and witches, hard times and good fortune, unlikely heroes and dastardly villains. They are tales of "Once upon a time" that still resonate in the psyches of contemporary men and women.

The contrasting courtly tradition of the bard and the troubadour takes us back to medieval times. For example, the Arthurian stories of the Mabinogion (based on fourteenth-century written sources) in Wales and the twelfth-century chivalric romances of Chrétien de Troyes in France are both widely believed to be based on much earlier oral stories and verses. Unlike folktales, these are stories of kings, queens, and nobles as seen through their own eyes (or perhaps as they would like to have been seen). They are tales of the heroic deeds of a ruling warrior class, largely divorced from the common people.

The same is true for the Icelandic sagas and for the eighth-century Old English epic *Beowulf* and even for the ancient Greek *Iliad* and *Odyssey*, attributed to the legendary poet Homer, and dating back as far as 800 years BCE. Scholars like Milman Parry[13] have shown how the language and structure of these long verse epics reflect the tropes, rhythms, and cadences of oral language. None of them, it seems, was the original literary product of a single creative mind. Rather, they represent crossovers between oral and written forms. In each case an author (or even several authors) of genius wrote down stories they were familiar with, stories that were originally told or sung by unknown bards.

Even restricting the search to evidence from the European tradition, we can trace the roots of storytelling back about 3,000 years. If we cast our nets a bit wider to include Asia and the Middle East, we can add at least another 1,000 years. The oldest known written story (based, it is believed, on a series of oral legends and poems about ancient Sumerian kings) is the epic of Gilgamesh; it too is a story of kings and heroes. Inscribed on 11 clay tablets and discovered in the ruins of Nineveh in 1853, it is believed to date back as far as 1700 BCE and its eponymous hero is thought to have been an actual ruler in Akkad around 2700 BCE.

But we should not assume, just because the surviving early written stories are heroic and courtly epics, that the common people were not also busy telling each other all manner of tales. Until relatively recently, writing was the preserve of the few; scribes, poets, and singers lived by the patronage of those rich enough to pay for their services. Naturally, they recorded the stories their patrons (often illiterate themselves) wanted to hear – stories about their own ruling warrior class. But everything we know about human nature suggests that folk of all kind have entertained and amused themselves throughout history with gossip, riddles and jokes, tales about their families and ancestors, fables about animals and the natural world, stories about their kings and queens, and creation myths of how things came to be.

These few pointers follow the trail of storytelling back 4,000 years in the history of humankind as far as the early Bronze Age, and there it runs cold. But our species' connection with story seems to be so profound that surely there must be something else, something that might explain the origins of story itself. I had the chance to explore this question more deeply when I met one of my great heroes, the radical anthropologist, linguist, and author, Hugh Brody – a man who has spent much of his life living and working alongside hunter-gatherer communities in the Arctic region and in southern Africa.

He explained that, in those communities, story is still the primary means of attributing significance and meaning to their experience of the world. Hunter-gatherers (the condition in which our species existed for

99% of its 2.5-million year history since the Early Stone Age) live in close and symbiotic relationship with their environment. To survive, they must learn to make sense of it in all its richness and complexity. Abstract logic and reason will not tell them at which waterhole, break in the ice, berry tree, or succulent plant their prey will appear on a particular day. Instead they rely on visions and dreams of what might happen and on stories of what they know to have happened before. Hugh told me that it was only with the arrival of agriculture in the Late Stone Age, which is reckoned to have begun about 9500 BCE, that humans developed the kind of analytical thinking needed to develop and exercise systems of control over their environment.

Today, we can access both forms of sense-making: story and logic. But while the capacity for logic is firmly imprinted in our minds, the need for story lies deep in our bones.

Bonus: *Atanarjuat, The Fast Runner*

We can get a glimpse of indigenous storytelling in an extraordinary Inuit film *Atanarjuat, The Fast Runner*, made at the turn of the millennium (and available on DVD). All those involved creatively in the making of the film – writer, director, and non-professional actors – were members of Inuit communities living in the High Arctic of northern Canada. In 2002, Hugh Brody wrote a review of the film for an online newsletter, *Open Democracy*,[14] in which he paints a wonderfully rich picture of the place of storytelling as it still is in hunter-gatherer societies and as it must have been since time immemorial:

> *Inuit watching Atanarjuat will not see a symbolic reality. They will see, rather, the enactment of an old story, a myth that has been passed down from generation to generation. Some of them – including the film's director Zacharias Kunuk – will have heard this story, or some version of it, as they lay in snow-houses or tents or houses built of sod and whalebone, with the glow of an oil lamp or candle the only light. Elders have told the story over and over to their children and grandchildren.*

And these elders are experts at storytelling, for their lives as hunters depend on the detail of stories. They know just the right word, use the perfect bit of hesitation, the exact imitation of the sound of a bird, or of the wind. They gesture in the shadows to evoke the movement of a seal or the thrust of a harpoon. They tell the story in their own way, to best effect. So that those who hear can do the same in their turn.

Great oral traditions produce great stories. Great storytellers keep these stories alive, make them real. And into the heart of such stories – the ones that survive through generations – are worked the steps each of its tellers will follow. The details, the riches of the narration, vary. But a central drama, a set of themes, becomes fixed – fixed, because these are themes at the heart of being human. So the story becomes mythic, and the footsteps become the trail leading to and from the wonders and mysteries of the world.

Summary

- Storytelling is a universal human phenomenon. The narrative form is deeply embedded in our lives and in our cultures – from traditional wonder tales to Hollywood epics. We are all touched by stories.
- We have two distinct and complementary ways of making sense of the world, which Jerome Bruner called the logico-rational/paradigmatic and the narrative modes. We can loosely equate these to the ancient Greek notions of logos and mythos.
- We have an in-built need to make sense of ourselves, our relationships, and our environment. As the Heider–Simmel experiment shows, we constantly create stories in order to attribute motivation and causality to events.
- Recent neuroscientific research by Vilayamur Ramachandra and others speculates about the key role of "mirror neurons" in our ability to

understand, learn from, and empathize with others. Is this how imagination works?

- Paul MacLean's earlier work on the triune brain emphasizes and gives an evolutionary rationale for the development of our emotional intelligence. Our limbic system is exquisitely attuned to our own and other's real feelings.
- Oral storytelling has particular power arising from the effect of hearing the spoken word. Walter Ong describes the physicality of all sound, especially "oral utterance." The shared interiority of listening to a speaker brings an audience into a unity.
- We can find written traces of oral storytelling as far back as the epic of Gilgamesh 4,000 years ago. It is highly probable that our Paleolithic forebears told stories just as surviving hunter-gatherer societies do today. We have stories in our bones!

Notes and References

1 Okri, B. (1998). *A Way of Being Free* (Phoenix: London, p109).
2 Bruner, J.M. (1986). *Actual Minds, Possible Worlds* (Harvard University Press: Cambridge, MA, p11).
3 Ibid., p13.
4 Ramachandran, V.S. (2012). *The Tell-Tale Brain: A Neuroscientist's Quest for What Makes Us Human* (WW Norton: New York).
5 Jonathan Gottschall has brought much of this material together in *The Storytelling Animal: How Stories Make Us Human* (2012) (Houghton Mifflin Harcourt: Boston, MA).
6 Ramachandran, V.S., op. cit.
7 MacLean, P.D. (1990). *The Triune Brain in Evolution* (Springer: New York).
8 Goleman, D. (1996). *Emotional Intelligence: Why it Can Matter More Than IQ* (Bantam Doubleday Dell: New York).
9 Brody, H. (2002). *Open Democracy*, http://www.opendemocracy.net/arts-Film/article_448.jsp, February 13.
10 TED talks are 10–15-minute video recordings of live presentations on a huge range of "ideas worth spreading" as it says on the home page of website www.ted.com.
11 Ong, W.J. (2002). *Orality and Literacy* (Routledge: London, p32).
12 Ibid., p73.
13 Parry, A. (ed.) (1988). *The Making of Homeric Verse: The Collected Papers of Milman Parry* (Oxford University Press: New York).
14 Brody, H., op. cit.

Chapter 4

The World of Stories

The universe is made of stories, not of atoms.

MURIEL RUKEYSER[1]

Muriel Rukeyser's poetic line begs an important question: surrounded by myriad different stories, what types of story should we tell as leaders? Over the years, many folklorists and writers have tried to categorize stories by origin, plot type, and genre. Personally, I'm less interested in trying to tame this wild proliferation of story than I am in finding a workable compass to help navigate the universe of stories in which we live.

From long experience, I've learned that we each have our own "home base" in the world of stories, particular types of story that we feel most comfortable telling and are therefore likely to be able to tell more confidently and authentically than others. This chapter will help you decide whether you are naturally a teller of *factual, fictional, or fantastical* stories and consider some key types of plot and what they have to offer to storytelling leaders.

Fact, fiction, and fantasy

Tell me the facts ma'am; just give me the facts.

APOCRYPHAL

It is ironic that this oft-repeated demand for the facts and nothing but the facts was made popular decades ago by a fictional character, Detective Sergeant Joe Friday of the Los Angeles Police Department, in the long-running US TV Series *Dragnet*. It is an objection that is sometimes raised to the whole idea of storytelling as a leadership practice. "Storytelling is just making things up," some people say. "We deal in facts and figures because they tell the truth."

My response when I hear this (and I've often heard it) is to invite my audience to engage in a live experiment to explore the gamut of fact, fiction, and fantasy in storytelling and then to decide for themselves how each of these three types of story can legitimately be used. I've done the exercise dozens of times with hundreds of leaders from all kinds of organizations with strikingly similar results. I've also found that when done in a group, it debunks the belief that "I can't tell a story." This is how the experiment goes; try it for yourself with a partner (or on your own) in response to the example stories below. The important thing is to speak the stories out loud and not just think about what they might be *if* you were to speak them.

In a group, I will ask people to stand in a circle and look around them to choose someone they are interested in. This is pretty much guaranteed to generate some nervous laughter, which is amplified when I tell them not to look at each other's faces for this purpose but a bit lower, and is followed by puzzled relief when I tell them to look at each other's shoes.

"Choose a pair of shoes that you are interested in," I say. "Catch the person's eye then go over to them and stand face to face, close enough for an intimate conversation. You are going to take it turns to tell each other the story of your shoes."

When the group has reformed into pairs, I invite them to introduce themselves if they don't already know each other, and then to listen as I tell them the story of my shoes as a prompt (listening to a story is the best way to allow one's own story to come to mind).

> *These are my shoes, I say (showing them to the audience).*
> *They are my lucky storytelling shoes; they are a bit unusual*
> *as you can see: the red laces are a little touch of my own.*
> *I was out shopping with my partner in Bath a year or two*
> *back. She wandered off for 10 minutes – she often does*

that – and when she came back to me she said, "I've found just the shoes for you, come and look." She dragged me protesting into the kind of shop that I don't normally go into and pointed at a small display of men's shoes tucked away in a corner.

I saw these very shoes and loved them at first sight. Then I saw the price: "I've never paid that much for a pair of shoes in my life," I said. "That," she replied, "is the problem. Never stint on shoes, your feet won't thank you." So I paid up and became the proud possessor of these stylish and comfortable, German-made shoes. Great, aren't they?

By this time, members of the group are ready to begin, taking it in turn to tell their own story and to listen (without interruption) to their partner.

1. Round One: Tell the story of your shoes: where they came from; whether or not you like them; anything else you would like to say about them. But do not embellish it or make things up. Take about a minute for your story.

In the hubbub that follows, people exchange straightforward factual stories about their shoes. Sometimes the stories are mundane ("I always buy Clarks because they are cheap and comfortable"), sometimes rather more exotic ("these purple pony-skin boots are my favorites; I wore them at a party last night and haven't been home"). Sometimes people cannot resist stretching the truth, but mostly they do their best to recollect the story of their shoes and tell it faithfully. "What did you learn about your partner?" I ask them. "Did you discover anything beyond the words they told you? What about my story? Although I didn't actually say so, you probably decided that I am rather vain and a bit of a cheapskate."

The point is this: when we tell a story – even a straightforward factual one – we always say more than we know we are saying. We reveal hidden aspects of ourselves to our audience. Showing our humanity may make us feel vulnerable but it is what makes us interesting, worth listening to, and (dare I say it?) a leader with whom others can empathize and connect.

So, how did you get on with your one-minute factual shoe story? Did you find it easy to tell? Did you enjoy telling it? How revealing of yourself were you? If you worked with a partner, what did you learn about him or her? Did you find that the constraint of keeping to the facts was comfortable or uncomfortable? In fact, how factual do you consider your story to have been? We'll come back to these questions later, but now it's time for the second round.

"Now choose another pair of shoes that you are interested in, catch the person's eye and stand face to face with your new partner, just like you did before. You are going to tell each other the story of your shoes, but this time I want you to exaggerate, to go beyond the boundaries of truth, make something up that could conceivably be true even though it's not. Just to get you started I'll tell you the *real* story of my shoes."

> *These shoes are indeed German and I did get them in Bath – though not quite how I told you before. These shoes are actually hand-made by the twin grandsons of Albert Schweitzer: Axel and Otto. You can't actually buy Schweitzer shoes in a shop; you have to be personally invited. If you achieve a certain standing in life then one day as you are walking in the street (as I was in Bath) your time will come; you will feel a discrete tap on the shoulder and hear the word Schweitzer whispered in your ear.*
>
> *That's exactly what happened to me. I was taken to a pop-up shop in a back alley where highly trained technicians took a full body cast and sent it off to Alex and Otto in their workshop high up in the Alps. Alex, who makes only left shoes, is a fast worker so two years later the left shoe was brought to my home by secret messenger. Unfortunately Otto works much more slowly, so it was another 18 months before the right shoe arrived. The waiting was agony and I had to remortgage my house to pay the bill. I won't tell you exactly how much they cost but I'm sure you'll agree they are worth every pfennig.*

Members of the group have now got a good idea what I'm asking them to do and invariably plunge in to telling their fictional stories.

The atmosphere becomes playful as members of the group vie with each other to invent fictional attributes and histories for their shoes ("I found these shoes hanging from a lamp-post at the end of my road"; "My Doc Martens are actually Oxford brogues in disguise"). There is often much laughter as people discover (or rediscover) the pleasure to be found in sharing the fruits of their imagination. "How was this different from the first round and how was it similar?" I ask them. "How do they relate to each other?"

The answers that come back reveal that the boundary between factual and fictional is easily blurred. The techniques applicable in telling the former translate easily to the latter. Even when the tellers are attempting to recall an experience accurately and tell it honestly, they have to draw on their imaginative capacity as well as their inevitably imperfect memory of the events in question. In this sense, fictional stories are imagined while factual stories are re-imagined from memory.

> 2. Round Two: Tell another story about your shoes. This time play with the boundaries of truth and fiction: exaggerate some feature of the factual story you told in the first round; invent something about your shoes and their origin; tell a story that could possibly have happened but did not. Take about a minute for your story.

What did you discover when telling your fictional story? How readily did you exaggerate and invent? What emotions did you experience: pleasure, embarrassment, guilt? How comfortable were you telling someone a story that you had made up? As a leader, under what circumstances might it be legitimate (or even necessary) to tell a fictional story? More of this soon. Time for the final round.

"Choose a third and final pair of shoes to talk to and stand face to face with your new partner. This time we're going to go beyond the bounds of what might have been and tell a story from that 'other place' – the magical world we all know from wonder tales and fairy stories – where anything is possible. I'll show you what I mean."

The first two stories I told you weren't quite right. But I am a storyteller and you deserve to hear how I really came by these shoes. Once upon a time (actually last August) my partner and I were returning home from a touring holiday in Spain on the Santander to Plymouth ferry. It's a huge ship; the buffet is gorgeous and the wine plentiful.

Well, I'm ashamed to say that I got rather drunk at dinner so afterward we went up on deck for some fresh air. After a while my partner went back in and I must have passed out because after she left I fell over the stern rail into the sea. Fortunately I missed the propeller but the churning waters dragged me down: once, twice, three times I went under. I was a goner; my life flashed before my eyes.

Suddenly a willowy shape with flowing hair and fishy tail swam into view. I called for help and reached out. Into my outstretched hands she thrust these shoes. "I'm drowning," I said. "What do I want with a pair of shoes, albeit ones as elegant and stylish as these?" "You misunderstand," she said. "These shoes have magic properties. Not only do they have unlimited buoyancy, they know their own way home. Hang on to them and they will take you there." She disappeared into the depths. I did the only thing I could and held on tightly to the shoes which did indeed save my life – just as the mermaid had said. An unlikely tale you may say, but the proof of it is that I am standing before you now safe and well, wearing those very same shoes.

With a multitude of fantastical images, the final round of storytelling begins with a chorus of "Once upon a time."

3. Round Three: Tell a third and final one-minute story about your shoes. This time I want you to explore the fantastical: the more-than-human world of magic where anything is possible. Give your shoes a mysterious origin and magical properties. Begin now "Once upon a time . . ."

Mild hysteria and much laughter usually accompany the stories. It can be difficult to make oneself heard above the din ("I told my boss these time-travelling shoes have a five-minute delay, which is why I'm always late for meetings"; "When I woke up the witch was gone but these four-inch stilettos were welded to my feet"). "What was it like?" I ask them. "What did it feel like to tell a fantastical story?"

As I anticipate, this generates a wide range of responses: "Easy." "More difficult." "It reminds me of being a child." "It reminds me of making up stories for my kids." "I enjoyed the freedom and the chance to play." "I loved it but I can't see how I could use this kind of story at work." The round of fantastical stories pushes people further and often brings out polarized comments: some find such tales easy and natural to tell while others prefer telling factual or fictional stories.

How did *you* get on in the final round? Are such stories part of your repertoire? Can you see how they might be used as allegories to engage an audience with their deeper meaning (well, perhaps not about your shoes)? The most useful thing to notice is in which of the three domains your home base is located. There are no rights and wrongs about this; it is just helpful to know so you can draw on that strength.

At this stage in the exercise, I often draw three overlapping circles on a flip chart for fact, fiction, and fantasy and take a straw poll of people in the group to locate their home bases. I haven't kept score religiously but the overall results from doing the exercise with several hundred leaders look something like this. About 50% prefer telling factual stories, 30% prefer telling fictional stories, and about 20% prefer telling fantastical stories. Where do you figure in this diagram?

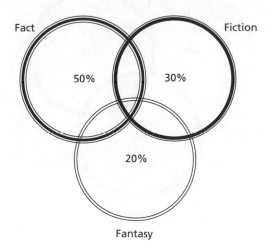

The exact proportions vary from group to group. I've found that a substantial majority of the senior civil servants I've done this with (as many as 75% in some groups) locate themselves firmly in the domain of factual stories. "We're civil servants," they say. "Of course we tell factual stories. That's our job." To which I reply: "Don't you ever talk about the future: where you are going; how you want things to be?" "Of course," they say. "We're leaders and leaders spend a lot of time talking about the future." And now I deliver the sucker punch: "Well, I've got news for you. The future hasn't happened yet. You're making it up. At best it's a fiction; at worst a fantasy. If you're going to paint a convincing picture of the future – one that people might actually buy into – then you need to imagine what it might be like and tell a good fictional story."

Another important phenomenon is revealed when I ask people to consider what kinds of story they most like to hear, read, or watch. Where is their home base located as consumers of stories? Is it to be found in the same domain as their preference for telling stories? Do they prefer biographies and autobiographies (fact), novels and whodunits (fiction), or sword and sorcery, Brothers Grimm and sci-fi (fantasy)? As story consumers, leaders have responded to these questions like this: about 25% prefer factual stories, 45% prefer fictional stories, and 30% prefer fantastical stories. What is your preference?

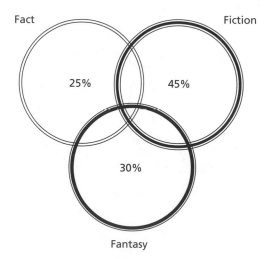

What can we learn from this? At the very least we can recognize that, in the midst of organizational life, there is a deep hunger for story of all kinds. As leaders, we cannot afford to ignore our basic human proclivity for stories and we can, perhaps, afford to be a bit more imaginative and daring in the types of story we tell, whether they be fact, fiction, or fantasy. Remember, as Mark Twain remarked:

> *Truth is stranger than Fiction, but it is because Fiction is obliged to stick to possibilities; Truth isn't.*[2]

Finding the plot

> *We have defined a story as a narrative of events arranged in their time-sequence. A plot is also a narrative of events, the emphasis falling on causality. "The king died, and then the queen died" is a story. "The king died, and then the queen died of grief" is a plot.*
>
> E.M. FORSTER[3]

Forster made this observation in 1927 in his collection of essays *Aspects of the Novel*. I beg to differ; for me a story does have a plot. Thus, I would say that "The king died, and then the queen died" is a mere chronicle, while "The king died, and then the queen died of grief" is a story. It is certainly true that any story worth its salt is more than a listing of events. Good stories have characters, drama, tension, motivation, action, conflict, and resolution. A good story well told – even a simple one – speaks to the human condition in ways that enable us to identify with it. Such a story offers a range of imaginative possibilities that engage our interest and concern.

If we accept that stories do have plots, then what kinds of plot do they have? A Canadian friend said to me in jest the other day, "There are only two kinds of story: either someone goes on a trip or a stranger comes to town." Of course, there is a bit more to it than that, but there is some wisdom at the heart of her remark. A story starts to get interesting when something happens to disturb the status quo and the possibility of something new and different arises.

Christopher Booker spent 34 years and 728 pages researching and writing his magnum opus[4] on why we tell stories and concluded (the title gives it away) that there are only seven basic plots which he characterized as: Overcoming the Monster, Rags to Riches, The Quest, Voyage & Return, Comedy, Tragedy, and Rebirth. Before him, Russian formalist scholar Vladimir Propp[5] analyzed all the Russian folktales he could find and declared that there were 8 character types and 31 story elements (plus variations) in different combinations and sequences that gave rise to all of them. Frankly, although both studies are of scholarly interest, they are not of much practical value to the modern-day storyteller or narrative leader.

There is, however, one way of looking at stories that has become widely known and highly influential, especially in the English-speaking world: Joseph Campbell's notion of the Hero's Journey[6], which – after a lifetime spent studying world mythology – he declared to be the "mono-myth," the essential pattern underlying all human adventures. The word adventure, incidentally, derives from the Latin word *advenire*, which basically means "stuff that happens." Campbell's ideas have been widely taken up by writers, storytellers, and screenwriters. George Lucas, for example, famously shaped his *Star Wars* trilogy on the Hero's Journey.

It is a useful and practical device for what we could call *leadership stories* though one that has become overused (perhaps because of our individualistic culture's fascination with the lone hero). We will explore it in more detail later in the book. For now, though, let me offer two caveats: first, we must not be too quick to make ourselves or our organizations the hero of our stories; second, heroic stories per se seem to be increasingly out of touch with our times, which are characterized more by a fall from grace than by a call to adventure. While the heroic protagonist triumphs through a combination of luck, magic, and courage, the post-heroic figure recovers what is most precious to him or her by exhibiting constancy, purpose, and fortitude. Post-heroic stories, reflecting the travails and trials of mid-life, may be more in tune with our current predicament than the youthful questing of the Hero's Journey.

When thinking about which of these two types of story is most fitting for you to tell, ask yourself where you are in your own journey through life and in what circumstances your organization finds itself. Starting out on the Hero's Journey might feel exactly right for a fresh new startup business (indeed I have helped to find such stories to publicize the work of young entrepreneurial university graduates) whereas leaders of established businesses undergoing crisis would do well to take a different tack.

For example, if leaders in the UK banking sector were to regard the recent widespread failure and disgrace of their industry as a well-deserved fall from grace, not merely as a temporary aberration or "blip," they might just begin to tell (and live) the kind of story that would regain public confidence and respect. At the time of writing, newly appointed Group CEO of Barclays Bank, Anthony Jenkins, has just announced a five-year program to transform the culture and values of the bank (his predecessor Bob Diamond having resigned over the LIBOR rate fixing scandal) from one focused on maximizing short-term profit to one that places customer service and colleague engagement on a level footing with shareholder satisfaction.[7]

Time will tell how well the Barclay's TRANSFORM program drives long-term sustainable change but it has the right "post-heroic" feel about it. As well as restructuring reward and bonus packages to reflect these desired behaviors, Jenkins and his team will need to find and share stories of the new culture in action to shift the way staff, customers, and the public perceive the bank. It is a massive leadership task, one important element of which is changing the story that the bank tells itself and the world about what it is, and living up to that new story.

When a heroic story *is* called for, it is often because we want to make someone else the hero. In the case of the entrepreneurial university graduates mentioned above, the object of the exercise was to show how the graduates themselves had established businesses and social enterprises through their own efforts (with the help and guidance of staff from various universities). The graduates, not the universities they had attended, were the real heroes of these stories. The message the universities wanted to convey was not "see how great we are" but "see how great we can help you become." In terms of the Hero's Journey, the universities positioned themselves appropriately as guides, helpers, and mentors in their students' stories. It is a subtle but important shift in perspective that placed the emphasis exactly where it needed to be.

Bonus: *Big Fish*

Director Tim Burton's 2003 film *Big Fish* tells the story of a man's life through the stories he told about himself. Albert Finney plays the old Edward Bloom and Ewan McGregor his younger self. Gliding back and forth through time, the dying Edward is reconciled with his estranged son Will (Billy Crudup) who gradually comes to understand that his father has become a character in the stories he tells.

The film begins with Will's voice over the opening scene:

> *In telling the story of my father's life it's impossible to separate fact from fiction, the man from the myth. The best I can do is to tell it the way he told me. It doesn't always make sense and most of it never happened. But that's what kind of story this is.*

And it ends with Will speaking again as the credits begin to roll:

> *That was my father's final joke I guess. The man tells his stories so many times that he becomes the stories. They live on after him. And in that way he becomes immortal.*

It is a wonderfully entertaining film that shows – in exaggerated form – how the stories of all our lives slide between fact, fiction, and fantasy. The stories we live and the stories we tell act upon each other to make us who we are.

Summary

- Given the enormous range of stories and story types available, a good starting point for deciding what stories we want to tell is to discover our "home base" in fact, fiction, or fantasy.
- Factual stories are about events that have actually happened. They are remembered or re-imagined from life and can be about yourself (autobiographical) or others (biographical).
- Fictional stories are about events that could possibly have happened or could possibly happen in the future. They are imagined, although

they may incorporate real-life details (most novels fall into this category).

- Fantastical stories go beyond what is humanly possible in the known world; they can be whimsical and amusing and they can sometimes offer powerful allegories for difficult truths (e.g., George Orwell's *Animal Farm*).
- Whatever our "home base" it is good to remember that there is a natural human hunger for stories of all kinds. People are probably more willing to listen to a leadership story than you think.
- Despite E.M. Forster's dictum, stories are much more than a chronicle of events; they have a wide variety of plots. Attempts to analyze plot types over the years are of scholarly interest rather than practical use.
- Two useful types of story to consider (whether fact, fiction, or fantasy) are the heroic (call to adventure) and post-heroic (fall from grace and renewal) quests. Consider carefully who should be hero of the stories you tell.

Notes and References

1 Rukeyser, M. (1971). *Speed of Darkness* (Vintage Books: London).
2 Twain, M. (1898). *Following the Equator* (American Publishing: Hartford, CT, Ch. XV).
3 Forster, E.M. (1927). *Aspects of the Novel* (Edward Arnold: London, p82).
4 Booker, C. (2004). *The Seven Basic Plots: Why We Tell Stories* (Continuum Books: London).
5 Propp, V. (1968 [1929]). *Morphology of the Folk Tale* (University of Texas Press: Austin, TX).
6 Campbell, J. (1972 [1949]). *The Hero With a Thousand Faces* (Princeton University Press: Princeton, NJ).
7 The *Guardian*, February 13, 2013.

Chapter 5

How Stories Work

If you tell me, it's an essay. If you show me, it's a story.
BARBARA GREENE[1]

The first time I heard a professional storyteller, as I described in the introduction to this book, I was entranced by the story that he told about the Banyan Deer. Within a few moments, I found myself inside the world of the story, moved by the plight of the characters and able to imagine scene after scene in graphic detail. I shared such an immediate and deep sense of connection with the story, the teller, and my fellow members of the audience that as soon as it finished I wanted to know how the story had caught me so profoundly. "How do stories work in this way?" I asked myself. "What is going on when a story is going on?"

A decade and a half of storytelling later and I have got some solid answers to these questions. It turns out that there are some clearly identifiable constituents of memorable stories and some key elements of engaging storytelling that can be learned by almost anyone willing to invest some time and effort. One of these secrets is embedded in the cryptic quotation under the chapter heading, from Barbara Greene, a writer of children's stories: to really engage our audience we must learn how to tell stories in ways that shift from *telling* them about the story to *showing* them (through our words and gestures) what happened in the story.

In my experience of coaching leaders to tell impactful stories, I have discovered that understanding and internalizing this crucial distinction is *the* single most important factor in becoming a good storyteller. For hundreds of the people I have worked with, this is when the penny drops; this is when they realize just how powerful stories can be and they see for the first time that the storytelling dynamics they have to master are within their grasp. If this chapter does its job then it will help you make this shift too.

In workshops, I like to explore the move from telling to showing by doing a two-part exercise that I created when someone asked me to show them the difference between a story and something that was not a story. You can try this on your own but it is better to do it with a partner because it is designed to distinguish the effects on the listener of communicating about the same subject in two quite different ways. The subject is train journeys – chosen because just about everyone has traveled by train at least once in their lives.

1. Part One: In the first exchange, you are going to have about two minutes simply to tell another person a list of all the reasons you can think of why it is a good thing to travel by train. Start now . . .

One person in each pair begins to give their list. They usually start with gusto but their energy quickly wanes and by the time two minutes is up some complain that they are losing the will to live. Here is my list, which is fairly typical of those offered:

* for one person it's often cheaper to go by train than drive;
* trains are much more reliable than they used to be;
* you can work, sleep, read, relax, and eat on a train;
* sometimes you meet people and fall into good conversations;
* you can charge up your cell/mobile phone or computer;
* train travel is more sociable than driving if you're in a group;
* you should go by train because it's better for the environment;
* we've got this entire expensive infrastructure, so why not use it?
* you can actually see the scenery out of a train window;
* it avoids having to drive and park in London;
* you can get a decent breakfast and even dinner on some trains;
* traveling by sleeper train is very romantic;

- trains are essential to get around if you don't drive;
- airport security is hideous so avoid it when you can;
- train travel is very safe.

How does my list compare to yours? If you did the exercise, how well did your energy and interest hold up as speaker and as listener? I generally find that even though I believe the reasons I give are both true and important, they do not really fire me up. The effect on most people is quite similar: interesting (at best) but not very exciting. But before analyzing it further, let's do the second part of the exercise and experience a very different type of communication.

2. Part Two: Think about the many times you have traveled by train and recall a particular journey that stands out as having been especially enjoyable. If that proves impossible, choose one that was memorably awful. Now take 2–3 minutes in turns to tell the story of that journey to your partner who will simply listen to you speak. Begin . . .

Let yourself go back in your own imagination to the particular train journey you are going to tell a story about, relive it as best as you can in your mind's eye, and share that memory with your listener. Your job as teller is to take your listener along with you on the journey as you relive it. Here, as an example, is the story of a memorable train journey that I sometimes tell:

> *In late August 2005, when the French Motorail was still running, my partner Chris and I drove our brand-new Morgan to Calais (via the Channel Tunnel). We arrived in France at about 5.00 p.m. to begin our holiday. That gave us about two hours to kill before putting the car on the train to Narbonne which is right down on the French Riviera. Perfect timing: we managed to locate a Carrefour and stocked up for the trip – a bottle of St Emilion, a crusty warm baguette, Bleu d'Auvergne, Saucisse de Morteau, peaches, and a couple of bottles of water. In the marshaling yard, I nervously handed the car keys to the valet and*

winced as I watched him rev up and zoom our very low-wheelbase car up some extremely steep ramps onto the rail truck along with half-a-dozen other cars. Abandoning Moggie to its fate, we found our couchette and, as the train pulled out of the yard, spread our picnic on the bottom bunk and tucked in. I remember Chris grinning at me with peach juice running down her chin: "Start as we mean to carry on," she said, and emptied the wine bottle.

By the time we were south of Orleans it was getting dark so we climbed into the bunks. Chris took the top one and I stayed down below. It was a warm evening so we opened the carriage window and we both dropped off to sleep quite quickly. It's about 1,000 kilometers from Calais to Narbonne and the train rattled along all night. It stopped several times (to drop off mailbags, I think) and each time I surfaced from sleep to the sound of workers on the platform calling to each other – in French, of course – and the clank and bang of couplings as the train jolted back into motion. We both woke up as it was getting light; Chris dropped her arm down from the top bunk and I reached up so we could hold hands. We arrived at Narbonne at about 7.30 a.m., washed in the tiny bathroom at the end of the corridor, then had breakfast in the station café as we waited for our car to be brought to us.

It was already very hot in the direct sunlight and I lent my hat to an immensely old man waiting with his equally ancient wife for their vintage Rolls-Royce to be unloaded from the train. "We do this every year," he said. "Good for you," I said, wondering how many more years they would be able to manage. Then the Morgan pulled up. The valet handed me the keys. I retrieved my hat, we said goodbye to the old couple, started up the car, and set off towards the coast. "I hope we're still doing this when we're their age," said Chris.

In a room full of people telling each other stories like this, the atmosphere quickly becomes noticeably intimate. Tellers and listeners lean toward each other; voices soften and take on a more musical quality; faces light up and hands gesture freely; often there is laughter and sometimes a few tears are shed. Something curious is happening as these simple personal stories are told, something that reveals the essential secret of how stories work.

The exercise lets us explore the graphic differences between the effects on both listeners and tellers of non-storied communication and of storytelling. In a group, I will ask people to tell me what they noticed about each of the two experiences and list their responses. I wonder how similar your observations are to the following comments which they typically make about the list of reasons why it is a good thing to travel by train:

> *Fragmented, disjointed*
>
> *Difficult to follow*
>
> *I didn't agree with all of the points*
>
> *Boring, I drifted off*
>
> *Some important information*
>
> *I wanted to know more*
>
> *It was hard not to tell stories*
>
> *It sounded good at the time*
>
> *I don't think I'll be able to remember them.*

What would you say about the experience of telling or listening to stories of particular train journeys (or perhaps of reading my story if you were not able to try the exercise for yourself)? Typical comments that people at workshops make about this experience include:

> *It had a good rhythm; I felt it was going somewhere.*
>
> *Very engaging, I could see the whole thing as if I had been there too.*

It made me think of train journeys that I (the listener) have made.

I enjoyed telling it; it made me feel good to remember that time.

I loved hearing about the people and the scenery in India.

It was very funny; she told it very well and it made me laugh.

There was a sense of anticipation and drama: would she be all right?

It made me want to travel by train more often!

It is a short distance from these and other similar reflections to Bruner's two modes of thought (the logico-rational mind and the storied mind) that we explored in some detail in Chapter 3. So, let's use the exercise to dig a bit deeper into the differences between telling and showing.

Information, argument, and story

> *A good story and a well-formed argument are different natural kinds. Both can be used as means for convincing another. Yet what they convince of is fundamentally different: arguments convince one of their truth, stories of their lifelikeness.*
>
> JEROME BRUNER[2]

The first part of the train exercise prompts people to provide a combination of information and argument in an attempt to convince their listeners that it is a good thing to travel by train. We use our logico-rational minds to inform (give the facts) and persuade (explain the reasons to) our listeners. And as listeners we receive information and argument with the same part of the mind.

We want to know the facts but we are going to use our critical judgment to check that they are accurate and relevant. The numbers have to add up before we will give them credence. We want to make sure we understand the reasons we are being given and they too will undergo inspection by our critical faculties before we will say "Yes. No. Maybe." The argument has to make sense.

This is familiar territory for most of us: the everyday stuff of business communication, the kind of thing that the techniques taught on any standard MBA course will equip us to do to a high level. So what can stories do that is so very different? Our storied minds (as evidenced by the comments in the previous section) enable us to do two things especially well. By evoking a particular experience in the form of a story, we can create memorable images that stir the listener's own imagination. At the same time, by allowing ourselves to be emotionally engaged with the experience about which we are telling the story, we can engage the listener's own feelings.

In the absence of feelings and imagination, the best we can achieve is a kind of intellectual assent to our proposition based on information and argument. When the proposition is routine and the stakes are low, that might be enough. But when the stakes are high and the proposition is demanding, a logico-rational cocktail of information and argument is unlikely to suffice. Have you ever been in the audience listening to a corporate "change management roadshow" as slide after slide packed full of data, graphs, and diagrams is flashed onto the screen to make the case for change and to show the shape of a bright new tomorrow? Have you ever been harangued by an incoming chief executive exhorting you to espouse yet another set of organizational values? If so, did it "do it for you?" I doubt it.

Maybe, like me, you've been on the other side of the fence, explaining why change is necessary, talking face to face at a "town hall" meeting or giving it your all from the roadshow podium? You gaze back at your audience and you can see that they just don't get it; the statistics are impeccable and the argument is irrefutable but they still don't get it. The temptation is to pile on more information (so they'll know) and to bolster the argument (so they'll understand) but it's a temptation to be resisted because that is exactly the point at which a story might be needed.

Commonly, the reason they don't get it (assuming that the numbers do add up and the argument does make sense) is that they (whoever "they" are) haven't been given any help to imagine what the proposed change might be like in practice or any opportunity to feel what it's like to imagine themselves as part of that future. Of course, the story has to hang together but if it's a good enough story and well enough told then it can help to create a genuine sense of inclusion and engagement with an organization's destiny. Let me give you a personal example to show you what I mean.

> *About 15 years ago, when I had only just encountered storytelling, I was involved with a multi-million-pound public service training organization (let's call it NTO). It had an excellent international reputation but was regarded by many in its home market as behind the times and as slow to respond to new developments. The various informal groups and formal steering committees set up to guide its programs rarely agreed about what was needed but continued to complain vociferously about what was being provided. For some months, I supported the Chief Executive as he tried to persuade staff at NTO's many locations to be a bit more innovative and risk-taking. With my help, he gave them the facts and figures and explained why change was necessary.*
>
> *People nodded but nothing changed so I went away for a couple of days with the Chief Executive and the Senior Management Team and we scratched our heads. "I think we need to show them what the future might be like," I suggested, wondering if what I was learning about story-telling could help. "I think we need to show them what might happen if we don't change and what might be possible if we do."*
>
> *"And how do you propose we do that?" said the Chief Executive.*
>
> *"I'm not sure exactly," I replied. "But I think we need to imagine the possibilities for ourselves first so we can paint a really concrete and convincing picture."*
>
> *We had all seen the lack of impact of our efforts to galvanize change and my suggestion was accepted. We spent the next day and a half imagining how all aspects of the*

organization might look in the future in terms of structure, funding, programs, research, resources, reputation, etc. The various possibilities clustered into two distinct scenarios: NTO as Market Follower (delivering a range of programs and products shaped by current customer and stakeholder demand) and NTO as Market Leader (using our expertise to develop programs and products that anticipated customer and stakeholder needs). I then took on the task of writing these up as two fictional future stories set five years ahead.

After a bit of practice, the Chief Executive and Senior Management Team took these two stories out on an organization-wide roadshow. "There are two futures for NTO," the Chief Executive would say and tell both stories. "It depends on all of us. What do you want to see happen?" With these two stories as catalysts for discussion, most people said quite heatedly that they wanted to see some variant of NTO as Market Leader. This was just what the Chief Executive had been waiting for: "OK, so what can we all do now to make sure that's what happens?"

I won't pretend that everything changed on the spot, but a dialogue had begun from which novel ideas and practical actions soon flowed. We had witnessed the limitations of information and argument to engage people and between us – with a bit of beginner's luck – we had stumbled upon the power of storytelling to unlock the imagination and energy of an organization (even one as innately conservative as NTO). The point is not that information and argument are unimportant. They are very important but, surprisingly often, they are simply not enough to move people to action.

With all this in mind, we can see that Annette Simmons' definition of a story (quoted in Chapter 1) contains two key words that tell us exactly what we have to do as storytellers to stir our listeners:

[A story is] . . . an imagined (or re-imagined) experience narrated with enough detail and feeling to cause your listener's imagination to experience it as real.

It is the particular details of a story that help to create memorable images in the minds of our listeners. Our imaginations work best when they are given something to latch on to – rather like the way (if you remember the experiment in your school chemistry lessons) that a super-saturated solution of salts will continue to sit in its beaker as a viscous soupy liquid until a single grain of sand is dropped in, when it instanta-neously crystallizes. That is what happens when we drop some details into our stories: they help to form crystal-clear images in our listeners' minds. Let me show you what I mean:

> *A few years ago I was coaching the Director General of a large Government Department to tell a story about an early leadership experience and he started to tell me about when – at the age of 14 – he had taken charge of his school library. "Tell me about the library," I said.*
>
> *"Old," he said. "Tall. Bookshelves covered the walls."*
>
> *"OK, I'm getting the general picture," I said. "Now give me a detail that will bring me into the room alongside you and let me see it though your eyes."*
>
> *His breathing slowed as he paused and thought for a moment. Then he turned back to me and said: "All of the bookshelves above the fourth row were covered in dust."*

Immediately, I could see the library in my imagination. Not just any library, but that particular library. He had remembered (re-imagined) the scene for himself and selected a detail that – for whatever reason – had significance for him. Because it was significant for him (had caught his inner eye even if he did not quite know why) he unconsciously spoke about it in a way that made it significant for me as the listener. Something subtle in his tone of voice and gesture enabled me to imagine myself inside his story.

This is just how it works: if the tellers do the imaginal (detail) and emotional (feeling) work of connecting deeply with the story, they will tell it and embody it differently. Because they are experiencing the story as real themselves, they can access and share the detail and feeling that will "cause the listener's imagination to experience as real." Notice that the storyteller's feelings are conveyed not merely by *telling* the listener what you feel ("I loved it; I was scared; I felt proud; I'm excited") but by connecting so deeply with the recollected or imagined scene that the particular details you share and your unconscious demeanor *show* the listener your feelings as you tell the story.

Once we grasp that it is the very particularity of stories that enables them to have general appeal, we are close to understanding how they work. They do not ask us to believe them, they ask us to believe *in* them – in the truths they contain – even when the stories themselves are not strictly true. Rather than telling us how the world works, they offer us glimpses of "narrative truth," which is close to what Aristotle called *phronesis*, that is:

> *[A] form of practical wisdom capable of respecting the singularity of situations as well as the nascent universality of values aimed at by human actions.*[3]

A good story lets us see ourselves reflected in the plight of its protagonists even if the actual circumstances they face are entirely outside our experience. Whereas information and argument both ask us to agree with them, stories make no such demand. Instead, they offer us vicarious experiences that invite our sympathy and understanding. That – in a nutshell – is the secret power of stories and why *Telling the Story* is the heart and soul of successful leadership.

Bonus: *An Inconvenient Truth*

Take a couple of hours to watch a master communicator at work: Al Gore's documentary *An Inconvenient Truth* (2006) interweaves information, argument, and stories together so brilliantly that it won him an Oscar, a Grammy, and a Nobel Peace Prize. If you have already seen it, then watch it again as an object lesson in getting a difficult message across. For example, mid-way in the film, having already presented a wealth of information and trends about global warming, he wants to make the point that we can change our behavior even though it may take time to acknowledge cause and effect. The camera cuts to a shot of Al Gore revisiting the family farm where he grew up and he tells the story of how his own father stopped growing tobacco:

> I don't remember a time when I was a kid when the summertime didn't mean working with tobacco . . . I used to love it. It was during that period when working with the guys on the farm seemed like fun to me.
>
> Starting in 1964 with the Surgeon General's Report, the evidence was laid out on the connection between smoking cigarettes and lung cancer . . . We kept growing tobacco.
>
> Nancy [my sister] was 10 years older than me and there were only the two of us. She was my protector and my friend at the same time. She started smoking when she was a teenager and she never stopped. She died of lung cancer. That's one of the ways you don't want to die. The idea that we had been part of that economic pattern that produced the cigarettes that produced the cancer was so . . . it was so painful on so many levels. My father – he had grown tobacco all his life – he stopped. Whatever explanation had seemed to make sense in the past just didn't cut it anymore and he stopped.
>
> It's just human nature to take time to connect the dots. I know that. But I also know that there can be a day of reckoning when you wish you had connected the dots more quickly.

As leaders, there many occasions when we need to use a story to stir the imagination and engage the feelings of our audience as well as giving them the necessary information and providing a clear rationale for what we are proposing. Combine all three to make your case convincing and engaging.

Summary

- The shift from *telling* people about a story to *showing* them what happened in the story (through words and gestures) is a key turning point in becoming a good storyteller.
- The train exercise demonstrates the imaginal and emotional impact of a story on the listener, compared to our rational response to non-storied communication in the form of information and argument.
- The logico-rational mind exercises critical judgment to establish the truth of something, while the storied mind is more intuitive and relational and is concerned with verisimilitude: realness or closeness to life.
- Communicating necessary information is important (the numbers have to add up). We process information by asking ourselves: is it relevant, accurate, up to date, sufficient, credible, etc.?
- Argument attempts to persuade by force of reason (the rationale has to make sense). We also process argument critically, testing each link in the chain to make sure that propositions are sound.
- Stories "land" differently and we judge them by different criteria (the story has to hang together). Ultimately we judge stories not by whether we believe them to be true, but by what they cause us to imagine and feel.
- The details and feelings in a story that are necessary to cause the listener's imagination to experience it as real arise when the storyteller him- or herself connects deeply enough with the recollected or imagined scene.

Notes and References

1 Attributed to children's author Barbara Greene.
2 Bruner, J. (1986). *Actual Minds, Possible Worlds* (Harvard University Press: Cambridge, MA, p11).
3 Kearney, R. (2002). *On Stories* (Routledge: London, p143).

Section Three

Narrative Leadership

Chapter 6

The Art of Narrative Leadership

There is nothing so practical as a good theory.

KURT LEWIN[1]

At first glance, Lewin's famous dictum could be taken for the throwaway remark of a detached academic refusing to dirty his hands with the messy business of life outside the laboratory or lecture hall. But Lewin (a social psychologist and the "godfather" of action research) was actually saying that good theory emerges from the study of what happens when we roll up our sleeves and try to change something. He was also saying that the primary test of a theory's value is determined by what happens when we try to put it into action. In this and subsequent chapters we will explore what narrative leadership looks like in action and what it takes to do it well.

So far, we have identified the limitations of regarding leadership solely as taking charge and making things happen; proposed that thinking of leading as participating in an ongoing process of meaning-making opens up new and creative possibilities for effective action; and explored the immense power of stories and storytelling to stir our imaginations and engage our emotions.

The case for narrative leadership (the conscious use of stories and storytelling to make meaning with and for other people) has been implicit in previous chapters. If leading is about meaning-making, goes the argument in Chapter 1, and telling stories is the primary way in which we give significance to and make sense of our experience, then it is not possible to reach our full potential as leaders (or indeed as human beings) without understanding how stories work and using them effectively.

A more explicit and pragmatic rationale is to be found in the manifesto of the Centre for Narrative Leadership,[2] which I co-founded with Sue Hollingsworth and Margaret Bishop in 2007:

> *On the surface, the rationale for developing the capacity for narrative leadership in organizations is quite straightforward. If, as leaders, managers or change agents we want to get our point of view across effectively, engage people's energy and commitment, inspire others and open their minds to new possibilities, we need to be able to tell a convincing story. As leaders we have to earn the right to ask for people's commitment by standing up and speaking out for what we believe in. Narrative leadership demands authentic stories told with skill, integrity and vulnerability. It also requires us to develop a deeper understanding of how stories work – to learn to see more clearly the sea of stories in which we swim.*

But that is not all there is to narrative leadership: our times demand a more critical stance toward both leadership and narrative. Narrative leadership will not make us good leaders although it may help us to lead; what we stand for – our values and the purpose of our leadership – is profoundly important. The manifesto goes on to say:

> *There is also a deeper rationale for working with narrative leadership. We live in a world bombarded by oppressive narratives, subliminal images, disguised messages, and political slogans. It is crucial for our future – especially at this time of urgent environmental, social and ecological challenges – that we develop skill and discernment in telling and listening to leadership narratives. We must learn how to differentiate between narratives that are self-interested and self-serving (and thereby diminishing of*

others) and those that come from a place of greater mutu-
ality and genuine engagement (and thereby potentially
life enhancing).

Chapter 1 claimed that stories matter because they shape who we are, how we relate to others, and how we make sense of the world. I asserted that stories are:

1. the primary way we make sense of our experience, giving meaning and significance to our lives and creating (and re-creating) our sense of self;
2. a vital means of building relationships, bringing groups and communities together (discounting others' stories can cause conflict and divisions);
3. a powerful force in the world, acting on our imaginations to shape, extend, and constrain our sense of what is desirable and possible.

We then explored these propositions for ourselves through some reflective exercises. They are the foundations upon which the art of narrative leadership is built and now we need to look at their practical implications. Assuming that we can rely on these foundations, what are we supposed to do about them? In short, so what?

I learned long ago that to develop real competence in any field of practice you need to have viable and congruent models of the phenomenon itself, of what causes it to change, and of the practices that enable and influence that change. Jumping straight from proposition to practice misses out a crucial step: without a clear understanding of *how* something changes we are merely guessing *what* we need to do to bring about change. If, for example, we do not understand how bowing and fingering techniques affect a violin's tonal qualities, we might as well counsel a budding violinist to improve his or her virtuosity by standing on one leg in a bucket of water.

Each of the foundational propositions of narrative leadership has an associated "theory of change" from which its practices emerge and it is important to state them clearly and explicitly:

1. Our sense of identity – who we are – changes when we change the stories we tell ourselves about ourselves.

2. Organizations, groups, and communities change when the stories, and storytelling dynamics (i.e., the processes by which stories are told and made sense of) between people, change.
3. Our view and experience of the world change as we question the prevailing meta-narratives and imagine new possibilities.

From these come three interrelated practices that together constitute the essence of the art of narrative leadership. We will focus on each of them in detail in succeeding chapters but for now, here is the overview:

1. Knowing one's life stories without being their prisoner – letting go of degenerative and dysfunctional stories and finding positive ones.
2. Building relationships and communities by creating and sustaining a healthy flow of stories between diverse people and groups.
3. Developing and telling authentic, compelling leadership stories that are grounded in reality and that help people connect with worthwhile purposes.

For the sake of brevity and memorability, we will give names to each of these three sets of practices. Let us call the first (after the inscription over the entrance to the ancient Delphic Oracle) *Know Thyself*; the second (plagiarizing E.M. Forster) *Only connect*; and the third (from the saying "If you stand for nothing, you'll fall for anything") *Stand for Something*.

It is tempting to think that if we just learn the techniques of storytelling we will be able to tell a compelling leadership story when we need one. But the three practices are intimately and inextricably connected. Unless we know who we are and what matters to us we cannot authentically stand for anything; unless we open ourselves to other people's stories we cannot expect them to be open to ours; unless we are willing to commit ourselves to something that is grounded in reality and helps people connect with worthwhile purposes we are merely peddling dreams or – worse – trying to manipulate others for our advantage.

The metaphor of a tree expresses the relationships between the three elements of narrative leadership in a lively and dynamic way: the roots of the tree represent the practice of Know Thyself; the branches and leaf canopy correspond to Only Connect; the trunk symbolizes Stand for Something. A tree draws sustenance from deep roots which anchor it firmly and enable it to grow; the stronger the root system, the greater its potential to support and feed a substantial trunk and an extensive canopy of interconnected branches, twigs, and leaves (through which it can absorb and convert light into chemical energy). A healthy tree is able to make the most of the resources and opportunities in its environment, contributing to the ecosystem as well as benefiting from it.

Like a tree, our leadership practice grows organically. As we come to know ourselves better, our roots deepen and we tap the source of our sense of purpose and vocation; as we reach out and connect with other people, we better understand what the world is calling for; nourished by a sure sense of who we are and what is needed, we can find the courage and determination to stand for what really matters. We flourish and grow as leaders by attending not just to one or two, but to all three practices together.

What is the alternative? Trees and people topple in the wind if they have weak roots; they wither if they do not put out branches and leaves; they remain stunted if they do not develop strong trunks. Know Thyself; Only Connect; Stand for Something.

Enough of models and metaphors you may be thinking. What does narrative leadership look like in real life; how can I imagine it for myself? Well, if you've read this far you'll have a shrewd idea that what we need now is a story to bring it alive. So here's a story that I've often told to leaders to illustrate the power of narrative leadership in action.

1. Story Reading/Listening: Read the story (or, better still, get someone to read or tell it to you). Let the story wash over you. You do not have to make any effort to understand or remember it. Allow time for your imagination to experience the images and for you to register the feelings that arise. Reread it or listen to it again if the story touches you.

Vinoba Bhave

On 30 January 1948, just months after India gained its independence, its great spiritual and political leader Mohandas K. Gandhi was assassinated, gunned down by a Hindu nationalist, Nathuram Godse. His death was mourned by millions who had never known him personally, and those who had known him were traumatized. Gandhi's intimates and members of his party retreated to their homes paralyzed by shock and grief.

After a few months, some of the most senior party members realized that for the sake of India something had to be done to re-galvanize Gandhi's followers. A small delegation went to the home of Vinoba Bhave who had been Gandhi's closest political associate. Bhave lived on a small ashram, following the master's precepts, growing the food he ate, spinning and weaving cotton for the simple dhotis he wore.

"Vinoba," said the leader of the delegation. "We have come to ask you to step into Gandhiji's shoes and lead our party."

Bhave was horrified: "No one, least of all me, could fill those shoes. It is not for me to lead you."

"Vinoba, you were close to Gandhiji and everyone respects you. We have canvassed opinion and it is clear that you are the only person who can lead us. Please reconsider."

No matter how much they pleaded and cajoled, he would not budge. In the end, seeing that they would not leave without some concession, Bhave agreed that he would go to Delhi and speak to a conference – a gathering of the party faithful – though he would not preside. "I'll go on one condition," he said. "You must delay the conference for six months because that is how long it will take me to walk to Delhi from here."

It was agreed; the delegation left and Bhave made preparations for his departure. He was well -known in his day and as he walked the hot dusty tracks and roads, he was joined by an ever-changing crowd of friends and well-wishers. Bicycles rattled by; bullock carts lumbered past; once in a blue moon a truck revved its engine and nudged through the crowd.

As Bhave passed from village to village he saw much poverty. He'd expected that, of course. But one day as he came close to a particular village he was shocked to see that some of its inhabitants were plump and prosperous whilst others were gaunt and hollow-cheeked with hunger. "What is the matter?" He asked them.

"We have no jobs and no money to buy food. We are starving," they said.

"Then why don't you grow your own food?" Bhave asked, gesturing at the fields, lush with grain and vegetables, at either side of the road.

"We are not permitted to own land. We are Dalits – untouchables."

That evening a crowd assembled in the village. It happened wherever he went, a combination of a political and spiritual meeting with a party to celebrate the great man's visit. After the usual pleasantries, Bhave told the crowd what he had seen and been told by the Dalits. "This division between the landed and the landless is wicked," he said. "I know Prime Minister Nehru. When I get to Delhi, I will speak to him. I will ask him to pass a law making it possible for these 'untouchable' people – who are your neighbours and mine – to own land." The villagers, even the most prosperous amongst them, agreed that this was just and proper. That night, after the party which went on longer than usual, everyone retired to bed and slept, well-pleased with Bhave's plan.

Everyone except Bhave, who tossed and turned all night long. The next morning, instead of setting off straightaway, he called the villagers back to their meeting. "I've been thinking," he said. "It's true that I know Prime Minister Nehru; it's true that I might be able to persuade him to change the law. But, my friends, it would take several years and it's also true – though sad to say – that even if a law were passed giving land to the Dalits, by the time the grants had made their way down from the capital to the regions, to the provinces, and to the districts and the villages, there would be precious little left for those who need it most. I wish I knew what to do."

It was then, as Bhave stood in silence, that a man at the back of the crowd spoke up: "I am one of the fortunate ones. I own a lot of land. I could spare some. How much do they need?"

It turned out that 16 Dalit families lived near that village. It took 5 acres support a family so 80 acres were needed.

"I will give them 80 acres," said the prosperous farmer.

"That is most generous," said Bhave. "But you should ask your wife and family first, it is their land too."

The farmer asked his family's permission. They agreed and the 80 acres were handed over to their Dalit neighbours then and there. The meeting broke up and Bhave continued on his way.

The next time Bhave came to a village where the landless untouchables suffered in the same way, he simply told the story of what had happened in the first village: 110 acres were given to 22 Dalit families. By the time he reached Delhi, he had told the story many times and 2,200 acres of land had been handed over. At the party conference, Bhave's sole act of leadership was to tell the story of his journey.

Bhave and hundreds of Gandhi's followers, inspired by what they had heard, went out from the conference and walked the length and breadth of India, repeating the story. In the next 14 years, those to whom they told it gave over 10,000,000 acres of land to the Dalits, without a single law being passed, without any red tape or bureaucracy.

Today this event is known as the Great Indian Land Reform Movement, one of the largest peaceful transfers of land in history. It began with a great man who had the humility to admit that he did not know what to do and the wisdom to tell the story of what happened when someone else – whose name is lost to us – stepped forward with an open heart.[3]

> 2. Reflection: Having either read or heard the story, take a few moments
> to jot down what stands out for you. What are your thoughts about
> Vinoba Bhave's leadership? In what ways are each of the three practices
> of narrative leadership (Know Thyself, Only Connect, Stand for Some-
> thing) manifested by Bhave?

I love this story about the power of story to change the world. It's a
story from life, about real people and real events, though it's also fictional
in the sense that it attempts to re-imagine what was inevitably a more
complex series of events, the actual details of which have become blurred
by time. It's a story, not a history, and it's in the nature of stories to focus
on iconic moments to convey the essence of something rather than foren-
sically to explore the limits of what we do and don't know about it. With
that caveat, I think that the story of Vinoba Bhave offers us a wonderful
object lesson in narrative leadership.

Several moments stand out for me when I tell the story: Bhave's insist-
ence on walking from his ashram to Delhi, echoing the epic walks that
Gandhi himself made in his lifetime; the silence that follows when Bhave
admits to the villagers that he doesn't know what to do; Bhave telling the
story of his journey to the conference (when perhaps his audience might
have been expecting a more direct display of leadership). I've told the
story dozens of times and these three moments consistently touch me.
Looking at the story through the lens of narrative leadership, all three
practices are evident. Let's look at each of them in turn.

Know Thyself: We can see, in the simplicity with which Bhave lived his
life congruently with his belief in social justice, the deep self-knowledge
arising from his spiritual practice. I am not suggesting that we all need
to live the celibate, ascetic life that Bhave chose, but I am saying that the
ground on which we stand as leaders becomes very shaky if the story we
tell is not the story we live. We have much more tolerance for each other's
foibles than we do for hypocrisy. Narrative leadership is about walking
the talk as well as talking the walk!

Only Connect: One of the most striking features of Bhave's ability to
connect with others is that he listens to them. He hears the delegation's

plea to act; he asks the Dalits why they are hungry; he tells the villagers "I wish I knew what to do" and waits. One gets the sense that Bhave opened his pores to let the world in and then responded to what came out of this profound listening. To make this possible, he relinquished his need to be seen to know what to do or to have all the answers. It takes an open mind and a generous heart to stand in this place of uncertainty where other people's stories are as important as our own. But that kind of inclusivity is the life blood of healthy communities: all cultures (including organizational cultures) in which a multiplicity of stories is not welcomed, sooner or later experience the rigidity and dearth of innovation that results from homogeneity.

Stand for Something: Bhave's commitment to social justice permeates the story. Having worked alongside Gandhi to throw off the yoke of British colonial oppression, he devoted much of the rest of his life to ameliorating the lot of the landless poor. The stories he told were not self-aggrandizing, heroic, or rhetorical masterpieces; they were simple tales of other people's generosity and wisdom. There is a lesson for all of us here: the impact of "leadership stories" often comes from their simplicity and authenticity (the teller's genuine commitment to the story) rather than from spectacular feats of speech-writing and oratory.

Narrative leadership is tough, not because it requires technical skill and virtuosity but because it demands the courage to acknowledge who we really are and what we care about, the generosity of spirit to value others as much as and sometimes more than oneself, and a willingness to embrace the vulnerability that comes from standing up for what we truly believe in. As Jacob Tas, Deputy Chief Executive at the charity Action for Children, and a long-time client of mine, said recently when I asked him to reflect on his experience of telling stories as a leader:

> *For me, the story that someone tells is the real deal and shows their inner human spirit. The leader who tells a story makes themselves open and vulnerable by telling what really moves them. This is at the heart of storytelling and leadership: show who you truly are.*[4]

Although rarely appearing in a job description, understanding and tapping the power of stories are vital skills for leaders in all walks of life.

When leaders pay insufficient or unskilled attention to the power of stories, things inevitably start going wrong. Ultimately the price of poor narrative leadership is failure. Here are some warning signs, some common symptoms of what we might call *narrative dysfunction*.

The story itself may be inappropriate or inadequate

- The dominant or prevailing story may be rigid and/or stuck in the past. If so it no longer offers a worthwhile or convincing vision.
- If circumstances change, the prevailing story may no longer hang together. At worst there is no coherent story – a condition of "narrative wreckage."
- The aspirations of the prevailing story can be too small to relate to people's hopes and fears, their human desire to make a contribution.

When the prevailing story is inappropriate or inadequate, there will be strong competing or conflicting stories, deliberate undermining of leaders, political infighting, and going behind people's backs.

The story (even a good story) can be poorly told

- Leaders may not have the confidence or skill to tell the story well. Even a good story needs to be well told if is to be convincing.
- In some organizations, the watchword is "just give me the facts" – storytelling is misunderstood, discounted, or devalued.
- Speakers forget that while facts inform, and argument persuades (or fails to persuade), it takes a story to inspire and engage.

Stories that are trite, poorly delivered, under-prepared, over-polished, impersonal, abstract, or just plain dull do not inspire.

Leaders may not live up to their stories

- A lack of congruence between the stories leaders tell and their behavior (the stories they live) is a recipe for disbelief and cynicism.
- If leaders distance themselves from the big-picture story or fail to commit themselves to it personally, their stories will fall on deaf ears.

- Trotting out official narratives (typically vision, mission, and value statements) at regular intervals invites and deserves a hostile response.

Narrative leadership requires integrity, honesty, consistency, and a willingness to stand up and be counted. Of course, such qualities are needed by leaders of all kinds, but there is something about telling a story that – as Tas says above – shows the inner human spirit. Not everyone is prepared to face this challenge: I've met a few people in leadership roles who have initially been too frightened of making themselves vulnerable (by showing others what they really care about) to drop their armor sufficiently to tell a story. Most of them overcame their fears and discovered that with a bit of help and support they were soon able to call themselves storytellers. Actually, I've never met anyone who couldn't learn to tell a story if they wanted to.

3. The Real Deal: What leaders have you encountered who were willing to make themselves open and vulnerable by telling (or showing) what really moved them? What leaders have you encountered who did not live up to the stories they told? What effect did both types of leader have on you?

Developing our capacity to lead

> *Education is an admirable thing, but it is well to remember from time to time that nothing that is worth learning can be taught.*
>
> OSCAR WILDE[5]

The basic elements of narrative leadership can be learned (indeed, despite Oscar Wilde's joke, many of them can be taught) but the qualities through which we exercise any form of leadership – including leading as meaning-making – develop in us over the course of a lifetime and are influenced by many factors beyond any leadership model or program.

It is outside the scope of this book to delve deeply into all the many – often competing – theories and models of adult development that underpin different approaches to leadership development. But, since I am inviting you to think hard about your leadership and potentially to change some of the ways in which you lead, it is important to say something about the process of development as it relates to narrative leadership before diving into the three practices in more detail in the next few chapters.

What are we talking about when we refer to "development?" It is something more profound than learning new skills, although that might happen as a consequence. If we conceive of leadership as meaning-making, then what we mean by development is the movement toward more complex, holistic, and integrated ways of coming to know and make sense of the world. Our values, beliefs, and motivations shape how we perceive the world and how we choose to act (and how we lead) in response to what we perceive. Although we each have unique constellations of values, beliefs, and motivations, they tend to cluster into observable patterns which Bill Torbert and colleagues call *action logics*.

I'm not a great fan of typologies, psychological instruments, or leadership profiles. On the whole I find them simplistic and self-referential, but so many leaders I've worked with have found action logics to be a useful framework that I'm going to use it here as a way of talking about leadership development. The Leadership Development Framework (LDF) identifies seven stages of development (action logics) which are briefly described in the following table which I've adapted from David Rooke and Bill Torbert's *Harvard Business Review* article "Seven Transformations of Leadership."[6]

Described as a holarchy rather than a hierarchy, each successive stage (from Opportunist to Alchemist) incorporates its predecessors so that development means expanding the range of possible action logics on which one can draw, rather than switching from one mutually exclusive modality to another. The percentage of the sample of leaders measured (using a variant of the Loevinger sentence completion test) as having their "center of gravity" in each of the action logics has been approximated from several different UK and US samples.

	Action logic	Main focus of awareness	Characteristics	%
Conventional	Opportunist	Own immediate needs and opportunities	*Wins any way possible.* Self-oriented; manipulative, "might makes right." Good in emergencies and sales opportunities	5
	Diplomat	Socially expected behavior	*Avoids overt conflict.* Wants to belong; obeys group norms; rarely rocks the boat. Good as supportive glue; helps bring people together	12
	Expert	Search for expertise, improvement, and efficiency	*Rules by logic and expertise.* Seeks rational efficiency. Good as an individual contributor	38
	Achiever	Delivery of results by most effective means. Success	*Meets strategic goals.* Effectively achieves goals through teams; juggles managerial duties and market demands. Well suited to managerial roles; action and goal oriented	30
Post-conventional	Individualist	Self, relationships, and interaction with the system	*Interweaves competing personal and organizational action logics.* Creates unique structures to resolve gaps between strategy and performance. Effective in venture and consulting roles	10
	Strategist	Links between principles, contracts, theories, and judgment	*Generates organizational and personal transformations.* Exercises the power of mutual inquiry for both the short and long term. Effective as transformational leaders	4
	Alchemist	Interplay of awareness, thought, action, and effect. Transforming self and others	*Generates social transformations.* Integrates material, spiritual, and societal transformation. Good at leading society-wide changes	1

Even from such limited descriptions you can probably identify your currently dominant action logic and that of other people you know well. Almost everyone experiences at least one shift (usually more than one) during their lifetime. The process of development does not follow a linear trajectory and it is likely to be a bumpy ride. Letting go of ways of perceiving and acting in the world that have served us well is not easy, even when we are striving to embrace something new. Perhaps that helps to explain the strikingly low proportion of people with predominantly post-conventional action logics.

Looking at the table, it is fairly easy to see that people with different dominant action logics are likely to tell leadership stories for different purposes and may be interested in different types of leadership story. There are no hard and fast rules about this because our appreciation of stories is broader than our dominant action logic might suggest: an Opportunist might be inspired by a symbolic tale; a Strategist might enjoy an insider's story about the latest big deal. Great leadership stories (like Martin Luther King's "dream" speech) transcend such categories because they appeal to something universal in the human condition.

Nevertheless, most of the time it pays to consider the nature of an audience and how they might respond to a particular story. Being aware of our own dominant action logic can help us lead (and tell leadership stories) more choicefully. For example, some years ago when I was initiating a new leadership development program, I told the story of *Jumping Mouse* – a Native American animal fable – to a large group of potential participants. I didn't expect it to appeal to everyone (and it didn't) but among the audience I could see the few whose faces lit up. They were the ones I wanted to recruit because I had caught a glimpse of their readiness to engage with the post-conventional action logic underpinning the program that I had convened and which we would collaboratively design.

Our willingness (and readiness) to develop is hugely affected both by internal personality traits and by external life circumstances. Chapter 7 will look at the way our self-stories both constrain and liberate us, and how we can take greater responsibility for our development as narrative leaders.

Bonus: Alchemy in Action

Like many people, I find the notion of the Alchemist *action logic* both elusive and fascinating. When looking for real-life examples, we often reach for a handful of extraordinary characters: Abraham Lincoln, Nelson Mandela, Gandhi, Aung San Suu Kyi. Their lives show us what it means to embody this kind of awareness as leaders. Perhaps what we most admire in them is the congruence between what they believe and how they live. The post-conventional action logics seem increasingly to demand this of us, which is both their challenge and their joy. There are several excellent "biopics" which show fictionalized versions of these characters: *Lincoln* (2013 – Abraham Lincoln), *Invictus* (2009 – Nelson Mandela), *The Lady* (2011 – Aung San Suu Kyi). As you watch them, see if you recognize the characteristics of the Alchemist described in the table: "*Generates social transformations. Integrates material, spiritual, and societal transformation.*"

When do you operate in these ways (whether or not it is your dominant action logic)? Who else have you seen behaving like an Alchemist? I know several people who perceive and act in the world from this logic. One of them is Lindsay Levin, the founder of Leaders Quest, a social enterprise that connects leaders in the developed world with grassroots leaders and others in developing countries. I was fortunate enough to go with Lindsay to Bangalore in 2009 where I took part in some of the life-changing (and action logic expanding) experiences that she and her colleagues have provided for thousands of leaders. Her work is driven by the belief that our time demands that we ask ourselves some tough questions: What are our responsibilities as leaders? What is the role of business in the world today? How can we combine profit with purpose? How do we build healthy communities from the grassroots up? How can we grow sustainably? How will we create value for future generations?

Lindsay is also a successful entrepreneur and businesswoman, wife, mother of three boys, and author of *Invisible Giants: Changing the World One Step at a Time*,[7] in which she shares her story and some of the formative experiences that led to the establishment of Leaders Quest. Lindsay would never claim to be an Alchemist, but she is one, and her book reveals the developmental journey she has taken.

Summary

• Narrative leadership demands much more than the ability to tell a compelling story; it challenges us to explore the purpose of our leadership and the values that underpin it. Why we lead will shape how we lead.

• The art of narrative leadership comprises three interrelated sets of practices, summarized as Know Thyself, Only Connect, and Stand for Something, through which we engage in making-meaning with and for others.

• Know Thyself is the root system of the tree; Only Connect is the canopy; and Stand for Something is the trunk. Unless we know who we are and what we stand for we cannot authentically stand for anything.

• The story of Vinoba Bhave offers real-life examples of all three practices in action. It is a story about the power of stories to change the world, which illustrates the importance of congruence between the stories we live and the stories we tell.

• There are three prime causes of narrative dysfunction: the prevailing story may be inappropriate or inadequate; the story (even a good story) may be poorly told; and leaders may not live up to their stories.

• If we think of leadership as participating in a process of meaning-making, then leadership development is moving toward more complex, holistic, and integrated ways of coming to know and make sense of the world.

• The seven action logics of the Leadership Development Framework provide a useful map of developmental possibilities. Expanding the range of action logics that we can access enables us to lead more choicefully.

Notes and References

1 Quoted in Marrow, A. (1969). *The Practical Theorist* (Knopf: New York).
2 The Centre for Narrative Leadership (www.narrativeleadership.org) is a not-for-profit network that brings leaders, storytelling practitioners, academic researchers, and organizational consultants together as a "community of inquiry" to share their practice and to play a role in developing the emerging field of narrative leadership.
3 I first came across a version of this story in *Soul Food*. I've written it here as I've come to tell it orally to leaders and other audiences. Adapted from *The Story of Vinoba Bhave* in Kornfield J. & Feldman C. (1996) *Soul Food*, (HarperSanFrancisco: San Francisco).
4 Quotation reproduced with the kind permission of Jacob Tas.
5 Wilde, O. (1894). "A Few Maxims for the Instruction of the Over-Educated," *Saturday Review*, November 17.
6 Rooke, D. and Torbert, W.R. (2005). "Seven Transformations of Leadership," *Harvard Business Review*, April.
7 Levin, L. (2013). *Invisible Giants: Changing the World One Step at a Time* (Vala Publishing: Bristol).

Chapter 7

Know Thyself

Those who do not have power over the story that dominates their lives, the power to retell it, rethink it, deconstruct it, joke about it, and change it as times change, truly are powerless because they cannot think new thoughts.

SALMAN RUSHDIE[1]

At various times in our lives, most of us ask: "Who am I and what am I here for?" Each of us has different answers and our answers are likely to change over time. You may already have thought long and hard about such questions, especially if you have reflected on the nature and purpose of your leadership. From the perspective of narrative leadership, we need to consider how our lives are shaped by the stories we tell ourselves about who we are and what we are here for, because knowing our stories is an essential prerequisite to claiming our personal authority and to making our unique and authentic contribution as leaders.

Following the logic of Rushdie's remark, if we gain power over the stories that dominate our lives then we empower ourselves. Knowing our self-stories (the iconic and foundational stories that shape our identity) we can begin to discern which of them sustain us and which of them constrain us; which of them represent values and ways of being that we want to live into and which it is time to let go of. It is not so much – as Socrates said – that the unexamined life is not worth living; it is rather that the examined life opens up more possibilities for developing our capacity for choiceful living and leadership. For example, Bill Torbert and colleagues at the Carroll School of Management at Boston College found that reflective autobiographical writing and storytelling was one of the most effective ways for people to extend their range of available action logics.[2]

In Chapter 6, Know Thyself was described as the roots of the tree linking the three practices of narrative leadership. Remember that stories were described as the primary way we make sense of our experience, giving meaning and significance to our lives and creating (and re-creating) our sense of self; that our sense of identity – who we are – changes when we change the stories we tell ourselves about ourselves; and that the first practice of narrative leadership is therefore knowing one's life stories without being their prisoner – letting go of degenerative and dysfunctional stories and finding positive ones. This chapter focuses on how we can explore our own stories and how our relationship to our own life story affects the way we live and the way we lead.

The storied self

> *People often summarise the events of their lives in a word or two and then forget what it is they have summarised. At first, the special titles they give themselves are convenient symbols or guides in an otherwise incomprehensible existence. But the details, the substance of life, may be lost. When the story is told again and substance and title reconnected, congruence is restored and a sense of wholeness regained.*
>
> ERVING POLSTER[3]

The well-established idea that we construct our sense of self from the stories we tell ourselves (and others tell us) about who we are implies that our identity is not fixed and immutable. However, just because our self-identity is not fixed does not mean that it is formless. Psychiatrist John Bowlby (whose early work on attachment theory has greatly influenced modern psychiatry) spoke of the need to develop *autobiographical competence.*[4] That is to say, the ability to form a coherent yet flexible life story grounded in our experience. When we explore our stories we are not reinventing either ourselves or the past (unless we are fantasists). Rather, we are re-imagining ourselves; we are coming into a new relationship with our stories. It is a subtle but important distinction; let me give you a personal example to show you what I mean:

> *In the 1990s, I trained in Gestalt Psychology at a well-known training institute in West London. On my first visit, I noticed a sticker on the inside of the front door which read:* It's Never Too Late To Have A Happy Childhood. *For several years, each time I looked at the sticker I was filled with hope that the process of therapeutic training I was going through would somehow rewrite my history in such a way that I would in fact have had a happy childhood. My continuing failure to locate this mythical happy childhood in my past only added to my woes. Then one day, toward the end of my training, I saw the sticker and realized that of course I could not rewrite history: it was too late for me to have had a happy childhood. Accepting this truth released me from an impossible struggle to rectify the past and enabled me to live much more fully in the present. Now, 20 years later, I see that my relationship with the stories of my childhood has changed again. Now I see the words in my mind's eye, realize how much lighter and more playful I have become in the past two decades, and I think that the sticker was right after all. It's never too late to have a happy childhood: I'm having one now.*

What happened in my childhood hasn't changed but the stories I tell about my childhood now are charged with a softer emotional energy. I hold them less tightly than I did. Some details seem more significant than they used to and others less. They do not trigger me as once they did; they have become stories that I have instead of stories that have me. The first step in gaining this new perspective was simply telling (and sometimes writing) the stories to get a little bit of distance and separation from them.

Once a story is "out there" we can begin to look at it from different angles; we can notice what we said and what we did not say; we can reflect on its tacit assumptions; we can consider how the story – as told – helps or hinders us now; we can imagine where the story might lead us and what other possibilities it opens up. We can think of ourselves as characters in the story: are we the hero(ine); the helpless victim; the compulsive rescuer; the curious or fearful bystander? We can interrogate the story for what it can tell us about what really matters to us: the values we want to uphold, the qualities we strive to display. We can invite others – a coach, for example – to help us think about the ways in which we might be using the story to reinforce a limiting view of ourselves.

As we tell more stories, we begin to get a sense of our autobiographical competence: are we holding our stories so tightly that we have become rigid and inflexible; are we still searching for coherence among fragmented stories; are there particular blockages we can dismantle or step around; are there hidden sources of strength and personal empowerment that we can draw on; are we living lives that make sense to us?

If our upbringing did not enable us to develop a reasonable level of autobiographical competence or we find ourselves stuck in the same old unhelpful story or we have experienced some trauma that haunts us (or even simply because we are curious), we might choose to work through these with a counselor or therapist. There are specialists in biographical and narrative coaching and narrative therapy, but almost all forms of coaching and therapy are designed to help us re-story our lives, to create new stories for us to live into. As psychologists Michael White and David Epston say:

> The narrative mode locates a person as a protagonist or participant in his/her world. This is a world of interpretative acts, a world in which every retelling of a story is a new telling, a world in which persons participate with others in the "re-authoring," and thus in the shaping, of their lives and relationships.[5]

The same principle holds good in non-therapeutic organizational settings too. Many of us seek to unlock our potential and improve our performance by exploring aspects of our life and work with coaches or mentors. Some of us belong to peer inquiry groups or action learning sets where we can share our experience and reflect on it with colleagues. Others write journals or sculpt or paint or meditate or run marathons as forms of personal inquiry; for Socrates, the route to an examined life was philosophical dialogue. I do not want to suggest that telling stories is the only way to come to Know Thyself, but it is a powerful and accessible way of getting under our own skins and an indispensable foundation for narrative leadership.

Being and doing

> *True vocation . . . is the place where your deep gladness meets the world's deep need.*
>
> PARKER PALMER[6]

If we think of leadership as participating in a process of meaning-making, then the degree of congruence between us and the context in which we lead becomes highly significant. All of us are more effective in some settings than others. In part this has to do with having the requisite knowledge and skills to operate in a particular domain (contrast the financial sector with fashion design, for example), but our ability to bring our whole selves to leadership also has to do with another kind of fit, which lies at the meeting place between who we are and what we are doing.

Some of us (not the author) find our vocation early in life: the call is clear and cannot be ignored. Others never find a sense of purpose beyond doing a good enough job to get paid. Many of us set out blindly in our youth on paths that we come to question. Even if our work gives us all the trappings of success and we are highly rewarded, we may still find ourselves asking (especially as we get a bit older): Does this really satisfy me? Is this the best way of making my unique contribution to the world? Is this really what I came here for?

We can try to ignore these inconvenient and potentially disruptive questions for a time but there is a high price to pay for living a life that is not ours. The underlying question is whether we are content to live out ready-made second-hand stories or whether we will commit ourselves to becoming the authors of our own lives. If the latter appeals to you, then you will find the three tried-and-tested story-based activities in this section useful as sources of insight and potential action.

They are designed to help you explore some of the stories with which you might respond to the twin questions that opened the chapter: Who am I? What am I here for? Remembering the results of the train exercise in Chapter 5, you will not be surprised when I say that that the stories we tell in response to such questions are usually much more interesting and revealing than any philosophical or abstract answer we might give.

I generally use these activities with leaders either in one-to-one coaching sessions or in small groups, as telling the stories to others – speaking them aloud – obliges us to give them form and substance. If you can do the activities with someone else (friend, colleague, partner, coach) then you are likely to find them more powerful. If you are doing the activities on your own, then I suggest that you take the time to write your stories down before reflecting on them.

Finding purpose

In his best-selling book *The Soul's Code: In Search of Character and Calling*,[7] James Hillman uses the metaphor of the acorn and the oak to help us think about who we are and what we are here for. Entertain the idea, he says, that perhaps we arrive in this world with our own unique potential just as the acorn comes into being with the full potential of the oak tree already within itself. Becoming an oak is the acorn's *telos* or destiny, though the course of its life is neither predetermined nor inevitable: many factors (such as environment, competition, disease, and predation) will determine whether or not it achieves its potential. Similarly, human beings come into the world latent with purpose though they may fail to achieve it or even to recognize it. Hillman suggests that our task in life is not so much to grow up as it is to grow down – into ourselves. It is a notion that sits well with the image in Chapter 6 of the practice of Know Thyself as the growing roots of narrative leadership.

The idea that we arrive in the world with our own unique destiny is a very old one, dating back well over two millennia to Plato's *Republic* and possibly beyond. That does not make it true, of course, but that is not the issue (it is an idea, not a belief). What matters is whether it is useful and – for some people at least – it can be. As adults, says Hillman, if we are uncertain about our sense of purpose, then it follows that our childhood is a good place to look for clues. He suggests that we ask ourselves the question: "What did I first want to be when I grew up?" The answer that comes back to us is important because it might just reveal the acorn that contains the oak.

1. Reflection: Take a few quiet moments to recall a specific time (probably in your childhood) when you first had an inkling of what you wanted to be when you grew up. Tell the story of that time to someone or write it down. What does the story tell you now, looking back on it?

Here is my response as an example:

When I was an 8 year old pupil at boarding school, I was obsessed with the Biggles stories by Captain W.E. Johns. I loved reading these stories of airborne adventures because they reminded me of my dad who had been a pilot. Indeed, I was so taken by them that I decided to write one myself. I spent my Saturday pocket money on a lined notebook and a new pencil, found a quiet corner and began to write. It was slow going and I managed a page and a half before stopping to read what I had written. But it was nowhere near as exciting as the books I had read. It didn't occur to me at the time that the real-life author of Biggles had the advantage of being an adult, just that my effort wasn't good enough. I cried with frustration and threw the notebook away.

Looking back on the story now, I realize that my childhood obsession with Biggles took a while to reveal its secret. At first I thought it meant that I wanted to follow in my father's footsteps as an RAF pilot (indeed, although I didn't join the RAF I did spend 30 rather puzzled years in uniform in the police service). I see it now as a signal that I would one day become a maker and teller of stories.

If you look beyond the obvious in your own story, what does it tell you about the purpose and meaning of your life? How are you manifesting these insights in your life and work? How do they find expression in the way you lead? On balance, does your story tend to affirm or disaffirm the choices you have made – and could still make – about the context in which you are exercising leadership and what you are leading for? Have you found and are you following your vocation? What would it take to live more fully the story you really want to tell about yourself and be told about you?

The way we lead is not separate from who we are and how we live. Narrative leadership suggests that we are at our most effective when we are being true to our values and purpose: when leading is part of our being and not just something we do; when – as Joseph Campbell put it – we are "following our bliss." If reflecting on the story of what you first wanted to be when you grew up posed challenging questions for you then the next activity, looking at some early leadership experiences, should throw more light on the issue of what really matters to you.

Adventures in leadership

If I were to ask you to tell me your values as a leader and you were to ask me to tell you mine, the chances are that we would say fairly similar things: hard work, fairness, loyalty, truth, courage, love, etc. Even if our lists were different, they would still be lists of our espoused values (or what we think we ought to believe) rather than our values-in-action (the values we uphold in practice) which may be quite different. We would not be deliberately lying to each other but we would probably be unconsciously deceiving ourselves.

To uncover what really matters to us as leaders we need to look at real-life examples of how we actually behaved in particular circumstances. Early experiences of leadership (probably before the age of 16) are particularly good because at that stage of our lives we are more likely to act naturally without consciously trying to adopt a particular style of leadership.

2. Reflection: Think back to an early occasion probably before the age of 16 (perhaps the first time) when you consciously acted as a leader. It could be in any context: family, school, social, work, etc. Tell the story of that time to someone or write it down. Ask someone else what qualities they think you displayed in the story and what it says about what matters to you.

My friend Sue Hollingsworth (one-time business executive and now a director of the International School of Storytelling) told me this story about an early leadership experience:

I went to an all girls school. When I was 15, a group of us were doing the Duke of Edinburgh's Award, part of which involves planning and taking part in an expedition. We had weekend training sessions for this in the Forest of Dean.

One December Saturday morning, a group of us were dropped in the middle of the Forest with a map, compass, a route we had to follow and the time we had to be at our final destination. We were told that we had to take it in turns to lead the group and map read and that if we weren't back within 30 minutes of the final time, the mini-bus would leave without us.

All started well, but then some of the girls misread the map when it was their turn to lead and we not only fell well behind on time but started to argue amongst ourselves. Late in the afternoon one girl slipped on the icy ground and went down with a scream, clutching a twisted ankle. At that same moment the map was thrust into my frozen hands: I was the last leader of the day. Organising someone to check the injured girl's ankle and strap it up, I peered through the gathering gloom at the map and saw straight away that we could never make it back to the mini-bus in time.

Then I spotted on the map a railway tunnel that disappeared into the hillside in front of us and emerged a short distance from the pick up point. If we could walk through that pitch black tunnel and avoid being killed by a train, there was a chance we might just make it in time. At that moment I realised it had all gone quiet and even my injured friend had stopped crying. I remember looking up and seeing a circle of eyes staring at me. It was then that I suddenly realised the responsibility of being a leader, that they were waiting for me to decide what we should do next and that it was my choice.

I chose to go through the tunnel. No trains came along but it was very frightening, expecting one to come through at any moment. We made it back in time and none of us ever told anyone what I had decided to do. It was many months later before I looked at the map in broad daylight and saw the word "disused" by the tunnel.[8]

When I listened to the story, Sue's courage and decisiveness stood out together with a certain gung-ho quality and determination to succeed. I recognize all these characteristics in the Sue I know today; they serve her well and (as is true for all of us) they also have a shadow side if carried too far. Two of my early leadership experiences (running a fishing club that never went fishing and organizing a collection at school for the Biafran famine) demonstrate a highly active imagination and a sense of moral purpose which are still characteristic of how I lead; but I know that, taken too far, they can sometimes cause me to ignore practical limitations and to adopt a somewhat "holier than thou" attitude.

It is fascinating how often the stories told by leaders who have done this exercise prefigure both the strengths and shadow sides of their more mature selves. Bringing to light the qualities and values that shape our leadership practice offers the opportunity for reflection and more choiceful action in the moment.

Reflecting on your own story, how did the qualities and values that someone else saw in you compare to what you perceived? How close are these qualities and values to your current sense of yourself? How do you manifest them as a leader now? What is the shadow side of these qualities and values? What would you say to your younger self if you could? What do you think your younger self would say to you if he or she could? What are the implications of this for you as a leader?

Developmental autobiography

The previous two activities invited you to glimpse aspects of yourself by looking at specific moments in your life that revealed something about your values and sense of purpose. It is also good to take an overview: to look at the overall pattern of your development as a leader. An excellent way of doing this is to write an autobiographical story tracing how and why your leadership style has changed over time. It is particularly helpful in relation to narrative leadership to explore how your range of action logics has expanded and where your current dominant action logic is located.

3. Reflection: Take another look at the table in Chapter 6. Which is currently your dominant action logic? Think about how and when you shifted from one dominant action logic to another. Write a brief autobiographical story tracing your development as a leader in terms of this framework.

Bill Torbert and his associates include some excellent examples of such developmental autobiographies in *Action Inquiry: The Secret of Timely and Transforming Leadership.*[9] If you find their Leadership Development Framework particularly engaging and want to go deeper then it is well worth completing their profiling instrument for a detailed readout, but, for the purpose of this activity, I have found that most people intuitively recognize the different action logics and can readily relate them to their own experience.

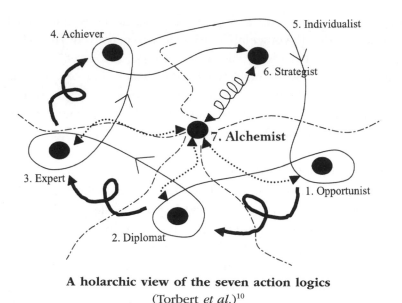

A holarchic view of the seven action logics
(Torbert *et al.*)[10]

Torbert *et al.* offer a wonderfully ingenious and ironically complicated diagram to illustrate the interwoven and looping nature of the interrelationships in the model. Please do not take it literally; it is included here simply to encourage you to feel free to describe your journey through the action logics in whatever way makes most sense for you. Be sure to include confusions, doubts, and difficulties: the shadow side of your journey as well as your sense of progress and expansion. The Leadership Development Framework is essentially an epistemological model describing different lenses through which we perceive and make sense of the world. Changing lenses – as anyone who wears spectacles knows – can be uncomfortable at first because we have got used to the limitations of the old lenses even though they may no longer be enough for our needs.

I have worked through the model with numerous groups of leaders and managers. While the details of everyone's developmental journey are unique, there are some typical features – summarized in the table below – that you might like to compare with the patterns revealed in your own developmental autobiography. Bear in mind that we expand the range of our actions logics in a holistic way rather than shift from one category to the next in an incremental linear fashion.

	Action logic	Main focus of awareness	Characteristic provocations for development
	Opportunist	Own immediate needs and opportunities	Archetypal teenager/student, moving outside parental control, without responsibilities to others, searching for identity, "trying things on for size"
Conventional	Diplomat	Socially expected behavior	Starting out on first job/new career, discovering and trying to meet other people's expectations, adopting culture of group/organization, "getting on by fitting in"
Conventional	Expert	Search for expertise, improvement, and efficiency	Expectation of contribution based on knowledge, gaining status from expert knowledge, acquiring a reputation for "knowing best"
Conventional	Achiever	Delivery of results by most effective means. Success	Acquiring managerial responsibility for meeting goals and targets, managing people cross-functionally, archetypal MBA student getting out of the silo, acquiring a reputation for "getting things done"
Post-conventional	Individualist	Self, relationships, and interaction with the system	Personal issues come to the fore, dissatisfaction with meeting other people's agendas, discovering unique interests and perspectives, desire to succeed by "doing things my way"
Post-conventional	Strategist	Links between principles, contracts, theories, and judgment	Moving into general management (or acting as advisor to top management), appreciation of breadth of interests, and ability to choose most appropriate means, acquiring reputation for "seeing the big picture"
Post-conventional	Alchemist	Interplay of awareness, thought, action, and effect. Transforming self and others	Significant life events provoke meta-perspective, near-death experiences, incarceration (Mandela), spiritual or shamanic initiation, loyalty to whole systems, ability to hold and transcend polarities, "being the change"

When you reflect on your developmental autobiography, ask yourself these questions: What triggered the changes in your dominant action logics? What benefits did the changes bring? What was hard to let go of and what were the costs of changing? What effect did the changes have on the way you exercised leadership? How well suited is your dominant action logic for your current and possible future roles?

In this chapter, I have suggested three story-based activities that fall within the first of the three interrelated practices of narrative leadership. Whatever methods we choose, coming to Know Thyself is the first step toward greater personal authority. With self-knowledge, you can decide for yourself. Are you happy where you are? Do you want to change? What is your next step? How can you best support yourself in making it?

In the next chapter, we will delve into the second practice of narrative leadership, exploring the rationale and method for using stories and storytelling to connect with others and build healthy organizations and communities. We will conclude this one with a traditional Indian story that, despite its simplicity (or perhaps because of it) has something profound to say about human nature. It seems that our individual character and the uniqueness of the contribution we can make comes as much from knowing and accepting our imperfections as it does from relying on our strengths. We may yearn to develop ourselves but we need not strive for perfection.

The Cracked Pot

A poor water-carrier went several miles each day to the well to fetch water for his rich master's household in two great earthenware pots that he carried on a yoke. One of the pots was cracked and by the time he returned it was half-empty.

This happened each day and the cracked pot felt ashamed that he was not doing his job properly. He decided to apologise and one morning just as the water-carrier was about to set off to the well, the cracked pot spoke to him.

"I'm sorry that I have a crack," it said. "You carry me back and forth every day and I let you down by not being able to hold all the water. I must make things very difficult for you. Forgive me."

"Forgive you? There is nothing to forgive," said the water-carrier. "Let me show you something." And that morning on his way to the well he stopped and said to the

cracked pot, "There . . . look out to your left. What do you see?"

"Nothing," said the pot. "It is hot, dry and dusty. A desert in fact."

"Now look out to the right hand side. What do you see there?" said the water-carrier. Beside the path, stretching as far as could be seen in both directions, there were flowers, plants, bushes, trees and vines.

"Yes," said the water-carrier. "They are there because of you; because of the water that drips out of you each day. Did you think I didn't know about your crack? You have made my difficult job much more pleasant and brought much beauty and joy to my life. Thank you my old friend."

The water-carrier looked at the pot and the crack seemed to take on the shape of a lopsided smile.

Bonus: *Groundhog Day*

Harold Ramis's (1993) comedy *Groundhog Day* shows us – in exquisite detail – the painful process of self-development. Bill Murray plays cynical and obnoxious TV weatherman Phil Connors, sent to Punxsutawney, Pennsylvania with his lovely producer Rita to cover the annual Groundhog Day celebrations. For reasons that are not explained, Connors gets caught in a time loop for an indeterminate period, waking up at 6.00 a.m. each morning in the same hotel bedroom, to the sound of Sonny and Cher singing *I Got You Babe*, to face exactly the same day over and over again.

At first, he behaves appallingly, stealing money, seducing women, driving maniacally. Worn down by the depressing repetition of life, bumping up against his limitations and his own character day after day, he tries to commit suicide (many times) but cannot escape the time loop. Eventually, he realizes that he has no option but to change his behavior and, as he does so, his personality slowly begins to shift. But I won't spoil the film for you by telling you the ending.

Groundhog Day is a classic. If you haven't already seen it then watch it to witness the slow, hard-won transformation of one person. If you have seen it before, watch it again just for the hell of it.

Summary

- Since the stories we tell ourselves about ourselves shape us so strongly, it behoves us to get to know them. What are our iconic stories? What do they say about what really matters to us or what we are in service of?
- If our stories remain hidden from us we live them out unconsciously. If we tell them and engage with them creatively then we can gain new perspectives about ourselves and what drives us, and open up new possibilities for ourselves.
- Developing autobiographical competence (the ability to form a coherent yet flexible life story grounded in experience) is an essential developmental task for all of us. Rigid or fragmented life stories can be problematic.
- When stories that we hold closely no longer serve us we need to re-story ourselves and to reinforce new self-stories by acting into our intentions, living congruently with the new stories as well as telling them.
- There are many opportunities for working with our self-stories; in the context of a coaching relationship, for example; with a biographical counselor; at a storytelling workshop.
- Writing a reflective account of our development as a leader over time using the Leadership Development Framework is a proven method of expanding the range of action logics we can apply in different circumstances.
- As well as autobiographical stories we can also draw on the wisdom of traditional tales and archetypal myths. However we choose to approach it, the imperative is the same – Know Thyself!

Notes and References

1 Rushdie wrote these words in an essay entitled "10,000 Days in a Balloon" reflecting on his time in hiding under the fatwa issued by Ayatollah Khomeini after the publication of his novel *The Satanic Verses*.

2 Torbert, B. (2004). *Action Inquiry: The Secret of Timely and Transforming Leadership* (Berrett-Koehler: San Francisco).

3 Polster, E. (1990). *Every Person's Life is Worth a Novel* (WW Norton: New York).

4 For an extended discussion of the notion of autobiographical competence, see Holmes, J. (1993). *John Bowlby and Attachment Theory* (Routledge: London).

5 White, M. and Epston, D. (1990). *Narrative Means to Therapeutic Ends* (WW Norton: New York, p82).

6 Palmer, P. (2000). *Let Your Life Speak: Listening for the Voice of Vocation* (Jossey-Bass: San Francisco, p16).

7 Hillman, J. (1996). *The Soul's Code: In Search of Character and Calling* (Random House: New York).

8 Story reproduced with kind permission of Sue Hollingsworth.

9 Torbert, W. and Associates (2004). *Action Inquiry: The Secret of Timely and Transforming Leadership* (Berrett-Koehler: San Francisco, pp95–101).

10 Ibid., p92. Reprinted with permission of the publisher. From *Action Inquiry*, copyright © 2004 by (Torbert, W et al), Berrett-Koehler Publishers, Inc., San Francisco, CA. All rights reserved. www.bkconnection.com.

Chapter 8

Only Connect

The most basic and powerful way to connect to another person is to listen. Just listen. Perhaps the most important thing we ever give each other is our attention.

RACHEL NAOMI REMEN[1]

It has become fashionable to tell leaders that they must learn how to tell inspirational stories, stories that will get their followers on board and galvanize them into action. Framed this way, storytelling becomes just another way to perpetuate the dominant heroic leadership discourse that we debunked in Chapter 2. There is a place for inspirational stories, but if they are to be more than window dressing or a con trick then they must be authentically rooted in the person of the leader *and* be meaningful for the audience to which they are being told.

It is vital to remember that storytelling is always relational. It requires both teller and listener and it happens in a context that is already replete with stories. Organizations, groups, and societies are "collective storytelling systems"[2] in which no one (including those in positions of leadership) can take for granted the right to have their stories heard. As leaders, it is the nature of our participation in these storytelling systems – especially our willingness to listen to other people's stories – that creates a receptive environment for our own stories to be heard.

If, as discussed in previous chapters, leadership means participation in an ongoing process of social meaning-making, then we cannot pretend to stand outside of the systems of which we are a part and try to manipulate them by imposing our stories (as the dominant machine metaphor of organizations leads us to believe). Instead we must act as intelligent agents within an evolving ecology of stories in which we ourselves are changed by listening to the stories of others just as others are changed by listening to ours. Our effectiveness as narrative leaders both depends upon and contributes to the quality and depth of our connectedness to ourselves, to others, and to the world around us.

In Chapter 6, Only Connect was described as the branches, twigs, and leaves of the tree linking the three practices of narrative leadership. Remember that stories are a vital means of building relationships, bringing groups and communities together; that organizations, groups, and communities change when the stories, and storytelling dynamics between people, change; and that the second practice of narrative leadership is therefore building relationships and communities by creating and sustaining a healthy flow of stories between diverse people and groups. This chapter focuses on some practical ways of achieving this in organizations and wider social settings and on some of the resulting benefits.

Creating communicative spaces

> *I define connection as the energy that exists between people when they feel seen, heard, and valued; when they can give and receive without judgment; and when they derive sustenance and strength from the relationship.*
>
> BRENÉ BROWN[3]

How can we use stories and storytelling to create the depth and quality of connection that Brené Brown is talking about when our ability to see, hear, and value each other is so often distorted by significant inequalities in power and voice? Differences in organizational position, age, class, gender, race, education, language, and personality are factors that make it easier for some, and more difficult for others, to speak out. If we put a group of people in a room and ask them to talk or share stories, some will jump in and others will hold back, some will take more than their fair share of time and others less, some will demand deference and others will defer.

To create the circumstances in which inequalities in power and voice are (at least temporarily) minimized we need to use a liberating structure, a process that gives all participants similar opportunities to speak and listen to each other. One of the most robust ways of doing this is the *story circle*: a turn-taking procedure in which small groups are invited to respond to a trigger statement with short stories. The form was developed by community workers in the United States as a way of bringing fragmented groups together in the wake of social breakdowns such as the notorious 1992 Los Angeles riots in which 53 people died and over 2,000 were injured.

It has since been tried and tested in a huge variety of organizational and social settings. I have used it scores of times in businesses, government departments, and charities; on leadership programs (from high flyers to top management); and in many countries. It works with as few as 5 people and as many as 400. It is simple, powerful, and effective and does not need slick storytelling skills to run. I will give you the essential guidelines followed by some examples of story circles in action.

Begin by establishing the theme or themes that you want people to tell stories about and frame the trigger statements carefully. Form circles, with 5–8 people sitting comfortably in each one; explain the following guidelines and demonstrate them with one of the circles so others can see. There is quite a lot to remember, so I sometimes post the guidelines on a flip chart or PowerPoint slide. The process is much easier to follow in practice than it appears on paper and it is well worthwhile spending time to clarify how the story circles will work and to take any questions.[4]

- Sit in a "good" circle without gaps so you can all see each other.
- If you don't already know each other say hello and give your names.
- You'll each have a maximum of three minutes to tell your story.
- Timekeeping (and a watch with a minute hand) passes round the circle.
- The person to the storyteller's right keeps time for them.
- Anyone can start, after which the story circle proceeds clockwise.
- Silence is OK – you can pause if you haven't used up your time.

- Tell stories, *not* theories, not analysis, opinions, lectures, etc.
- The essence of the story circle is the quality of your listening.
- Trust that your story will come up spontaneously as you listen.
- Don't take notes or hold papers and computers etc. in your lap.
- You'll want to discuss the stories but please don't. Just listen.
- Pass if you're not ready – the circle will come back round to you.

You are now ready to introduce your pre-prepared trigger, which needs to be carefully phrased so it evokes stories (not answers to a question). Choose themes that everyone present can relate to and are likely to have some experience of. To get you started, here are some that I use:

1. Tell a three-minute story about a time, person, or event when someone unexpectedly helped you in your life or work.
2. Tell a three-minute story about a time, person, or event when you were inspired to do your very best work.
3. Tell a three-minute story about a time, person, or event when you failed to do your best and later learned from your failure.
4. Tell a three-minute story about a time, person, or event that led to you doing the work you do today.
5. Tell a three-minute story about a time, person, or event when you faced and overcame an obstacle in your life or work.
6. Tell a three-minute story about a time, person, or event when you faced a moral dilemma in your life or work.
7. Tell a three-minute story about a time, person, or event when you realized that something had to change in your life or work.
8. Tell a three-minute story about a time, person, or event when you were a member of a high-performing team.
9. Tell a three-minute story about a time, person, or event when you experienced excellent (or terrible) service from someone.
10. Tell a three-minute story about a time, person, or event when you witnessed great leadership in action.

Once you have introduced the trigger, it helps to relax people if you can tell them a story yourself before they start. It shows that you are willing to do what you are asking of them; it also models how to tell a simple story and gives them time for their own stories to begin to emerge.

Then invite the circles to begin and keep an eye on how they are managing until they settle down. When all the circles have finished a round of storytelling, give them a few minutes to discuss what they have heard before introducing a second round if desired. If you have time, start with a gentle round using neutral/positive triggers such as themes 1 or 4 before diving in deeper in a second round using more challenging triggers like 6 or 7.

The process does ask people to behave in some counter-intuitive ways: for example, by listening quietly to the stories and not slipping into conversation and by potentially cutting short what promises to be a particularly interesting story. You may be asking, "Can't we just ask people to tell a few stories?" Of course, we can; sharing stories spontaneously and informally also helps us connect, especially when everyone feels equally free to speak their minds. But there are many circumstances in which the liberating structure of the story circle, specially designed to minimize inequalities of power and voice, is a better option. To see why, let's look at a few real-life examples of what story circles can do.

Example A: On the fast track

A few years ago, a colleague and I facilitated a group of 12 engineers, members of a fast-track management training scheme in an engineering company. In two story circles, they each told stories in response to the trigger: Tell a three-minute story about a time, person, or event that led you to doing the work you do today for XYZ Company.

They told stories of mentors in the company who had helped them get on; of inspired school teachers who had encouraged them to become engineers; of following in the footsteps of parents and grandparents; of breaking the mould to become the first person in their families to go to university; of being one of relatively few women engineers in the company; stories of their hopes, doubts, fears, and gratitude for the opportunities they had been given. Some were "natural" storytellers, some were a bit vague and lacking in detail, some artful, others artless, but all had a story to tell and all were heard by their colleagues with rapt attention.

Afterward, one of them said in tones that suggested a sense of wonder, "We really opened up to each other didn't we? We all work in the same business and we have been together on this training scheme for two years but I look round the room now and for the first time I feel that I actually know these people and that they know me."

Following this intervention, the Program Director reported that the experience had helped this disparate group become a cohort of potential leaders on whom the company could call for special projects that required effective joint working.

Example B: Global network

A group of 18 members of a global energy company traveled to London from Africa, Asia, Australia, Europe, North America, and South America for a three-day semi-structured workshop to explore and make recommendations to the Chief Executive on current and future "people issues" in the business. They had been selected to represent a broad cross-section both functionally and geographically. Although some of them were in regular email contact, few of them had met before in person. To justify the expense of bringing them together, it was essential that they were quickly able to relate well to each other so they could get down to work. After brief introductions, they formed into three story circles and told two rounds of stories. The first round was told in response to a similar trigger to the one used with the engineers in Example A and the second round in response to: Tell a three-minute story about a time, person, or event when you faced an obstacle in your work.

They found it such an effective way to connect with each other that when the Chief Executive joined them on the final morning of the event, they repeated the process with him as a member of one of the circles. In his closing remarks, he said that in all the years he had been attending such events, this had been the first time he had been made to feel genuinely part of the group. "I loved the story circle," he said. "When I wasn't telling my stories, it gave me a wonderful opportunity to listen without feeling any pressure to fill the space with my own words. You'd be surprised how rare that is for someone in my position."

Example C: Inclusion and exclusion

Dealing sensitively and respectfully with a hugely diverse workforce and client base is a serious matter for the National Health Service and it takes the issue very seriously. As part of a session on "equalities and inclusion" members of the NHS Top Leaders Programme were asked to share their own experiences by telling stories in response to the trigger: Tell a three-minute story about a time when you were (or felt yourself to be) excluded from a group that mattered to you – or included in a group that mattered to you.

Senior clinicians and managers in the story circles shared some very powerful and moving personal stories (including one from an oncologist who told of his sense of exclusion by colleagues who avoided him when his wife was dying of cancer). Instead of "equalities and inclusion" being discussed abstractly as an issue of policy to be managed, the stories brought them vividly to life as something in which everyone is potentially implicated as both victim and perpetrator and is therefore obliged to consider the effects of their actions on others and to take responsibility for their own behavior: in effect, "they" became "we."

What all these examples have in common is that the story circles opened up spaces for people to engage with each other more personally and with less distortion caused by inequalities in voice and power than they might usually experience. Sociologist Jurgen Habermas made a distinction between the goal-focused "instrumental action" prevalent in the system-world of organizations and what he called "communicative action" focused on reaching mutual understanding, which is more typical of our everyday life-world. He argued that in our post-modern age, system-world and life-world have become decoupled and that the economic power and efficiency of the system-world is such that its ends-driven logic has a propensity to overwhelm the more communitarian logic of the life-world.[5]

In other words, the inherent logic of organizational (and institutional) life – even when its ostensible purpose is to do good in the world – tends to drive out the qualities and values that matter most to us in our day-to-day lives. Unless we can create communicative spaces – such as story circles – in our organizations to reconnect the two worlds and to reassert the primacy of the life-world, it is almost inevitable that the short-term achievement of economic goals will continue to trump the long-term consideration of our human needs. The unintended social and planetary consequences of this are already apparent: significant climate change, massive environmental degradation, multiple species extinctions, and a global economic crisis to name a few. An alien observer would probably liken us to the apocryphal frog boiling to death rather than jumping out of the pot as the water heats up.

I'm not sufficiently foolish or grandiose to claim that telling a few stories will save the world but I do say that it becomes harder not to notice the effects of our actions as leaders when the logic and values of the life-world are embraced and when we really connect with each other at a human level in the midst of organizational life. As Remen says, "When we know ourselves to be connected to all others, acting compassionately is simply the natural thing to do."[6]

Listening to the story

> *I like to listen. I have learned a great deal from listening carefully. Most people never listen.*
>
> ERNEST HEMINGWAY[7]

Many of us believe, like Ernest Hemingway, that we are good listeners. Few of us are, and sufficiently few that when we come across someone who really listens – as if we were the only other person in the room and with the possibility that what we say might actually change what they think or how they behave – we often call them charismatic. Paradoxically, in a book called *Telling the Story*, I am about to suggest that listening to other people's stories is as important (perhaps even more important) than telling your own.

Rather than argue the point, let's test this proposition with a small experiment. Since it is about listening, you will need a partner, but it only takes a few minutes and it will give you both some useful insights.

1. Listening Exercise: One person (A) recalls a pleasant holiday memory and tells the listener (B) all about it for a few minutes. While A continues to speak, B changes the quality of their listening. Stage One: B listens intently, making good eye contact, nodding, etc. Stage Two: After a minute or so, B progressively withdraws their attention. Stage Three: B increases the level of their attention to where it was in Stage One. When all three stages are finished, reverse roles and repeat the exercise.

Even though the exercise is set up so that you know what is coming and even though you are simply talking about a pleasant holiday experience, the effects of being listened to (and not listened to) are extraordinarily powerful. I have seen grown men and women shaking their heads in frustration and near despair as their listening partner glazes over and looks away or even checks their mobile phone. But it is also interesting to note how quickly connection can be re-established when the listener's attention returns to the speaker.

I did this exercise recently with a conference room full of nurses, midwives, and allied health professionals. They knew that listening to patients is fundamental to good health care; they knew it was a vital part of their roles. They also knew that in practice their attention was often partial and easily diverted. They laughed ruefully as the exercise reminded them what a difference good listening makes and how easy it is to forget to listen in the heat of the moment. The lesson for leaders is clear: creating a healthy flow of stories requires good listening as much as it requires telling good stories.

Conversation matters

> *Let us make a special effort to stop communicating with*
> *each other so we can have some conversation.*
>
> MARK TWAIN[8]

The practice of Only Connect reminds us that real engagement with others can only be accomplished through an engaging process. It is rarely achieved by inspirational rhetoric and it cannot be finessed by sleight of hand or foisted on people. All too often, leaders attempt to "get their people on board" without having involved them in the process of deciding where to go or even of helping them understand how and why they have decided to follow a particular course of action. They attempt to communicate their position rather than have a conversation in which they too might be changed.

One of the fundamental tenets of narrative leadership is that organizations, groups, and communities only change when the stories and storytelling dynamics between people change. A more open process – especially one involving an exchange of stories – is more likely to result in a substantial shift in understanding and attitude than a slick presentation because it enables people to participate in creating an ongoing dialogue about the past, present, and future.

David Green (an Australian colleague at Narrative Leadership Associates) recalls an example of working in this way some years ago with a central state agency in his home country.

> *It began when he facilitated a two-day meeting of the executive team to draft a strategic vision to put before their staff. The director of corporate development had already prepared the ground over some months with research, presentations, and a staff working group – all of which fed into the workshop. On the second day, the executive team agreed on a statement which captured their strategic intent, and also agreed that additional wordsmithing would not essentially improve it further.*
>
> *It was what happened next that made the difference. With David's prompting they realized that it was the personal meanings which each staff member attached to the statement that would decide whether it would be "real" for them, and lead to a shared commitment. After some discussion, they came to accept that rather than try to sell the vision, each staff member needed to create their own unique picture of the*

way forward. These would be concrete instances of events and behavior (vignettes and stories) and those images would hold the attachment to the vision for each person.

Over the next few weeks, they each sat down with several groups of about 20 staff at a time, with one of their executive colleagues, and led exploratory conversations of up to two hours, in order to elicit and share the meanings/ images that each person had of the "vision-in-action." Working together, they created not a single, monolithic story but a whole ecology of stories which brought the vision alive for them all.

By resisting the temptation to follow a more conventional form of dissemination in favor of a more open process they were enacting a more engaged and participative culture, not just espousing one. Like Mark Twain, they came to realize that the nature of the conversation matters as much as its content.

Whose stories count?

The whole family sat down to eat in the restaurant. The adults conversed about the weather, the news, and other weighty topics, ignoring 9-year-old Rosie who stared at the ceiling and twiddled her thumbs. The waitress passed round menus to everyone and when the orders were taken, she came to Rosie last.

"And what would you like?" she asked.

"A cheeseburger and Coke please," said Rosie.

"Nonsense," said her grandfather, "she'll have roast chicken with vegetables like the rest of us."

"And water to drink," said her mother.

The waitress jotted down the family's orders on her pad, then glanced over at Rosie as she walked away from the table. "Would you like ketchup or mustard on your cheeseburger?"

"Ketchup please," Rosie called out. Then she turned to her family and added: "At least she thinks I'm real!"

APOCRYPHAL[9]

This small family drama illustrates perfectly a phenomenon that gets played out in groups, organizations, societies, and nations. Some people's stories count more than others. It happens to all of us at some time or another but for some people and some groups it happens much of the time. They become marginalized, shoved to the edge of our awareness. In extreme (but sadly not rare) cases they become "others" or even "non-persons."

As mentioned in Chapter 1, we only have to think of the "troubles" in Northern Ireland in the late twentieth century to see what happens when groups within a community no longer give credence or legitimacy to the stories of other groups. The stories of one group were not just disagreed with by the other; they literally held no meaning or significance for each other. Because they were disconnected in this way, the most extreme Protestant Loyalists and Catholic Nationalists had no understanding or empathy for each other's plight. Northern Ireland's long history of violence, poverty, and social injustice drove a wedge between them. Failure to listen to each other's stories was both a cause and effect of this deep-seated social division.

Conversely, as President Nelson Mandela and Archbishop Desmond Tutu of South Africa realized, when they established the post-apartheid Truth and Reconciliation Commission in 1995, healing bitter divisions requires that we can once again tell our stories to each other and be heard. The Commission – for all its difficulties – was a conscious exercise in storytelling across boundaries. The justice it sought was restorative, characterized by a search for truth and the granting of amnesty, rather than retributive for which proof of guilt and imposition of punishment would have been required. It was a bold move that brought witnesses, victims, and perpetrators face to face. Since then, over 25 nations[10] have instituted truth-seeking commissions, the best of them modeled on the

South African original. Here is Archbishop Tutu explaining its underlying principle of *ubuntu*:

> *In the South African experience it was decided that we would have justice yes, but not retributive justice. No, the Truth and Reconciliation Commission process was an example of restorative justice. In our case it was based on an African concept very difficult to render into English as there is no precise equivalent. I refer to Ubuntu. Ubuntu is the essence of being human. We say a person is a person through other persons. We are made for togetherness, to live in a delicate network of interdependence . . . I need other human beings in order to be human myself. I would not know how to walk, talk, think, behave as a human person except by learning it all from other human beings.*
>
> *For ubuntu the* summmum bonum, *the greatest good, is communal harmony. Anger, hatred, resentment all are corrosive of this good. If one person is dehumanised then inexorably we are all diminished and dehumanised in our turn.*[11]

These examples graphically make the point that we exclude people at our peril. The consequences may not be as severe as they were in Northern Ireland or South Africa, but we cannot expect people to join us in our endeavors unless we make room for them and their stories. Creativity occurs at the margins where diversity and interchange with other organizations and systems are greatest. If, as leaders, we occupy central positions (systems self-organize to ensure this happens) we must make particular efforts to connect with those at the margins: front-line staff, overseas outposts, customers, supporters, competitors, opponents. To avoid isolation we must shrink distance and welcome difference. If we cannot physically meet then we must find other ways to share our stories: by Skype, YouTube, Facebook, whatever it takes to connect.

To bring this closer to home, think about whose stories count most in the organizations, systems, and communities of which you are a part. You might want to jot down your responses when you have had time to reflect. Here are some trigger questions to help you focus.

2. Reflection: Whose stories are given most weight? Whose stories do not get heard? What kinds of story are listened to and what kinds ignored? What kinds of story need to be told? Whose stories do you need to hear? How could you enable this to happen? When could you use a story circle?

Only Connect is represented by the branches, twigs, and leaves of our metaphorical tree because creating and sustaining a healthy flow of stories between diverse people and groups is another source of nourishment. If Know Thyself gives us access to our unique qualities, values, and destiny, then Only Connect opens us to others and to the world. Whole-hearted engagement with these two practices will define the purpose of our leadership and, as we will explore in the next chapter, enable us to Stand for Something that is authentically ours and of our time.

Bonus: *Local Hero*

Bill Forsyth's Scottish–American comedy drama *Local Hero* came out in 1983 just as the UK was entering the Thatcherite era. The storyline has Peter Reigert (MacIntyre) as a hot-shot oil company executive from Houston being sent to the fictional Scottish village of Ferness to buy the whole place from the local inhabitants to put an oil refinery in its place. As he falls in love with the landscape and way of life, the locals gleefully anticipate becoming millionaires.

It is a meeting of two worlds: the system-world of Knox Oil and Gas and the life-world of a remote fishing village. It shows beautifully how the different logics of these worlds infiltrate each other so that they both change. In contrast to *Avatar*, James Cameron's CGI-laden, culture-clash blockbuster, *Local Hero* avoids obvious stereotypes of "goodies" and "baddies," preferring to reflect the complexity and subtlety of this meeting. Watch it on DVD and enjoy Burt Lancaster as the wonderfully eccentric Felix Happer, star-gazing owner of Knox Oil and Gas, stealing the limelight to the sound of Mark Knopfler's haunting and lyrical soundtrack.

Summary

- Storytelling is always relational; every story needs both teller and listener. Leadership stories are told in "collective storytelling systems" where they compete for attention and must earn the right to be heard.
- Contrary to what the dominant machine metaphor of organizations suggests, we cannot stand outside the systems of which we are a part and try to manipulate them by imposing stories.
- Our ability to connect (to be seen, heard, and valued) in many circumstances is distorted by inequalities in power and voice. The liberating structure of story circles can help to minimize these inequalities.
- The inherent logic of the system-world has a propensity to overwhelm the more communitarian logic of the life-world; communicative action (focused on mutual understanding) reasserts the primacy of the life-world.
- Connecting through stories is at least as much about listening to other people's stories as it is about telling our own. Not being listened to has a powerful, visceral negative effect.
- Some stories are louder than others: stories of the powerful may be given more credence than those of the weak. Whose voices are muted or ignored in the systems that you are a part of?
- As leaders we nourish ourselves through both the roots of Know Thyself and the branches, twigs, and leaves of Only Connect. We need both if we are to Stand for Something that is authentically ours and of our time.

Notes and References

1 Attributed to Rachel Naomi Remen, Professor of Integrative Medicine, University of California, San Francisco.
2 Boje, D. (1991). "The Storytelling Organization: A Study of Storytelling Performance in an Office Supply Firm," *Administrative Science Quarterly*, **36**: 106–126.
3 Attributed to Brené Brown, author of *The Gifts of Imperfection* (2010) (Hazelden: Center City, MN).
4 I am indebted to Theresa Holden of Holden Arts from whom I learned the story circle technique and whose original guidelines I have adapted here.
5 Habermas, J. (1987). *The Theory of Communicative Action, Vol. 2, Lifeworld and System: A Critique of Functionalist Reason* (Beacon Press: Uckfield, pp381–383).
6 Attributed to Rachel Naomi Remen.
7 Attributed to Ernest Hemingway.
8 Attributed to Mark Twain.
9 Adapted from "The Story of Molly and the Cheeseburger" in Kornfield J. & Feldman C. (1996) *Soul Food*, (HarperSanFrancisco: San Francisco, p81).
10 Argentina, Brazil, Canada, Chile, Colombia, Czech Republic, El Salvador, Fiji, Ghana, Guatemala, Kenya, Liberia, Morocco, Panama, Peru, Philippines, Poland, Sierra Leone, Solomon Islands, South Africa, South Korea, Sri Lanka, East Timor, Uganda, Ukraine, and USA.
11 Archbishop Desmond Tutu (2004). "The Truth and Reconciliation Process – Restorative Justice," Longford Lecture, February 16.

Chapter 9

Stand for Something

> *If I am not for myself, who will be for me? If I am for myself*
> *alone, what am I? And if not now, when?*
> HILLEL THE ELDER, C.50 BCE[1]

This well-known aphorism, from the Jewish tradition, pinpoints what it means to Stand for Something; if what we stand for as leaders (in our actions and in our stories) is to bring real value then surely it must be authentically ours, relevant for others, and shaped by what is needed by our time and circumstances. This means that if the trunk of the metaphorical tree of narrative leadership is to grow straight and true, we must draw up strength from the roots of Know Thyself and spread the branches, twigs, and leaves of Only Connect far and wide for nourishment. Narrative leadership – the conscious use of stories and storytelling to make meaning with and for other people – is inherently personal, relational, and contextual.

If the stories we tell as leaders are going to engage or even inspire listeners, instead of being received with justifiable scepticism, then there are some very important things to remember. We must be clear about the ground we are standing on when we claim that something matters. The truth is that if our story does not matter to us then, however skilled at storytelling we are, it will not matter to anyone else either. The story needs to be authentic and compelling, but you do not need to be a brilliant storyteller or especially charismatic; it is much more important to find genuine points of congruence between who you are and what you are saying. Ask yourself: How are you personally involved in the bigger story you are telling? In what ways is your life touched by what you are asking people to do?

Stories are a powerful force in the world, acting on our imaginations to shape, extend, and constrain our sense of what is desirable and possible; our view and experience of the world changes as we question prevailing narratives and imagine new possibilities. Therefore, the third practice of narrative leadership is to develop and tell authentic, compelling stories that are grounded in reality and that help people connect with worthwhile purposes.

This chapter will look at how the stories that leaders live and tell define their leadership, and it will also look in some detail at two particular examples of telling stories to Stand for Something.

Leading minds

Any book on storytelling and leadership must acknowledge the groundbreaking work of Professor Howard Gardner of Harvard University who researched the phenomenon of leaders-as-storytellers in his analysis of twentieth-century leaders *Leading Minds: An Anatomy of Leadership*. Drawing on the lives and works of Margaret Mead, J. Robert Oppenheimer, Robert Maynard Hutchins, Alfred P. Sloan, George C. Marshall, Pope John XXIII, Eleanor Roosevelt, Martin Luther King, Margaret Thatcher, Jean Monnet, and Mahatma Gandhi, he declared:

> *The ultimate impact of the leader depends most significantly on the particular story that he or she relates or embodies and the receptions to that story on the part of audiences (or collaborators or followers) . . . What links the eleven individuals [named above] and the score of others . . . whose names could readily have been substituted for them, is the fact that they arrived at a story that worked for them and, ultimately, for others as well. They told stories – in so many words – about themselves and their groups, about where they were coming from*

and where they were headed, about what was to be feared,
struggled against, and dreamed about.[2]

Gardner's leaders occupied the world stage – their stories and their actions are writ large in history. Because they were public figures, their lives and work are very accessible so we can easily look at them from the perspective of narrative leadership. Gardner used the term "leader" to mean "persons who, by word and/or personal example, markedly influenced the behaviors, thoughts, and/or feelings of a significant number of their fellow human beings."[3] The primary way his leaders exercised influence was, he says, by relating and embodying stories, particularly – but not exclusively – identity stories: who we are and where we are going. So far so good, but in what follows we should note that his study sought to understand the means by which his chosen leaders influenced people rather than to judge the nobility of their ends.

Some of them he classified as "direct" leaders of organizations or nations, some as "indirect" leaders, exercising influence over intellectual domains. This is a useful reminder that narrative leadership is not restricted to formal leadership roles within defined systems but is open to anyone who is trying, in Gardner's words, to "influence the behaviors, thoughts, and/or feelings of a significant number of their fellow human beings."

Gardner uses the ideas of story and storytelling quite loosely to mean a drama that unfolds over time: a journey in pursuit of certain goals in the course of which there will be resistances and obstacles to overcome. The story is sometimes told explicitly (as in Margaret Thatcher's "the lady's not for turning" speech); at other times it is implied in the words and actions of the leader (as in Gandhi's non-violent protests and marches). Gardner also makes the point that these stories are told in the context of prevailing counter-stories of why things should not change (or why the leader's story does not make sense).

Let's look briefly at Gardner's analysis of the stories of three of his leaders: Margaret Mead, Margaret Thatcher, and Mahatma Gandhi.[4] I have chosen them because of their different spheres of influence: Mead was a thought leader and ground-breaking anthropologist, Thatcher a controversial and radical politician, and Gandhi an iconic spiritual figure and non-violent agitator for social justice.

	Mead	Thatcher	Gandhi
Identity story	As human beings, we can make wise decisions about our own lives by studying options that many other cultures pursue	Britain has lost its way in defeatism and socialism. We must reclaim the leadership from "them" (socialists, union troublemakers, and the "wets") and restore earlier grandeur	We in India are equal in status and worth to all other human beings. We should work cooperatively with our antagonists if possible, but be prepared to be confrontational if necessary
Counter-stories	We Americans are special, and we have little to learn and much to fear from the examples of other cultures	Imperial Britain was a mistake and certainly should not be reinstituted. Despite its flaws, the socialist/Labour way is still the best	There is inherent inequality between colonizer and colonist. Might is right. If one is going to be confrontational, one must be prepared to be violent

In each case, by a combination of their explicit stories and their implicit embodiment of those stories, these leaders exercised tremendous influence, reframing the discourse within their domains in ways that – for good or ill – have left lasting legacies. Although Gardner is not so much concerned with the particular stories that these leaders told as with the general pattern of their stories over time, there are some significant parallels with narrative leadership. First, he reminds us that leaders tell their stories into a contested space; second, he stresses the importance of leaders (especially "direct" leaders) embodying their stories; third, he shows that, despite their power to influence, all stories are of their time and have their limitations.

	Mead	Thatcher	Gandhi
Areas of failure	Never set up an enduring organization or a viable program; analysis of Samoa may have been flawed; her progressive ideas lost currency when the society took a more conservative turn in the 1970s and 1980s; her personal life became fragmented	Eventually followed her own dictates without even taking into account the views of others; at the end of her tenure in office, political failures were largely self-inflicted; did not achieve many of her goals for Britain, though she did change the nature of the debate	India was and remains wracked with conflict; to some extent, more successful outside of India, family life was not harmonious, Gandhiism is more of an ideal than a reality

Stories are a powerful way to make meaning, but meaning – in human affairs – is not fixed and leaders who stake everything on a single story eventually lose touch with the times (which is why Know Thyself and Only Connect are ongoing practices) and fall from grace. When we choose to Stand for Something – as Gardner's leaders did – we must express authentic commitment to a certain position while also, if we are wise, knowing that it is essentially transitory. As storytellers, we must believe *in* the story, that is to say, believe in the essential message of the story, without falling into the trap of believing the story itself (always the product of imagination or re-imagination) to be an absolute truth. It is a tricky balance, and leaders best able to hold this paradox are likely to be those whose range of action logics (described in Chapter 6) extends beyond the conventional Opportunist, Diplomat, Expert, and Achiever into the post-conventional Individualist, Strategist, and Alchemist.

We will stay up in the leadership stratosphere just a little longer and bring things up to date by looking at the impact of Barack Obama's storytelling mastery, before coming down to Earth again and turning our gaze onto the kinds of leadership stories that we ourselves might be called upon to tell. At the time of writing, Obama had just been returned to the White House for a second term as President of the United States, a country in which the whole electoral process can be seen as a battle between competing stories.

In 2008, Obama defeated his opponent because his optimistic story of the future caught the imagination of a sufficient number of voters to ensure victory. The story he told of embodying change seemed absolutely congruent with the story he had lived: a journey from humble beginnings – a peripatetic mixed-race family – to Harvard Law School and the US Senate. In contrast, his Republican opponent Senator John McCain, trailing in the polls, invoked the figure of "Joe the Plumber" to persuade white working-class voters to vote for him, but the story was soon seen as a folksy gimmick; it lacked traction and McCain's audience slipped away.

Described by Christian Salmon in his excellent book *Storytelling: Bewitching the Modern Mind*,[5] as "the first elected president of the digital age," Obama followed a campaign strategy based on a highly sophisticated understanding of the "collective storytelling system" that is the US electorate. He told his own identity story (this is who I am) and wove it into a wider historical narrative in *Dreams from My Father: A Story of Race and*

Inheritance[6]; he declared his aspirations for the future of the nation (this is where we are going) in *The Audacity of Hope: Thoughts on Reclaiming the American Dream.*[7] In writing and speaking he consistently used positive and coherent language and metaphors to frame the debate and – crucially – he used the viral power of the Internet to build the audience for his stories. Obama's potential as an epic hero was spotted by the scriptwriters of influential drama series *The West Wing* when he was still a Senator; they based the character of successful presidential candidate Matt Santos on him: a case of art imitating life imitating art?

But even a brilliant storyteller like Obama can lose the plot. In 2011, after three years in office and facing the battle for re-election, Obama talked about the power of storytelling to *Vanity Fair* journalist Michael Lewis who recounted:

> *Obama was especially alive to the power of a story to influence the American public. He believed he had been elected chiefly because he had told a story; he thought he had had problems in office because he had, without quite realizing it, ceased to tell it.*[8]

In 2012, Obama's story once again spoke powerfully to the heterogeneous US electorate. Only time will reveal the substance of his legacy but we can certainly agree with Salmon's conclusion that Obama is "the embodiment of a new generation of politicians . . . who use signs and symbols rather than programs and promises . . . in order to inspire new ways of thinking about and changing the world."[9] Narrative leadership, it seems, is an idea whose time has come.

What is your story?

> *80% of success is showing up.*
>
> WOODY ALLEN[10]

It is not just politicians and public figures who need to Stand for Something. In whatever walks of life we exercise leadership, we are called upon to show up. Not just turning up, as Woody Allen's joke implies, but really showing up: declaring who we are, where we are going, and what we believe in. Telling a story enables us not just to make a declaration, but to show this with enough detail and feeling to bring it alive for our listeners. By bringing ourselves to our leadership stories, by allowing others to see our passion and vulnerability, we manifest what Arthur Frank calls "mundane charisma," the capacity to enlarge the sense of human possibility among those whom our everyday stories and actions affect.[11]

The source of this charisma does not lie in great oratory, good looks, or a commanding presence (indeed they can prevent an audience from seeing and hearing the real person) but in our willingness to tap into what really matters to us and taking the risk of reaching out to others and sharing it with them. The gesture is less one of trying to win an audience over than of inviting them into your story. Let's look at two substantial examples of this in practice to show you what I mean. The first example is from the public sector and the second from a business environment; one concerns a chief executive and the other a group of regional managers.

Stranger in a strange land

When Customs and Excise was merged with Inland Revenue in 2005 to become Her Majesty's Revenue & Customs (HMRC) with well over 100,000 staff, UK ministers decided to look outside the Civil Service for a leader capable of bringing the two organizations together and delivering new levels of efficiency in HMRC's cost base and revenue collection. The word went out: "Find us a captain of industry."

And find a captain of industry, they did. The new Chairman of HMRC, David Varney, had been a senior executive with Shell Petroleum, Chief Executive of BG (British Gas), and Chairman of mobile phone operator 02. His dynamism and experience of industry were considerable; his inexperience of the ways of Whitehall was offset by appointing career civil servant Paul Gray as his deputy. A dream team, one might say.

My company had been asked to coach the group of HMRC executives in storytelling and narrative techniques, as they settled into their new roles and began to think about how they could inspire staff from both predecessor organizations to make radical changes to working practices. My colleague Sue Hollingsworth and I spent many days in HMRC's headquarters at 100 Parliament Street and, after a while, we realized that, even at senior levels, most people didn't really understand what sort of person David Varney was or why he had taken the job. This wasn't helped by his frequent references to the business world and his tendency to rely on rather gung-ho sporting metaphors (he'd previously been involved with Formula One Racing and with the World Cup-winning England rugby team) to get his points across. Our impression was that although he was getting on with the job and getting things done, at a personal level he'd not yet "landed" in his new role.

Sue and I decided to tackle this at our next coaching session. "So David," we said. "Why *are* you here?"

"I could put my feet up," he replied. "I could just sit on the verandah drinking gin and tonic, but that's not my style. I've had a good career and I thought I could put something back."

"There has to be more to it than that," said Sue. "You probably don't need to work at all. Why are you *really* here David?"

"Well," he said. "It could be because my parents believed in the possibility of progress and taught me that we need taxes to pay for a decent society."

"That sounds more like it," I said. "But can you tell us the *story* of how and when they taught you that?" He sat back thoughtfully in his chair. After a few moments he leaned forward with a gleam in his eye and began to speak.

> *I was born just after the Second World War. We didn't have much money. My dad worked as a labourer; mum stayed at home. I'd come back from school each day and she'd say "How did it go today?" and I'd show her my marks. "Good David. Very good. But I think you could do even better." She knew that hard work was important. She and Dad both thought that the world could be made better.*
>
> *We lived in London and Dad would go miles to find work. He never shirked; always worked hard. Sometimes, if he wasn't too far away, I'd get on my bike and cycle over to wherever he was working and we'd walk home together. Those were special days. One day when I was 12 or 13*

years old, we walked home together through Docklands.
It was a bomb site – literally a bomb site – with piles of
rubble and craters half-full of water all around us. Dad
stopped and put his arm round my shoulders, "Take a
good look son," he said. "It won't always be like this. Cities
and roads will be rebuilt; industries will get back on their
feet. Things will get better. One day, in this country, we'll
have proper schools, homes and hospitals for everyone."

David paused, obviously moved, and looked us in the
eye. "That's why I'm here," he said. "Because at HMRC we
collect the money that makes all those things possible.
That's why I'm here."[12]

We told David that it was a great story: authentic, simply told, and
heartfelt. That same evening, at a formal dinner in the City, he told it to
a gathering of the good and the great. Within hours the story had spread
far and wide through HMRC. When Sue and I went back to 100 Parliament Street a few days later, the effect on David Varney's colleagues was
palpable: now they understood why this outsider had joined them and
had learned something about what drove him. He had arrived.

> 1. Challenge: What circumstances and events shaped your values? If you
>   wanted to let people around you know why you have taken on your
>   particular leadership role, what would you tell them? What story could
>   you tell from your life that would *show* them what you stand for?

If you find yourself drawing a blank in response to this challenge, you
might want to go back and reread Chapter 7 or have a conversation about
it with someone who knows you well.

Inch by inch

Often, as leaders, we are asking other people to see things another way
or to do things differently; change (even the change needed to preserve
something) is the stock in trade of leadership. Unsurprisingly, when

change is asked of us, we want to know how the person asking for the change is implicated in it. We do not like being "done to" or told by some remote figure that change is needed and will be good for us. We want to know that we are in it together.

A few years ago, I was asked to work with a regional management team of a utility company who were facing exactly that challenge. To remain competitive in a deregulated market the company needed its engineers to work more flexibly and to higher standards for no additional reward, but how could it convince them this was necessary? The company knew that it had to do more than just roll out the standard company-wide communications package and that the engineers needed help.

By the time he contacted me, the regional director (we will call him Andrew)[13] had decided that the answer was to tell an inspiring story: the four members of his team would run a series of "town hall" meetings attended by every employee in the region; they would show a video clip from *Any Given Sunday* in which Al Pacino as an American Football coach fires up his underdog team in the locker room before the big match; then they would each tell an inspiring personal story to connect the film clip with the productivity and quality message they were trying to get across. The film clip was a given; the rest was up to me and the team.

On the plus side, Andrew knew that information and argument would not be enough and that some kind of story was needed to engage his "heard it all before" engineers. On the minus side, I was not at all sure about the wisdom of using the film clip, though I was confident I could find some way of working with it. We agreed that I would work with his four team members as a group on the first evening and coach them individually the next day before getting everyone together to run through their stories and give each other feedback.

I showed the film clip to Andrew's team and asked them what they thought about using it. Randy said he liked it and that he thought most of the engineers would as well. The other three were more sceptical: Jon asked how football was relevant to digging holes in the road; Lucy and Ann said that it was too loaded with testosterone for them to engage with as women. I told them that Andrew would not budge on using the film clip and that our job was to find a way to respond to it authentically and to find personal stories making the same point – that the business would only succeed (and in the long term only survive) if they and their teams did everything they could to improve their productivity and quality of service.

Together, we created a structure that would enable them to use the clip as a springboard for their own stories. They would show the clip at their "town hall" meetings and then say something like:

> *That was Al Pacino, playing a character based on the legendary coach Vince Lombardi – in the film* Any Given Sunday. *When I first saw it, I felt . . . I wonder how it affected you? Al Pacino talked about the inches – the things that matter – the differences that make a difference in our lives. It made me think of a time when . . . It made me think about some of the tough things we need to do in our business to face the future and come through successfully.*

Their overnight homework was to think of a personal story from their own experience that reflected this theme: a difference that made a difference. The next day I spent a couple of hours with each of them, selecting, honing, and practicing their stories; the day after that they told their stories in front of Andrew and their colleagues as a dress rehearsal before taking them out on the road and telling them for real. The stories they told were authentic and every bit as powerful – in their context – as David Varney's was in his world.

It was Jon's turn first:

> *When I first watched the clip, I'll be honest with you, I wondered what on earth it had to do with us. I'm not a sports fan; I never watch football. But then I began thinking about what it means in our business to do that little bit extra that makes all the difference. You probably all know that I started out in this company as an engineer – like most of you – and I remembered a time way back when I was the supervisor on call one Christmas Eve. It was 1985, a white Christmas, snow over most of the northwest. The power went down outside a small town right on*

the edge of our area; you know how it is when water and ice get inside those old cables.

The crew got the call at mid-day and they were still at it at 5.00pm so I thought I'd go and see how they were getting on. The roads were icy and it was a hell of a drive, even with snow chains. The guys were still digging when I got there, tracking the cable back to find the fault. It was pitch dark and freezing cold. I asked the foreman how they were getting on. "She's in there somewhere," he said. "We'll get her. It's only a matter of time."

"You should be packing up soon," I told him. "It's Christmas Eve. Time to be home with your families."

"We're not going anywhere until we've got this fixed. We're not leaving these folk without power on Christmas Day." He jerked his thumb towards the town. "They've got families too."

So I asked him what I could do to help and he told me to get the burner out of the wagon and make some coffee. I stayed with them until they fixed the fault. It was gone midnight, the stars were out and the snow was thick on the ground. We said good night and went on our way. I got home at about 3.00am, crept upstairs to bed and fell asleep.

That night taught me a lesson about what we can be at our best. I've never forgotten it. In a strange way it was one of the best Christmases I've ever had.

Lucy stood up next. A diminutive young woman without Jon's long association with the company to draw on, she had to find another tack. Rather than attempt a "war story" she connected with her audience by sharing something personal (which if not quite a full-blown story, still had plenty of detail and feeling):

Well that's the film clip and I know what you're thinking: we don't play football and I'm not Al Pacino. You're right; we don't and I'm not. Although it just so happens that Al Pacino and I are almost exactly the same height. My sport isn't football; it's rock- and ice-climbing. It's also a team sport in which inches matter: stretching for ledges and handgrips; gauging the length of a pitch; knowing exactly how high to climb until you need to belay on a piton. Above all, it's a sport in which you have to trust your colleagues. When I'm out on an icefall in the Rockies, hanging off a rope, I want to know who's on the other end of it. I want to look them in the eye and know that they are going to do their job properly and I want them to look me in the eye and know the same thing. And I want it to be the same for us; I want you to look me in the eye and know that I will do my absolute best for you just as you would for me and for everyone in the team.

Ann managed a project team of technical specialists. The project was due to finish within six months when the whole team would either take voluntary redundancy or be reassigned to other work via the company "talent pool" – an HR holding bay sometimes referred to as the Sargasso Sea. In our coaching session we agreed that it would not be appropriate for her to use the film clip and that she would speak with all her staff in more intimate groups of 8–10 rather than in a "town hall" meeting:

You've probably heard by now about the film clip that Jon, Lucy and Randy are showing to their teams. Well, I've decided not to show it here because we're in a very different position. They are fighting for an unknown future and we know what our future as a team will be. In 6 months' time the project will be delivered, we'll have done our work and our team will be disbanded. We've worked well together and I have no doubt that we'll continue to work well together for the next 6 months. It's what happens afterwards that concerns me and I'm sure it concerns you too. The good news is that we don't make anyone redundant compulsorily; the less than good news is that we will all (including me) be put into the "talent pool" for reassignment.

Today, I want to have a conversation with you about what this means, how to manage the process and how to give yourself the best possible chance of getting reassigned

*to good jobs. But first, I want to tell you that I've been
through this process before 3 years ago and it wasn't
handled well. I wasn't properly prepared, I didn't know
what I was entitled to and what I could do for myself. It
was a real low point in my career and I am absolutely
determined that it won't be like that again for you or for
me. I'm going to give you a few minutes to talk it over with
the person next to you and then we'll gather up all your
questions and begin to answer them. If you've already
been through the talent pool process we want to learn from
your experiences too. OK?*

Randy decided to play it straight with the film clip and to call on his
family history to engage his audience of engineers:

*I love football and I loved the locker room pep-talk. The
bit that really got me was when he talked about things
being taken away. That's what I see happening to us: new
competitors coming into the market trying to take it away
from us. I joined this company 17 years ago, straight out
of college. My father Alex worked in this company as an
engineer all of his working life. Some of you knew him,
worked alongside him. This company is part of my family
history and I don't want anyone to take it way from us.
We know the challenges are real. We know what we have
to do to meet them. That's what I've come here today to
talk with you about. I'm up for this fight and I want
to know if you are too.*

These are not perfect stories: Lucy's would have been better if she had
used a specific climbing incident; Randy's and Ann's could have done with
a bit more detail; but they were all "good enough" and they improved
with each telling. The film clip provided a starting point (except for Ann
and even she was able to capitalize on the fact that she was deliberately
not using it) from which they could launch their own stories. Each of
them showed – authentically – how they were affected by what they were
asking their teams to do. Because the stories were real, they were easy

to tell and they rang true. The hard work in the coaching sessions – as it so often is – had been digging around for the right stories to tell.

2. Challenge: Gandhi is reputed to have said, "We must be the change we want to see in the world." Take a few minutes to think of a situation in which, as a leader, you are asking others to do something differently. What story could you tell to *show* how you are enacting the change you want to bring about?

Whatever kind of story you tell, it is best shared with others in a way that is open and inclusive, and that has room for their stories as well so they can see themselves in it. Remember too that "victory narratives" are dull and not very credible. People are much more interested in and inclined to believe stories that are rooted in reality, that acknowledge difficulties and struggles while also offering something better. Ultimately the qualities of the teller count much more than the content of the story, and those qualities shine through when you know what you stand for and when you Stand for Something!

Bonus: *The Man from Hope*

In 1992, US presidential candidate Bill Clinton made a 12-minute film about his life, originally for delegates at the Democratic National Convention. Clinton was born in a small Arkansas town called Hope and the film was called *The Man from Hope*. His mother Virginia, half-brother Roger, daughter Chelsea and wife Hilary appear alongside him. He and Hilary acknowledge past "problems" in their marriage; he is shown as a teenager in 1963 meeting President John F. Kennedy; and references to both Martin Luther King and Bobby Kennedy are woven into the story.

Some 20 years later it seems a bit saccharine and clichéd. But we are looking at it with hindsight. At the time – before the digital age – the film was seen by millions. It showed Bill Clinton as a man of the people, someone who represented the American dream of rags to riches, a politician who still "believe[d] in a place called Hope." It is well worth watching as a powerful example of political storytelling: he says, "this is where I've come from, this is who I am, and this is what I believe in" and all of it hangs together beautifully.

At the time of writing, a good-quality recording could be found at http://www .youtube.com/watch?v=X_u5R9ZQofE.

Summary

- Be clear about the ground you are standing on when claiming that something matters: the truth is that if your story does not matter to you then, however facile or skilled a storyteller you are, it will not matter to anyone else.
- Howard Gardner claimed that the primary way his chosen leaders exercised influence was by relating and embodying stories, particularly – but not exclusively – identity stories: who we are and where we are going.
- The stories we tell have most impact when they are congruent with the stories we live. For example, in the 2008 US presidential election, Barack Obama was seen to embody the positive story of change encapsulated in "Yes We Can."
- By allowing others to see our passion and vulnerability in our deeds and stories, the "mundane charisma" of ordinary leaders enlarges the sense of human possibility among those whom their stories and actions affect.
- Telling an iconic story of a time that shaped our values and sense of purpose can help others understand who we are and what we are leading for. We should avoid blowing our own trumpet in such stories.
- When we are asking others to change, we can tell stories showing that "we are all in it together." Finding an authentic point of connection and the right story to tell is crucial – real stories are convincing and easy to tell.

- When you Stand for Something, the leadership stories you tell do not need to be told brilliantly to have impact: the qualities of the teller count more than natural eloquence or technical proficiency as a storyteller.

Notes and References

1 Attributed to Hillel the Elder (traditionally said to have lived from 110 BCE to 10 CE).
2 Gardner, H. (1996). *Leading Minds: An Anatomy of Leadership* (HarperCollins: London, p14).
3 Ibid., p8.
4 Ibid. Excerpted from Appendix 1, pp308–325. Adapted from "The Eleven Leaders Viewed along the Principal Dimensions of Leadership" in Appendix 1 of Gardner H. (1996) *Leading Minds: An Anatomy of Leadership*, (HarperCollins: London).
5 Salmon, C. (2010). *Storytelling: Bewitching the Modern Mind* (Verso: London).
6 Obama, B. (2004). *Dreams from My Father: A Story of Race and Inheritance* (Broadway Books: New York).
7 Obama, B. (2006). *The Audacity of Hope: Thoughts on Reclaiming the American Dream* (Crown: New York).
8 Lewis, M. (2012). "Obama's Way," *Vanity Fair*, October.
9 Ibid., p159.
10 Attributed to Woody Allen, *New York Times*, August 13, 1989.
11 Frank, A. (n.d.) "Between the Ride and the Story: Illness and Remoralization," Unpublished paper, University of Calgary, http://people.ucalgary.ca/~frank/ride.html (accessed April 22, 2013).
12 Story reproduced with kind permission of Sir David Varney.
13 I have omitted the name of the utility company, used pseudonyms for the members of the management team, and reconstructed the stories to enable the inclusion of these excellent real-life examples of stories that Stand for Something while maintaining client confidentiality.

Section Four
Storytelling

Chapter 10

So You Want to Tell a Story

> *If stories come to you, care for them. And learn to give*
> *them away where they are needed. Sometimes a person*
> *needs a story more than food to stay alive.*
>
> BARRY LOPEZ[1]

In the practice of Know Thyself the stories we tell someone else are actually being told for our own benefit and we are primarily interested in their content rather than their form or the skill with which they are told. Nor do the stories we share in the practice of Only Connect need to be polished or artful; the openness and depth of our self-disclosure and the quality of our listening are much more important than the glibness of our storytelling. The quality of our storytelling matters more when we consciously tell stories in order to Stand for Something or to influence others.

Storytelling is both a natural human activity and a performative art. We already have most of what we need to be good storytellers and we can make even better use of our innate ability by learning a few basic techniques from the world of professional storytelling about constructing and telling stories. Like any art form, we can spend a lifetime honing our knowledge and skills, but this book – although it will offer some useful tips and practical exercises to develop your storytelling prowess – is not intended to turn you into a professional storyteller.

Instead, we will concentrate on those aspects of storytelling that are most relevant to narrative leaders by addressing the questions I am most commonly asked by people wanting either to start telling leadership stories or to improve the impact of their storytelling. There are three elements to consider: *repertoire* (how do you know what stories to tell, and where do you find them?); *composition* (how do you put your story together?); and *performance* (how do you tell the story well?). The next two chapters will focus on composition and performance; this one will look primarily at repertoire and we will consider these questions:

- Should I tell a story or not?
- When should I tell a story?
- What kinds of story work best?
- Where do I find stories to tell?

Should I tell a story or not?

If we are trying to decide whether or not to tell a story, we need to think about what stories do well and compare that to what effect we want the story to have. Remember that a story is *an imagined (or re-imagined) experience narrated with enough detail and feeling to cause your listener's imagination to experience it as real* and that a story – as opposed to information and argument – has a unique capacity to stir the imagination and feelings of listeners. If we want to enable our audience to experience something as real then a story can potentially help us. If *all* we need to do is to give people information or make a logical case for something then a story might amuse our audience or enliven our presentation but it is not absolutely necessary.

All too often (especially in corporate life) leaders fail to understand that when an audience "just don't get it," it is probably not because the numbers do not add up or that the argument does not make sense, but because they have not enabled people to imagine or to feel what "it" is. That is exactly the point at which the right story can make all the difference. Often, an example is all that is needed; let me give you one now.[2]

Shortly after a narrative leadership workshop for the UK Cabinet Office Top Management Programme, one of the participants – a senior official in the Department of Health – told me that he had subsequently been invited to address a group of 50 Department of Health officials about the importance of equality and diversity issues when treating patients in the National Health Service. He had spoken on this subject numerous times before – given people the damning evidence and made a strong case for action – but had never really engaged his audience. Following the workshop he had decided on this occasion to tell a story to make his point. I asked him to tell me the story just as he had told them. "Well," he said, "it's a true story. It's in the public domain now because there was an inquiry. I said something like this":

> *A few years ago, a man – let's call him Michael – was admitted to hospital after he had a stroke. Michael was 43 years old and had severe learning disabilities. He had difficulty communicating with people he was not familiar with or making his needs known. The stroke had left him unable to swallow but somehow the medical team did not make a decision about alternative feeding until he had been in hospital for 18 days. Soon after that, Michael became too ill to undergo the procedure to insert a feeding tube and he subsequently died. His parents complained that he had, in effect, been starved to death whilst in the care of the National Heath Service. I very much doubt if any of those doctors or nurses charged with looking after Michael went into work wanting to provide sub-standard care. If they had been challenged they would have said, "Of course we provide good quality care for everyone." So how did we – the system – let Michael and his parents down so badly?*

I asked him how the story had gone down with the audience and he told me that instead of looking down at their notebooks as so often happened at these events, they had been on the edge of their seats: "They were looking straight at me and leaning forward as if they wanted to know more. Some of them shook their heads in dismay; the sense of indignation in the room was palpable. Afterwards, some of them came up to me and asked how they could spread the word."

He had intuitively realized that although the case he had been making for health professionals to take better account of patients with disabilities was sound, he needed a story – a particular concrete example – to make the issue real for his audience. Most of us have been in similar situations, trying our best to inform and persuade to little avail, when what we needed to do was illustrate our point with a story.

> 1. Reflection: Take a few moments to recall an occasion when you have tried unsuccessfully to get your point across using information and argument. What stories could you have used to make it real for your audience?

If we have the luxury of a little time to think ahead then we can make a conscious decision whether or not a story is called for and plan accordingly. If we do not already have a suitable story in our repertoire then it can take some time and effort to find the right story and make sure we can tell it well enough (not perfectly) to do the job.

> 2. Reflection: Take a few moments to look ahead to a future occasion when you might want your audience to imagine and feel something as well as understand it. What stories could you use to make it real for them?

Are there times you should definitely not tell a story? Well I can't think of many occasions when it wouldn't be helpful to illustrate your point with a real-life or imagined example, particularly if you're talking about something outside of your audience's direct experience when they may need your help to make it real. Conversely, when something is part of your audience's direct experience they may need to be jolted out of the abstraction and detachment that tend to come with professional expertise.

On the other hand, if you're confident that all your audience actually needs is information or logical explanation then a story is not required and may not be welcome. Imagine that you're driving and can't find your destination. I'm walking along on the pavement and you pull up beside me and wind down the window: "Could you tell me the way to the train station, please?" "Good question," I reply. "I really should know the way. My grandfather was an engine driver on this line. That was many years ago, of course. They were all steam engines in his day. Wonderful things, steam engines. Why, I remember once he took me to the shunting yards. I was only 5 years old. I kept hold of his hand as he walked me across the tracks, trains going in every direction . . ."

Even if you were a steam train enthusiast on your way to a rally, I would probably have lost your attention. Not because my story didn't have the potential to be interesting but because I was telling the story for my own benefit (for the pleasure of reminiscing) and not being sensitive to your needs which were different from mine: you simply wanted to know how to get to the station.

The golden rule in the context of narrative leadership is to be clear why you are telling a story. Narratologist Roger Schank asserts that in the moment of telling a story we always have implicit goals, which he divides into three categories. *Me-goals* are directed toward meeting our own needs: to achieve catharsis, get attention, win approval, seek advice, or describe ourselves. *You-goals* focus on the impact of our stories on our listeners: to illustrate a point, make the listener feel something, transport the listener, transfer information, summarize significant events. *Conversational goals* are intended to influence the ongoing process of communication: to open a new topic, change the topic, continue the conversation, respond to someone else, be argumentative, distract attention away from other topics.[3]

Any and all of these implicit goals are legitimate (and potentially effective) in the appropriate context. For example, the stories that we explored in Chapters 7, 8, and 9 covered most of the me-goals and you-goals as well as the conversational goals of opening a new topic and responding to someone else. It is rarely appropriate for leaders to tell cathartic stories simply to make themselves feel better (although genuine expression of emotion and self-disclosure may be exactly what is needed).

In short, there are no hard and fast rules about when to tell and when not to tell a story. It is more a matter of using stories for what they do best (stirring the imagination, engaging emotions, making things real); ensuring that the stories you tell are appropriate for the context; and telling them well enough to hold your audience's attention. Whatever the circumstances, it does not pay to be self-indulgent, rambling, or long-winded!

When should I tell a story?

The previous section offered you a test to help you decide whether or not to tell a story: ask yourself, "Do I need to make this real?" It's a principle, not a rule, and as you gain confidence and experience in applying it, you'll develop a more intuitive sense of when a story is needed. Your "storied mind" is a more reliable guide in these matters than any rule-driven checklist. Having said that, it *is* possible to anticipate a range of circumstances when telling a story is likely to be helpful. Here are brief descriptions of 20 I've come across that are worth thinking about from the perspective of narrative leadership and tucking away in your back pocket. You'll notice that I've stayed away from sales and brand stories for which there are many other sources.

1. *Honoring achievement:* stories about individuals to honor their service and achievement when they move on or retire; stories about the outstanding achievements of particular groups bringing to life what they have done and why we should celebrate and be inspired by them.

2. *Focusing on purpose:* stories about those whom we serve – clients, customers, patients, members, etc. – foregrounding their experience to remind us what our organization or institution exists for; these stories exemplify the benefits to others of doing our work well and the costs of doing it badly.

3. *Remembering our roots:* foundational stories of how our group, organization, institution, or movement came into being carry great emotional weight and resonance; knowing our history helps us develop a sense of belonging to something bigger than ourselves in which we can play a part.

4. *Encouraging good practice:* sharing examples of good practice and telling "appreciative stories" shows other people how to do things better; research by John Seely Brown and colleagues[4] at Xerox revealed how peers often use this kind of knowledge exchange to share solutions to technical problems.

5. *Demonstrating values in action:* catching people doing things right and telling their stories enables others to think about what they might do to put espoused values into action. To show quality of service in

action, a senior executive I once worked with in HMRC used to tell the story of a local manager who had used her own initiative and money to set up a crèche for claimants and children so they did not have to queue for benefits in the rain.

6. *Warning about bad practice:* stories about things going wrong bring us up short and can cause us to reflect on how to improve our practice; a report containing specific examples of how badly some NHS patients were treated in certain hospitals has prompted calls for reform of medical and nurse training.

7. *Anticipating change and transition:* in uncertain times a story that shows that "we know what to do when we don't know what to do" helps to maintain confidence; the CEO of a retail sports fashion chain I once worked with told the story of yachtswoman Dee Caffari preparing her boat for stormy waters as a way of alerting the staff to the prospect of difficult market conditions.

8. *Imagining possible futures:* making sense of what the future might hold is a key leadership task; stories that imagine possible futures enable us to take a creative leap and consider what we need to do to get there; the stronger the image of the future, the more it can drag us out of the gravitational pull of the present; building such detailed scenarios is an essential part of long-range strategic planning (remembering of course that any story of the future is a fiction).

9. *Introducing radical ideas:* a "what if" story is a good way of playing with speculative ideas without committing prematurely to a new course of action; this kind of creative storytelling is commonly used to drive social and technical innovation; the Japanese inventor of the personal stereo asked himself, "What if I could listen to my favorite music in public without disturbing other people?"

10. *Telling people who you are:* iconic stories that reveal who you are and why you are here are important for people claiming leadership roles; Bill Clinton's 1992 video *The Man from Hope* is a classic example of this kind of storytelling from someone on the world stage; the stories told by David Varney and the utility company managers in Chapter 9 are also excellent in their own ways.

11. *Sharing hopes and dreams*: these stories are extensions of the "Who am I" stories mentioned above; they demand a willingness to let down

our defenses and be vulnerable – few things are more sensitive to share than our hopes and dreams for the future; the practice of Know Thyself will help us get in touch with our authentic sense of purpose and help us avoid clichéd, commonplace, aspirational stories.

12. *Claiming helpful associations:* by telling stories about people we admire – our heroes and heroines, be they humble or grand – we associate ourselves with them and their qualities; we are not claiming to be like them, just that we have learned from them or would like to be more like them in some way; Barack Obama used such stories quite legitimately to associate himself in voters' minds with both President Kennedy and Martin Luther King.

13. *We're in this together:* as the utility company managers' stories in the last chapter showed, authentic personal stories that connect your fate with the fates of those you are asking to change is a powerful way of establishing common cause; Shakespeare gives us a wonderfully dramatic fictional version of this in the inspirational words he puts into the mouth of Henry V before the Battle of Agincourt, when he is asked by the French herald if he will desert his men and be ransomed, to avoid what looks at that time like certain death. Henry refuses the offer outright and casts his lot in with his soldiers:

> Come thou no more for ransome, gentle herald.
> They shall have none, I swear, but these my joints,
> Which if they have as I will leave 'em them
> Shall yield them little . . .

14. *Normalizing experience:* when someone is surprised, delighted, disturbed, made anxious, or upset by an experience, responding with a story showing that you have had (or perhaps someone you know has had) a similar experience or similar feelings can settle them; think of it as putting "war stories" to good use.

15. *Encouraging other people to tell their stories:* we know that listening to personal stories prompts a storied response so we can invite other people to tell their stories – if that is what we want to do – by opening the space with a story of our own; there were numerous examples of this phenomenon in Chapter 8.

16. *Naming the elephant in the room:* an allegorical story can depersonalize issues and give people a common language to resolve tricky

issues and interpersonal conflicts; as a consultant I once told a board that they reminded me of courtiers scheming and conniving for the favors of the monarch of a medieval kingdom; the characters I named became the jocular means for them to talk about conflict in the team.

17. *Apologizing, showing contrition:* offering an "unreserved apology" is not the same as saying "I'm sorry" and saying that we are sorry is not the same as showing that we are sorry; remedial action and recompense speak louder than any words, but telling a real-life story showing that we have accepted responsibility for our actions and are taking active steps to ameliorate their adverse consequences is an important step on the way.

18. *Acknowledging disaster or tragedy:* in the face of tragedy or disaster, the human needs of the life-world reassert themselves; when serious illness, bereavement, desertion, and accidents happen, we need to share stories about our experience; we need the loving attention of our friends and colleagues and we make time to say what needs to be said.

19. *Making a point memorably:* if we have a vital point that we want to be sure people will remember, using a story to illustrate it is much more effective than simply telling people that it is important; working as a consultant in an oil and gas company, I noticed that every significant meeting I attended began with someone telling a "health and safety" story to remind everyone in the room of the ever-present hazards of the petrochemical industry.

20. *Entertaining ourselves and others:* we don't always need an ostensible reason for telling stories, gossip, jokes, and anecdotes beyond the fact that they can be highly entertaining; we are the storytelling animal, we cannot help telling stories, and, when told well enough, we love to hear them too.

This isn't a comprehensive list, of course. I'm sure you can think of many other occasions when a telling story is likely to be useful and appropriate. We'll look in depth at some of these opportunities for narrative leadership in future chapters. For now, I'll leave you to compare what I've said about these 20 situations with your own experience, and turn to the next big question.

What kinds of story work best?

For a story to work well it has to fulfill three conditions. You have to be OK telling it; your audience have to be open to it; and it has to meet the needs of the situation. Finding a good enough fit with all three is a matter of judgment rather than an exact science. The image that comes to mind is the ancient Celtic triple spiral. There is a famous one carved into the entrance stone of the Newgrange megalithic tomb in Ireland.

We can imagine that each of the three loosely drawn spirals represents one of the three conditions we want our story to satisfy. As long as we pay attention to all three, our story will work well. Fortunately we are used to making this kind of complex judgment (although we may not have done so before in relation to storytelling). It all boils down to three key questions about the *situation*, the *audience*, and *you*:

1. What is the point I want to get across?
2. What are my listeners open to hearing?
3. What stories do I feel confident telling?

Getting to the right story is an iterative process and you will probably loop round the questions more than once. But putting the needs of the situation first, the capacity of the audience second, and your own preferences third is more likely to guide you to the best option than working inside out from what stories you feel comfortable telling.

Situation: The previous section listed 20 situations in which telling a story is likely to be helpful. If you look back over them you will see that in each case the reason for telling a story (the underlying intention) determines what it is that you want the story to make real for your audience. And that is the point of your story: to bring something alive in the hearts and minds of your listeners rather than to impose a particular meaning or moral, which is a surefire way of turning your audience off. Remember that when you tell a story with enough detail and feeling, your listeners have a realistic imagined experience. Ask yourself what the situation calls for – what kind of imagined experience might make the difference that is needed.

For example, to honor an achievement, we want our story to enable the audience to have an imagined experience of things like the exceptional effort, particular abilities, unusual dedication, good fortune, courage in overcoming difficulties, determination to succeed, etc., that led to the achievement, so we look for a story that exemplifies these. We can apply a similar thought process to any situation to get a sense of what it calls for and to clarify what imagined experience we want to give our audience.

Audience: Next, we want to think about our audience; how well do we know them? If we know them well, then we will already have a good idea of what they are interested in and receptive to, in which case we can decide whether to go for a safe bet or stretch their comfort zone with a story they might find a bit challenging. If we do not know our audience personally then we can use the Leadership Development Framework described in Chapter 6 to guide us. Stories told from within the dominant action logic of the audience are likely to go down well, but we might also choose to tell a story that speaks to their potential to act from a different action logic that we believe to be more appropriate and effective in the circumstances.

For example, to encourage an audience whose dominant action logic is Expert to excel within a technical problem-solving mode, I might tell them the story of how Nobel Prize-winning Physicist Richard Feynman discovered the cause of the *Challenger* Space Shuttle disaster (a rubber seal that fractured when cold, allowing highly explosive propellant to escape and ignite). Or, I might draw on the well-known story of the NASA "backroom boys" who devised the jury-rigged CO_2 scrubber that saved the lives of the crew of Apollo 13.

If, on the other hand, I wanted to encourage my group of experts to apply more of an Achiever action logic, I might tell the story of the Ford Edsel launched in 1957 after an unprecedented amount of market research and technical R&D. The Edsel offered innovative features such as warning lights for low oil level, parking brake engaged, and engine overheating, as well as a push-button transmission gear shift in the center of the steering wheel, ergonomically designed controls for the driver, and self-adjusting brakes. It also had advanced safety features such as seat belts (which were rare at the time), and child-proof rear door locks that could only be opened with the key. Everyone thought it was a surefire winner – everyone except the car-buying public, who looked at the whole package and saw that it was a complete turkey. The Edsel has passed into automotive legend as the *Titanic* of cars because no one took responsibility for making sure that the Ford Motor Company achieved the most important thing – a car that people would actually buy.

A well-told story can offer glimpses of what it might be like to operate from a different action logic in a much less threatening way than a direct injunction to do things differently. Our capacity to appreciate stories defies rigid categorization, so we must use the model with caution and not jump to conclusions that limit our options or underestimate our audience's ability to engage imaginatively with the whole range of action logics.

You: Like our audience, our own dominant action logic will also give us a tendency to prefer particular types of story and it is as well to know which, so that we can check whether or not our natural preference also meets the needs of the situation and the audience. We might need to stretch ourselves as well as our audience!

The post-conventional action logics of Individualist, Strategist, and Alchemist tend to be more self-reflexive and adaptable than the Opportunist and the conventional Diplomat, Expert, and Achiever. Rules and categories are less fixed from a post-conventional perspective and post-conventional storytellers are therefore likely to be comfortable telling a wide range of stories, though everyone (as we discovered in Chapter 4) also has a "home base" in fact, fiction, or fantasy.

Don't let the model over-complicate things. We know what kinds of stories we feel comfortable and confident telling. Over time we can expand our repertoire and learn to enjoy different genres. There's just one golden rule to remember: if you don't connect emotionally with a story – if it doesn't make sense to you – don't tell it, no matter how well it seems to fit the bill, because you won't be able to bring it alive for your audience.

Where do I find stories to tell?

The world is made of stories but where do they come from? Where can we go to find a story when we want one to tell? I've often heard a plaintive cry of "but I haven't got any stories to tell" in workshops and coaching sessions. The problem is never that we haven't got any stories, it's that we don't necessarily know where to look for them. The good news is that there are only five pots of stories to look in (though you might have to rootle round a bit to find the ones you want).[5]

Official stories are handed down to us to tell on behalf of the organization or system within which we work. They are the sanitized and approved stories that toe the "party line" – risk free because HR, Legal, Finance, and the CEO's Office have checked them to within an inch of their lives, but unlikely to convince anyone of anything. If we are obliged to tell them, then we need to find other stories with which to frame them and add a personal dimension to make them real for the audience. There is never a shortage of official stories.

Our own experiences provide a wealth of stories: childhood memories, doing something for the first time, giving and receiving help, triumphs and disasters, unexpected events, meeting new people, falling in love, standing up for what we believe in, compromising our values, joining a team, visiting other countries. All our significant memories are stored as stories or proto-stories waiting to be told. Exploring these memories through the practice of Know Thyself is an invaluable way of accessing these stories and building a repertoire. David Varney's story is a good example of this.

Other people's experiences provide us with second-hand experiences we can draw upon. It is often much more effective to put other people in the spotlight; let them be the heroes and heroines of your stories. In Chapter 6, I told the story of Vinoba Bhave to show narrative leadership in action. We constantly learn from other people – those we know personally and those we know of but have never met. Tell stories based on their experiences and let your audience know how they have affected you. This is where the practice of Only Connect pays dividends in terms of stories you can tell.

Fictional stories like the "what if" story or the "possible futures" story or the "I have a dream" story generally require some forethought and preparation, although they can arise spontaneously in the heat of the moment. I gave an example of a fictional "future story" when I described the NTO Market Leader and Market Follower scenarios in Chapter 5. It is fine to tell fictional stories (any story about how things might be is a fiction) but not to pass them off as actual experiences.

Borrowing well-known stories taps into a vast pool of material that already exists in our common culture. Novels, traditional stories, television drama, radio serials, theater, and films offer a fantastic treasury of stories that you can draw upon. Choose iconic moments that are known to a fair proportion of your audience and you've got a ready-made story that you don't even have to tell in full. If it's not well known you may have to play an excerpt (as the utility company managers did with *Any Given Sunday*). I've used this technique in writing this book, particularly in the Bonus sections at the end of each chapter.

As a leader, I once used a scene from *Indiana Jones and the Last Crusade* to make my point for me: "Remember the moment when Indiana Jones steps off a ledge into the ravine and a glass bridge appears under his feet? The bridge only appears when you step off. That's what trust is about and that's what we need in this project."

3. Borrowing Stories: Think of a challenging situation ahead of you in which you want to communicate a strong message. What moment(s) from literature, drama, film, etc., could you use to make the point for you? What would you need to say to make the link between you, the "borrowed story," your audience, and the situation you/they are facing?

You probably found that the stories you were invited to think of in this chapter didn't come to mind fully formed. You may just have had glimpses of a few possible stories that you might want to tell. Don't be put off; that's often how it works. The frameworks and exercises in the next chapter will enable you to develop these fragmentary thoughts and memories into fully fledged stories. You'll also find that the process gets easier as you begin to build a repertoire: you'll become more aware of the richness of your own stories; you'll pick up on other people's stories; you'll notice stories all around you; and one story will lead on to another.

Bonus: *Made in Dagenham*

The film *Made in Dagenham* (2010) is a fictional account of real-life events: a strike by women fabric workers at Ford's Dagenham car factory in 1968. The women, angered by their re-grading as unskilled workers and the fact that women were not entitled by law to the same pay as men for equivalent work, vote to come out on indefinite strike until their demands for equal pay are met. The film depicts women – led by women – fighting for their rights. At a critical moment, shop steward Sally O'Grady reluctantly steps forward at the Trade Union Congress, to ask for the support of male colleagues, many of whom are initially quite unsympathetic.

She wins them over with a story about a friend of hers, an ex-serviceman who had recently died. It speaks to the situation (fighting for what is right); it is a story that her audience could relate to (many of them had also fought in the war); and it is one that she could connect with and tell with feeling (it was about her best friend's husband). The scene is well worth watching. Her two-minute speech is a brilliant example of narrative leadership.

Summary

- Storytelling in the context of narrative leadership is often quite low key, though there is a performative element to storytelling in formal settings. We can easily supplement our innate ability by learning a few basic techniques.

- There are three essential elements: repertoire (knowing what stories to tell and where to find them); composition (learning how to put our stories together); and performance (telling a story for maximum effect).
- The key question to ask when deciding if you are going to tell a story is whether or not you need to "make something real" by sparking your audience's imaginations and stirring their feelings.
- We can anticipate many situations when a story of some kind is likely to be useful. The list of 20 such situations given in this chapter is indicative rather than definitive; trust your intuitive "storied mind" to guide you.
- The different action logics in the Leadership Development Framework can help us choose what kind of story to tell: we might want our story to speak to our listeners' dominant action logic or to challenge it.
- The stories we tell come from five potential sources: sanitized and approved official stories handed down to us to tell; our own experiences; other people's experiences; fictional stories; and borrowed stories already in the common culture.
- The speech made by the character Sally O'Grady to the Trade Union Congress in the film *Made in Dagenham* is a great example of telling a very effective story that fits the situation, the audience, and the teller.

Notes and References

1 Lopez, B. (1990). *Crow and Weasel* (North Point Press: San Francisco, p48).
2 I first shared this example in an earlier book, Mead, G. (2011). *Coming Home to Story: Storytelling Beyond Happily Ever After* (Vala Publishing: Bristol).
3 Schank, R. (1995). *Tell Me a Story: Narrative and Intelligence* (Northwestern University Press: Evanston, IL).
4 Brown, J.S., Denning, S., Groh, K., and Prusak, L. (2005). *Storytelling in Organizations* (Elsevier: Amsterdam).
5 Adapted from Schank, R., op. cit.

Chapter 11

A Good Story *Well Told*

> *But the love of a good story, of terrific characters and
> a world driven by your passion, courage and creative
> gifts is still not enough. Your goal must be a good story,
> well told.*
>
> ROBERT MCKEE[1]

Robert McKee is a Hollywood script consultant, screenwriter, and screen-writing teacher whose Story Seminar has attracted over 50,000 students (including 35 Academy Award winners and 170 Emmy Award winners)[2] since it was first offered in 1984. There is not much he does not know about how to put a good story together. His best-selling book *Story: Substance, Structure, Style, and the Principles of Screenwriting* is a treasury of excellent advice for creative writers on how to tell stories and I recommend it for anyone wanting to dive in deeper than the limitations of this book allow.

As leaders, though, we are more interested in the practical effect of our stories than in winning Oscars and our goal is correspondingly modest: a good enough story well enough told. Fortunately, although few of us have the talent to write award-winning novels, plays, and film scripts, we all have the ability to tell a good enough story well enough to engage an audience. The previous chapter focused on repertoire – choosing what stories to tell and knowing where to find them; this chapter will focus on composition – how to structure and tell your chosen story for maximum impact.

We will assume that you have already decided that you want to tell a story; that you have identified one that you think might work; and that you have some time to prepare before actually telling it. At this stage it is probably quite rudimentary: not so much a story as an idea of what the story might be about. What do you do now? What are the key things to think about – the essential steps that will make all the difference – when you are putting your story together?

Remember that a story is an imagined or re-imagined experience narrated with enough detail and feeling to cause your listener's imagination to experience it as real. If nothing happens, it is not a story (it is more likely to be an opinion or a description); something has to happen and it has to happen to someone (not to anyone and everyone); furthermore, it has to happen somewhere and sometime. Stories always involve particular characters and events and are always located in time and space. A story's power to engage our feelings and imagination comes from its specificity; we are much more interested in what happens to a particular person than what tends to happen to people in general. It is for this reason that a traditional storyteller might begin: "Once upon a time, there was a king and a queen." The storyteller will not say: "On the whole, there was royalty." The former heralds the possibility of a story, whereas the latter announces the probability of a lecture!

The process of preparation is similar whatever kind of story we have chosen to tell: an official story handed down to us to tell (if we must); a story from our own experience; a story from other people's experiences; a fictional story; or a borrowed story already in the common culture. The balance between imagining and re-imagining (recalling) the specifics of the story will vary depending on its source, but the elements we need to consider are exactly the same. The mnemonic CASTLE may help to keep them in mind:

Characters
Action
Structure
Texture
Language
Emotions

In the rest of the chapter, we'll look at each of these elements in turn and apply them in practice by developing a leadership story step by step, from an idea of what the story might be about, to a fully fledged ready-to-tell story. It's one from my own experience that I called to mind when asked by a colleague if I knew a story about much-needed help arriving unexpectedly. I scratched my head for a few minutes and then replied:

> *When I was a student, the professor let me dictate some of my exam papers so they could be marked because my writing was illegible.*

It was the half-remembered germ of a story; I knew it would need some work to make it interesting and memorable. As I prepared the story – which I now regularly tell in narrative leadership workshops – all the elements in the CASTLE mnemonic came into play. To demonstrate the process I'll take each element in turn, though in practice they tend to overlap and merge as different images and memories spring to mind, blending into one another like splodges of paint on an artist's palette. Afterward, I'll reveal the whole picture – the story as I tell it now.

Characters

We have to care about what happens to the characters in a story for it to engage us at all. For that to occur we need to know something about them: what is special or unique about them; what are their circumstances; what do they want or need? Desire is the motivating force of stories; it provokes the characters into action and moves the story along. In this story there are two characters: me and the professor. What can I say about them that might be important for putting the story together?

> *The Professor: he was quite distinctive and very distin-guished in his field, with a fearsome reputation; he was not one to tolerate incompetence or folly. These are the details I recalled (re-imagined) about him:*
>
> * *Professor James Holt (Reading University)*
> * *World expert on Magna Carta*
> * *Stocky, sandy-haired, wore horn-rimmed glasses and brogues*

- *About 50 years old at the time and still alive today*
- *Blunt Yorkshireman with northern accent*
- *Pronounced the letter "R" as if it were "W"*
- *Went on to become Master of Fitzwilliam College, Cambridge*
- *Visiting Fellow at Emmanuel College, Cambridge after retirement*
- *Knighted in later life – Sir James Holt.*

Me: I needed to think back to the summer of 1972 when I took the Final Examinations for my History BA at Reading University. Who was I then? What did I most desire?

- *21 years old, shoulder-length hair, bearded*
- *Proto-hippy (but quite conventional underneath)*
- *Dropped out for a year but returned to finish degree*
- *Had crammed but was ill-prepared for examination*
- *Knew that my handwriting was unreliable*
- *Accepted for Police Graduate Entry Scheme*
- *Needed to pass degree to take up job offer*
- *Failing would have been huge blow to pride.*

I won't necessarily use all of this detail when I tell the story but recalling (re-imagining) it helps me connect emotionally with those long-ago events, and I can definitely use some of it to flesh out the characters. It may seem strange to think of ourselves as characters in our own stories, but that's who we are to our listeners.

The 21-year-old me is the protagonist of this story and I'll tell it from his point of view, but the real hero is Professor Holt who let me dictate some illegible exam papers so they could be marked, so it's important that I present him as a real person, a character not a caricature.

Action
The next thing to look at is what happened, not the minutiae but the key moments in the action. Because I've got time to think about the sequence of events, I can check that they're in the right order and that I'm not leaving anything out that a listener will need to understand what's going on; I want to be sure that one thing leads naturally to another when I

come to tell the story. As I do this, I also begin to recall (re-imagine) a lot more descriptive detail, but I'll come back to that when we look at Texture.

- *It's examination fortnight, June 1972*
- *On day 1 write the first of 10 three-hour papers*
- *I struggle more and more with handwriting*
- *By day 6 it starts to crumble into a wild scrawl*
- *I carry on knowing that my answers are illegible*
- *I finish the last exam knowing that I have failed*
- *I tell no one and wait for the axe to fall*
- *I am summoned to Professor Holt's office*
- *He tells me that some of my papers cannot be read*
- *He tells me to dictate them to his secretary*
- *She types them and they are then marked*
- *I pass the examination and get my degree*
- *I join the police as a graduate entrant.*

A chronicle of events like this gives us the bare bones of a story on which we can hang all the rest. Making sure that we know the sequence of key events is the single most important thing to give us confidence in telling a story. The CASTLE process is designed to help you engage deeply with the story so that you know it (whatever its source) so well that you can tell it as easily and naturally as the train stories were told in Chapter 5.

Many novice storytellers confuse knowing a story with remembering a story; they write it out word for word and memorize it. When it comes to telling the story, they recite it from memory; most of their attention is directed toward trying to remember the words. It is not surprising they often worry about losing the thread. But you can only forget something when you have to remember it; if you know the story you cannot forget it.

There is another good reason not to write your stories out and commit them to memory. As mentioned in Chapter 3, oral language is different from written language; what reads well on the page will not necessarily sound good to the ear. I sometimes write down stories that I have told (to share them in written form as I do in this book) but I never write them out in order to tell them. I will make notes, draw sketches and doodles, jot down names, dates, and places, but when it comes to telling, I set all that aside and just tell the story in the moment as best I can.

Structure

We have to get the basic sequence of what happened right for a story to make sense but a chronological list of events (even a richly detailed one) is not enough to make a satisfying story. To satisfy us, the story needs to take us somewhere; it needs to feel whole and complete. Aristotle understood this and it was he who first said (writing about the dramatic arts in his *Poetics*) that:

> *A whole is that which has a beginning, a middle, and an end . . . Well-constructed plots should not therefore begin or end at any arbitrary point but should employ the stated forms.*[3]

Ask anyone what they know about the structure of a good story and they will tell you that it must have a beginning, a middle, and an end, though they may not be quite certain what this means in practice beyond starting, talking for a bit, and then stopping. To understand better what it really means, imagine that instead of telling a story you are the pilot of an airliner. You get your passengers on board (get their attention), you take off (the beginning of your story), you fly the plane to your chosen destination (the middle of your story), you land safely with all your passengers in good shape (the end of your story).

Just as we appreciate a good clean takeoff and a smooth landing when flying, we want the beginning and ending of a story to have a comfortable angle of ascent and descent: not too shallow or it drags; not too steep or it jolts and jars. Unlike flying, which we generally prefer to be free of dramatic incidents, we do want some drama in our stories, so we like the middle to have some ups and downs, some twists and turns.

As a rule of thumb, the beginning needs to give us enough context to locate the events of the story in time and space, and tell us enough about the protagonists and their circumstances to interest us in their fate. As listeners, we do not need very much information to catch on, so a lengthy preamble is quite unnecessary and makes us wonder if the story will ever get off the ground. On the other hand, if we do not give enough information to orient our listeners and grab their attention we are likely to take off with an empty plane.

What does the beginning of the example story need to include? I want to find a hook – maybe something about help arriving when you most need and least expect it; early on it should locate the story, which happened at university in 1972; and, finally, I am going to set up the drama by including something about having to pass the examination but fearing that my handwriting will let me down.

The middle section is the meat of the story. It is where the most dramatic moments occur, when the main characters try to obtain what they want/need and meet the difficulties and obstacles that stand in their way. It shows us the qualities they are called upon to display, what help they receive (if any), and how they overcome – or fail to overcome – the challenges they face. If we have set up the beginning of the story well enough, our listeners will care about what happens to them; tension and anticipation build because they do not yet know if the protagonists will reach their goal.

In the example story that we are putting together, the middle section includes me in the examination room, starting well but then seeing my handwriting become increasingly illegible; knowing that I must have failed; being summoned to see the professor; and his arranging for me to dictate my papers to a typist.

The end section of a story provides a release for the dramatic tension that has built up. We want to know whether or not the protagonists finally achieved their goal and the consequences of achieving or not achieving it: What has changed as a result of the struggle? What has been learned and by whom? A story that does not provide such a resolution is not a whole because (though it may have finished) it has not yet ended. Writers of serials deliberately use the cliffhanger technique to leave their audience wanting more, but we are unlikely to do that in the time-bound context of narrative leadership.

The end of the example story needs to let listeners know that my papers got marked, as a result of which I passed my degree and was therefore able to take up the offer I had received to join the police as a graduate entrant. As well as this factual information, it could also say something about my gratitude for the professor's generosity and the difference it has made to my life.

Texture

We give texture and color to a story by including specific sensory details: impressions of what we would see, hear, touch, taste, and smell if the events of the story were actually unfolding around us. With a factual story we can draw on our memories for these details, while for fictional or fantastical stories we either have to import them from other experiences we have had or imagine them from scratch. Most of us emphasize visual imagery but descriptions of sounds, tastes, smells, and tactile sensations are also powerful stimulants for the listener's imagination. A story with too little detail is flat and uninteresting; one with too much detail gets bogged down and loses impetus. Judging how much is just right takes a bit of practice – your listener's level of interest will give you the best feedback.

For the example story, I can recall (re-imagine) a fair amount of detail, though I may not use it all every time I tell the story.

- *Professor Holt was a Yorkshireman; had a booming voice but spoke with a lisp; was stocky; had sandy-colored hair; wore horn-rimmed glasses, heavy brogues, and leather elbow-patches on his tweed jacket.*
- *I was 21 years old; had shoulder-length hair and a beard; wore flared "hippy" trousers; felt ashamed when I "failed" the exam and blushed.*
- *It was a hot summer; we all sweated in the examination room; Professor Holt's study was crammed with books and medieval documents; the message summoning me to see the professor was delivered to my pigeonhole.*

These are the kinds of detail that will help to bring the story alive in a listener's imagination. Specific sensory details distinguish one experience – one story – from another; they make it *your* story not just any old story.

Language

I will say more about the language of storytelling when we focus on the business of actually telling stories, in the next chapter. However, one important aspect to consider when putting stories together is how we treat speech (i.e., what characters said). Using direct speech rather than reported speech at key moments brings listeners into the presence of the story. To see what I mean, contrast the following two passages:

> *The bride agreed that she would stay faithful to the groom.*

> *"Do you promise to keep yourself only unto James as long as you both shall live?" – "I do," said Rosalie.*

The latter (direct speech) shows you what was actually said, whereas the former (reported speech) tells you about what was said. Direct speech is a form of sensory detail that we can use to powerful effect when telling a story, but it takes much longer and slows the story down. Using direct speech all the time can be wearing for the listener and hard to remember for the storyteller, so it is best to use it sparingly. A good rule of thumb is to reserve it for the most dramatic moments – the turning points – in a story when you want to slow things down and bring the audience close.

The key turning point in the example story occurs when the professor tells me that I cannot be awarded a degree if my examination papers are unreadable and then offers me the opportunity to dictate what I have written so that they can in fact be marked. If I use direct speech here, it will be more dramatic than reported speech and it will also give me an opportunity to have a bit of fun with the professor's lisp. My memory of this encounter is a vivid one, but it happened more than 40 years ago so I cannot remember his exact words, but allowing for some poetic (and storyteller's) license, I come up with this, which is the essence of what he said and the manner in which he spoke:

> *Some of your scwipts are unweadable. If we cannot wead them, we cannot mark them. And if we cannot mark them we cannot award you a degwee. Fortunately for you, I'm interwested in whether you can think, and not whether you can wite. Take the scwipts to my secwetawy and dictate what you have witten. We'll get them typed and see what you had to say, shall we?*

Emotions

Bringing such details to mind takes us into the world of the story and helps us connect with it emotionally. I can feel echoes of the anticipation, anxiety, frustration, shame, relief, and gratitude that I felt at the time. It is easy to see how this happens with stories from our own experience, but we can also feel strong emotional connections and reactions to fictional stories: theater, film, opera, poetry, and literature all thrive on our imagination's capacity to provoke such feelings.

If we want to make something real for our listeners then – as well as telling them what happened in our story – we also have to take them on an emotional journey. Thus, the final element to consider when putting a story together is its emotional palette: both the range of emotions expressed and how they change during the story. It is helpful to name these emotions (to ourselves) as I have done above for the example story – anticipation, anxiety, frustration, despair, shame, relief, and gratitude – so we can differentiate them.

When we tell the story we can negotiate the emotional terrain better if we have already mapped the broad sweep of the emotional journey. A simple way of doing this is to chart the shifts in the protagonist's emotional state (in terms of overall positive–negative feelings) throughout the story. Doing this for the example story made me realize that its trajectory was more complex than a simple – "things got worse then they got better" – U-shaped curve.

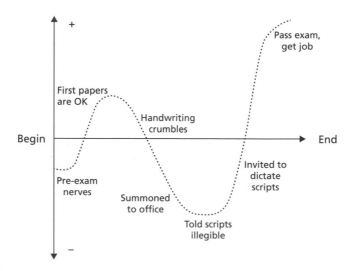

Things started off badly with pre-exam nerves; got a bit better with some good early papers; then got a lot worse as my handwriting crumbled, realized that I'd failed, and was summoned to the professor's study. They reached the low point when he told me that my papers were unreadable and couldn't be marked. Suddenly there was new hope when I was invited to dictate the illegible scripts; and finally I was euphoric when I learned that I'd passed the exam and got the job.

Feeling better because the early exam papers went well turned out to be a "false dawn" and it is not strictly necessary to include it for people to get the gist of the story, but it makes the subsequent descent into despair steeper and more dramatic so it probably needs to stay in when I tell it.

This kind of preparation helps to ensure that we have all the elements of a good story in place: distinctive characters an audience can care about; a logical sequence of events; a robust structure with a beginning, middle, and end; detailed and memorable images; appropriate and dramatic use of direct speech; a clear and compelling emotional journey. Putting them all together resulted in the following story (written down as I tell it and not written out in order to learn it).

The first two lines introduce the theme of the story and are only necessary if the context in which the story is being told has not already highlighted the theme. The coda in the final two paragraphs gives the story a nice twist, brings us back to my bad handwriting, and reflects my very real sense of gratitude to the professor who had helped me.

Better late than never

Sometimes help comes unexpectedly when you most need it. When it does you never forget the person who helped you.

At 21, I was a hippy – flared trousers, shoulder length hair, the lot. I was at university studying English History. Despite my appearance, I was desperate for a career in the police service and I'd been offered a place on the Police Graduate Entry Scheme. All I needed was to pass my degree. When it came time for Finals, it was all or nothing

– no assessed work – it all came down to 10 (three-hour-long) written exams in a fortnight. I'd crammed hard and I was as ready as I'd ever be. But the trouble was my handwriting; it had always been shaky and I didn't know if it would stand up to 30 hours of exams.

The first few papers weren't too bad. I hit the jackpot with a few stock questions and I began to feel more confident about passing. But although I knew what I wanted to say, my handwriting began to crumble. By Paper 7 (Church Architecture in the Middle Ages, as I recall) it had become an illegible scrawl. Even I could hardly read it; the examiners didn't stand a chance. I knew I'd failed but I carried on anyway – I couldn't think of anything else to do.

After the last exam, I went out with my mates to drown my sorrows. Then I waited for the axe to fall, as I knew it would. Three days later there was a message in my pigeon-hole (no mobile phones back then) instructing me to attend the Head of Department's office at 9.30 a.m. the next day. I'd been expecting something like this. Decent of them to tell me in person, I thought. Even so, I couldn't sleep.

At the appointed time, I knocked on the door of the professor's study and waited. Professor James Holt was a blunt Yorkshireman who spoke with a slight lisp; a world expert on Magna Carta (I'd taken his seminar); and noto-rious for not tolerating fools – gladly or otherwise. Flower power and student revolution had passed him by; he wore heavy brown brogues and had leather patches on the elbows of his tweed jacket. All in all, he was not a man to be trifled with!

"Come in," he boomed through the door.

I entered his study, my heart pounding. The inner sanctum, the holy of holies: walls lined with gold-embossed volumes; medieval exchequer records scattered on a vast oak table; student papers and PhD theses waiting to be read, piled in great heaps in front of him on the desk.

"Geoffwey," he said. "We seem to have a pwoblem."

I stood nervously. I hadn't been invited to sit down.

"Some of your scwipts are unweadable. If we cannot wead them, we cannot mark them. And if we cannot mark them we cannot award you a degwee."

I had nothing to say ("Tell me something I don't know," I thought). He handed me the four illegible exam scripts. I felt so ashamed I actually blushed.

"Fortunately for you," he said, "I'm interwested in whether you can think, and not whether you can wite. Take the scwipts to my secwetawy and dictate what you have witten. We'll get them typed and see what you had to say, shall we?"

"Thank you very much," I said. "I will."

I couldn't believe my luck. The papers got typed. I got my degree (and joined the police). That was the last time I saw Professor Holt, although I've often thought about what he did for me.

Two years ago, I tracked him down – Professor Emeritus Sir James Clarke Holt, Honorary Fellow of Emmanuel College, Cambridge – and wrote him a letter telling him what a difference his generosity had made to my life (to my police career, to further academic study, but above all to my confidence and self-belief). He never replied.

He probably couldn't read my handwriting.

Castles in the air

If you have built castles in the air, your work need not be lost; that is where they should be. Now put the foundations under them.

HENRY DAVID THOREAU[4]

The CASTLE process has brought the half-remembered incident from a couple of lines – *When I was a student, the professor let me dictate some of my exam papers so they could be marked because my writing was illegible* – to a story told with the kind of detail and feeling that I know (because I've now told it many times) brings it alive for an audience.

As storytellers, we create worlds out of words; we make the invisible visible; we stir the feelings and stimulate the imaginations of our listeners to give them a vicarious experience of something real, whether it's fact, fiction, or fantasy. We can all make castles in the air, but it takes a bit of work to do it well and the CASTLE process will help you put solid foundations under them.

Here is a two-part invitation for you to try it out for yourself.

1. Preparation: Bring to mind a story from your own experience that you would like to tell. Take 30 minutes to work through the CASTLE process, jotting down notes under each heading.

2. Reflection: Read through your notes and notice how much richer and more detailed the story is becoming. You will be telling the story in the next chapter so keep your notes – but resist the temptation to write out the whole story!

For new stories, taking the time to work through each step is invaluable. Even with stories you know well, it is a good idea to strip them down to the basics and rebuild them now and again. It helps a frequently told tale stay fresh; often you will find a new angle, or interesting details that have got lost through familiarity. And it is not just for novices: experienced and so-called natural storytellers also find it hugely beneficial to limber up and exercise their storytelling "muscles" from time to time.

Bonus: The Simple Shapes of Stories

Novelist Kurt Vonnegut (1922–2007) was fascinated by what he called the simple shapes of stories. His Anthropology Masters Degree thesis, which explained these shapes (various forms of the emotional journey map used in this chapter), was rejected by the University of Chicago because, as Vonnegut said, "it was so simple and looked like too much fun." Academia may have rejected them but these shapes are really useful for storytellers. You can see Vonnegut having a lot of fun with them in a five-minute film made in 2005 at a public lecture in New York, in which he draws and explains the shapes of three popular types of story that he calls: Man in a Hole, Boy meets Girl, and Cinderella. Watch the clip on YouTube at http://www.youtube.com/watch?v=oP3c1h8v2ZQ.

Summary

- Use the CASTLE technique as an aid to composition; it takes less time to do in practice than you might think and it is a great way to stimulate your memory and imagination when you are putting a story together.
- **Characters:** Who are the main characters in your story; what is special or unique about them; what are their circumstances; what makes them interesting; what do they want or need?
- **Action:** What happens in your story; what are the key events; where and when do they happen; in what sequence do they occur; are there any other events that your listener *needs* to know?
- **Structure:** A satisfying story is a "whole" with a beginning, a middle, and an end. As a storyteller you have to get your passengers on board, take off smoothly, arrive somewhere (after a bit of drama), and land safely.
- **Texture:** We give texture and color to a story by including specific sensory details – impressions of what we would see, hear, touch, taste, smell if the events of the story were actually unfolding around us.

- **Language:** Use direct speech rather than reported speech at key moments to bring listeners into the presence of the story – but remember that it slows things down so reserve it for dramatic moments.
- **Emotions:** We need to know the emotional palette of our story and the way that feelings shift over time; chart the "simple shape of the story" to help you take your listeners on a compelling emotional journey.

Notes and References

1 McKee, R. (1999). *Story: Substance, Structure, Style, and the Principles of Screenwriting* (Methuen: London, p21).
2 http://en.wikipedia.org/wiki/Robert_McKee (accessed May 1, 2013).
3 Aristotle (1996). *Poetics* (Penguin Classics: London, p13).
4 Thoreau, H.D. (1987). *Walden: Or, Life in the Woods* (Houghton Mifflin: Boston, MA, pxli).

Chapter 12

On Your Feet

Many are ready to die in battle, but few can face an assembly without nerves.

THIRUVALLUVAR[1]

It is said that many people fear public speaking more than they fear death. With me, it is singing: if push came to shove, I would probably choose singing in public rather than death, but it would be a close-run thing. The prospect of telling a story fills some people with a similar sense of dread. There is indeed a performative element to storytelling, but in the context of narrative leadership it is often a low-key affair that unfolds quite naturally in small-group settings.

It does need a certain degree of self-confidence to claim the space to tell a story but – as we saw in the stories of the utility company managers in Chapter 9 – simplicity and sincerity count much more than technical skill or natural aptitude as a storyteller in securing a sympathetic audience. There is a much greater readiness for stories in the system-world than we might expect.

Having looked at aspects of repertoire and composition in the previous chapters, we will focus on what we can do to improve our performance as storytellers – not as professional storytellers on stage but in the everyday context of our work as leaders. This is where the stories we have been gathering and putting together see the light of day; where we have to find the words we need to tell them. If we have prepared well (e.g., by using the CASTLE technique) then telling the story is a natural – if challenging – progression. The challenge comes because our first efforts at telling a new story always fall short of the as-yet-unarticulated perfect stories still lurking inside our heads as possibilities.

Getting over this hurdle is not difficult but learning what works for us and for a particular story necessitates trying things out in practice. It is the same with any art or craft: knowing *about* it is important but not enough; it is knowing *how* to do it that really counts. If you've learned to drive a car, you'll know just what I mean. Many years ago, when my stepfather put "L" plates on the family car and took me out for my first lesson, he told me to turn right at a corner. I did so but had not realized from my study of the Highway Code that I had to turn the steering wheel back to center afterward, so we just kept turning. He averted disaster by grabbing the steering wheel and straightening us up, and I learned an invaluable lesson on what I had to do to keep a car on the road.

You will find that doing the exercises in this chapter – with a partner when recommended – will pay huge dividends. The exercises will help you develop your storytelling skills, build your confidence, and tell your stories with impact. Actors say that there are no mistakes in the rehearsal room, just discovering different ways of doing things, all of which have something to teach. I encourage you to approach the exercises in that spirit, as if you were in a rehearsal room preparing for a performance.

Story coaching

If you're preparing a story to tell at a major event and you have enough time and resources you might choose to work with a professional story-telling coach; you'll get expert feedback and advice on how to improve your story and the way you tell it. Frequently, though, you won't be in that position so it's good to know that peer coaching can also be a great help. We don't have to be expert storytellers to know what we like about a story and how it affects us.

This section will provide some really effective non-expert ways of helping you tell stories better. First, some guidelines for your coaching sessions, which I've adapted from Doug Lipman's excellent book *The Storytelling Coach*,[2] to give you the best chance of success:

> *Be bold and be generous:* Take the risk of stretching yourself with your stories and of being honest with your feedback. Holding back in the rehearsal room will not prepare you for the performance.
>
> *Create the container:* Work privately, somewhere you will not be interrupted and agree up-front how much time you have got. Make an explicit agreement that the work you do together is confidential.
>
> *Exchange of value:* Stick to the clock and if you are taking turns, make sure the time is fairly allocated between you. If only one of you is going to be coached, find some way to recognize and reward the coach for his or her help.
>
> *Ask for feedback:* Tell your listener exactly what you want information, suggestions, and feedback on. The listener's opinions about storytelling in general will not help you, so take responsibility for getting what you need.
>
> *Make the goals explicit:* The storyteller (not the coach) is responsible for deciding why the story is being told and what effect the storyteller wants it to have. The more explicit the storyteller is about the goals, the more the coach can help.
>
> *Listen open-heartedly:* As coach you can only help the storyteller if you allow his or her story to touch you. Use your critical faculties but remember that you are there to help and not to judge the storyteller.
>
> *Emphasize the positive:* Most of us underestimate what is working well in our stories; we are generally better at spotting what is not working so well. As coach, make sure your feedback is both specific and appreciative.

Actually, these are pretty good guidelines for most types of coaching conversations; use them with your partner to get the most out of doing the exercises in this chapter. We will begin with six story coaching techniques for you to try out. Most of them are derived from exercises originally developed by Ashley Ramsden and Sue Hollingsworth at the International School of Storytelling. You will find the techniques explained in much more detail than space allows here, with many other storytelling tips and exercises, in their excellent book *The Storyteller's Way*.[3]

I have chosen ones that I have tried and tested over the past decade in a wide range of organizational and leadership settings. If you are working your way through the book, you can base these activities on the story you put together in the last chapter, but you could use any story that you want help with, one that you have told before or perhaps one that you know but have not yet told.

The first technique helps to bridge the gap between the semi-formed stories in our heads and the words that come out of our mouths. It breaks the ice by taking the story less than seriously and can be very funny to do. Use this technique if you have never told your story before or you want to get to know it better.

1. Gossip the Story: The storyteller and coach imagine themselves as two old friends on a park bench; one has a story to tell and the other wants to hear it but cannot resist butting in with comments and questions. The storyteller tells the story as if it was a piece of gossip – a story someone else has told him or her – and responds to the comments and questions as they arise (with anything except "I don't know") but also persists with the story until it is told. Allow 12–15 minutes to gossip a 5–7-minute story.

Of course, the resulting story is not fully formed but it has been given a chance to breathe. Now it has become an oral story, we can use other coaching techniques to craft and enhance it. For the remaining activities, tell your story to the coach as if you were actually telling it to your intended audience; aim for five minutes or less and do not exceed seven minutes.

2. Images and Feelings: When the story has ended, the coach reports what images in the story caught his or her imagination (and which of the senses they stimulated) and then reports what specific feelings the story evoked (and the strength of their emotional response).

The coach's feedback gives the storyteller valuable information about how vividly he or she is re-creating the experience in the listener's imagination through the use of detail and feelings. The more precise the feedback, the more helpful it will be. Having highlighted the moments when the story feels most alive, the coach can also identify parts of the story that would benefit from stronger images or greater emotional expression. You can incorporate as much or as little of the feedback as you want in future tellings.

3. Impact on Listener: When the story has ended, the coach reports what insights were gained from listening to the story; what the story meant to him or her; and what he or she might do differently as a result of having heard it.

The coach is just one listener so you should not rely absolutely on this feedback, but it gives some indication of the story's potential to make an impact on the intended audience. It is helpful to discuss this in the light of your explicit goals, that is, why you want to tell the story.

4. Heart of the Story: When the story has ended, the coach reports what he or she sees as the nub (or heart) of the story, and what if anything seems to be unnecessary or extraneous.

Most of us go off the point sometimes, or say too much by way of a preamble in the run-up to a story, or too much by way of explanation afterward. We are especially prone to do this when we are uncertain about the effect of the story and we want to make sure that the audience gets the point. Paradoxically, doing any of these things actually tends to dilute the impact of the story, so it is very helpful for the coach to act as a sounding board in this regard.

> 5. Beginnings and Endings: When the story has ended, the coach and storyteller review the beginning and ending of the story; the storyteller can use this feedback to craft the actual words he or she will use to take the intended audience across these two "thresholds" – into and out of the story.

In Chapter 11, we discussed the importance of the beginning and ending of the story as part of the CASTLE technique for putting stories together. The takeoff and landing are critical moments and it is worth spending some time and effort to craft them. Try various ways of wording them until you have a beginning that catches your audience's attention and an ending that leaves them satisfied. You will need something different from "Once upon a time" and "They all lived happily ever after" but you are trying to achieve a similar effect.

> 6. Action and Description: As the story is being told, the coach pays particular attention to the balance between action and description: is the story moving along at a good pace; is there enough detail to create vivid images? The coach intervenes: "tell me more about that" or "what happened next?" as appropriate. Allow 12–15 minutes to practice a 5–7 minute story.

Balancing action (what happens) with description (sensory detail) is not a precise science; we each have our own style. I tend to err on the side of detail so I particularly benefit from being told when a story I am telling needs to move along a bit quicker. The Action and Texture elements of the CASTLE technique provide the raw material to draw upon, but getting the balance right in practice comes from paying attention to your audience and their reactions.

You will find that using a selection of these techniques as a rehearsal space will hone your story ready for telling to an audience and rapidly improve your storytelling confidence and skills. The rest of the chapter builds on this foundation by responding to some of the questions leaders commonly ask me about the practicalities of telling a story. Just as a good story is a whole, so these questions are related to each other, although, for ease of understanding, we will take each of them in turn:

* How do I get people to listen to a story?
* How do I hold their attention?
* How do I make sure I can be heard?
* How do I find the right language?

Some people spend years training in the performing arts; there is an extensive literature on all aspects of performance and many short courses and workshops are available if you want to dive in deeper. I will restrict myself here to a few practical tips and techniques that anyone can use, and that make a substantial and immediate difference.

Introducing stories

Every language has got its own way of introducing a story.
PHYLLIS KLOTZ[4]

And that includes the language of leadership and organizations, in which some might feel that the words "let me tell you a story" are out of place. In the system-world, we are perhaps more used to trading information and swapping logical arguments than listening to stories. But we *do* tell and listen to stories in the system-world and we have our own ways of introducing them.

In everyday conversation we are remarkably skilled in knowing how and when to introduce brief anecdotes and examples. Most of us (the pub bore and the chronically shy excepted) take for granted our innate capacity to pick up cues and play the conversational game. It is the more performative aspects of storytelling that we are generally less used to handling. To tell a substantive story – something longer than a brief anecdote – we have to step outside conversational mode. For this to happen, we have to agree that one person will speak for an extended time and that everyone else will listen. In other words, we have to shift from conversational mode to storytelling mode.

If we just lurch into a story without negotiating the shift, there is a danger that we will leave our audience behind. Traditional storytellers sometimes use the method of call and response to make sure they bring their audience along with them. "Cric," calls the West African griot. "Crac," yells the audience. Back and forth it goes, three or four times, establishing the contract between the storyteller and the audience: "I will tell you a story" – "And we will listen."

Clearly we are not going to use a traditional call and response like this in an organizational setting, but we do need to achieve a similar effect. The easiest and most effective way I know is to use a simple phrase like: "Let me give you an example." "I'd like to tell you how I came to this conclusion." "Let's imagine what this might look like in practice." "This reminds me of a time when . . ." "This is what happened when . . ." "I heard about something like this," etc.

This kind of low-key signal triggers the expectation that you want to shift out of normal conversational mode and tell a story even though you have not labeled it as such. To check their interest and to encourage them to assent to your proposal, make eye contact with your audience and "gather them in." This is the moment when – to continue the analogy of storytelling as flying a plane – you have to get your passengers on board and seated, ready for takeoff. Once you sense that they are willing to listen, take a breath and start your story.

7. Observation: Find an opportunity to take a back-seat in a conversation and notice the different ways people claim the attention of others; if the conversation moves into storytelling mode, how was the contract between teller and listeners negotiated? Could it have been done better? How?

Holding their attention

> *As we let our light shine, we unconsciously give other people permission to do the same. As we are liberated from our own fear, our presence actually liberates others.*
> MARIANNE WILLIAMSON[5]

The contract we establish with people to listen to us telling a story is a conditional one; an audience will listen for as long as the story holds their attention. The more relevant the story and the better we tell it, the greater the impact it will have. The work you have done on repertoire will help you choose the "right" story; the effort you have put into composition will help you bring it to life; and the time you have spent rehearsing your story will improve your performance.

Together these activities build a solid platform on which to stand as you tell the story to your audience; good preparation is half the battle when it comes to holding people's attention with a story, maybe more than half the battle – but it is not the whole battle. The rest is down to the confidence and manner of the storyteller, something we might call "presence." The good news is that although presence is often spoken about as some kind of mysterious gift given to some but not to others, that is not the case. If we want to develop our presence and hold people's attention better, there are a few tricks of the trade that make all the difference.

Storytelling is an embodied act. We use our breath and our bodies to make sounds and gestures, and our gaze to see and be seen by an audience. Breath, bodies, and gaze are the visible and audible signs of presence; how we use them strongly influences how others experience us. Performing artists know this and many of them undergo rigorous training and long hours of practice to improve their physical and vocal abilities. I've been fortunate enough to have come across some great teachers and I'm going to draw on their expertise to give you some key practical tips and techniques that you can use to hold people's attention when you're "on your feet" telling a story.

Breath: Breathing is a good idea under any circumstances. Most of the time, though, we give very little thought to how we are breathing or how we can use our breath to support ourselves. Many of us – especially when nervous – constrict our breathing, using our upper chests instead of our bellies to breathe. Breathing more fully keeps us in touch with our feelings (from which shallow breathing cuts us off) and supports our voice – both of which are helpful when telling a story. Our breathing patterns are deeply ingrained; it takes professional coaching and regular practice to make lasting changes, but there are a couple of things that we can do without too much effort.

First, when you are preparing to go "on stage," spend two or three minutes beforehand in a private space, breathing slowly and deeply, allowing your lungs to fill and empty. If you are doing this properly, you will notice your belly expanding and contracting as you breathe in and out.

Second, breathe out before you start to speak. This sounds counterintuitive but it relaxes your body and you will sound and feel more at ease; your voice will actually drop a note or two. Do not worry about the in-breath, your body will take that automatically when it needs to. Once you have begun to speak, just let yourself breathe naturally.

Body: Holding a lot of tension in our bodies is uncomfortable for us and off-putting for our audience. Many actors and other performers use physical warm-ups to release nervous tension and loosen up their bodies before a performance. We may not have the time or inclination for such elaborate preparations but – as with the breath – there are a couple of quick, easy, and effective techniques that will help you to feel more relaxed and grounded.

First, check how hunched your shoulders are. If you are feeling nervous then they are likely to be raised (as if locked in a permanent shrug). Consciously lower them and you will feel a release of physical tension. It will also allow your body to breathe more fully, move more freely, and project your voice more effectively.

Second, check your overall posture. If you are standing, unlock your knees and stand with your feet apart, pointing slightly out; this will help you stay balanced and mobile. If you are sitting, uncross your legs, plant both feet firmly on the floor, and sit up straight. There is much wisdom in the injunction to keep one's feet on the ground.

Gaze: The human gaze is a subtle and complex phenomenon; it is partly to do with where we direct our visual attention and partly to do with the quality of that attention. We both see and feel seen through our gaze; lovers proverbially gaze into each other's eyes as if they were indeed the windows to the soul; good screen actors can convey a huge range of emotional responses through their eyes. We find it hard to trust someone who refuses to look at us yet we soon feel uncomfortable when stared at. When telling a story we do not want our audience to feel uncomfortable and we do want them to trust us, so how can we use our gaze to help build rapport and hold people's attention?

First, remember that the most important times for the audience to feel that they are in a safe pair of hands are the beginning and end of your story (that is why the captain of an airliner personally speaks to the passengers just before takeoff and again just before landing) so make a point of looking around your audience at those times. You can practice doing this in a coaching session, if you like.

Second, be interested in how your story is going down while you are telling it. Seeing the audience and allowing yourself to be seen by them is the most reliable way of making sure you stay connected. If you have a solid relationship with the story (through your work on repertoire and composition) and with the audience (through the ways you use your breath, body, and gaze in performance) then you create the best possible circumstances to achieve what you want, which is for the audience to forge a strong relationship with the story.

Doug Lipman describes the combination of these three relationships as the storytelling triangle and says:

> *As a storyteller . . . you are powerless to force the audience to create a relationship with the story. You can try to influence that third relationship through the [two] relationships that involve you directly, but you can only prepare, suggest, offer and then hope.*[6]

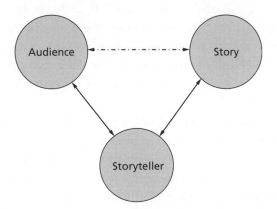

It is a useful reminder for us to put our energy into what we can control when performing and to put our trust in the story. The more you can relax and enjoy the experience of telling the story, the more likely your audience are to connect with it.

> 8. Feedback: The next time you tell a pre-prepared story to an audience, try these ways of using your breath, body, and gaze and see what difference they make; ask your storytelling coach to sit in the audience and give you feedback afterward on what difference he or she thought using the tips made to your performance.

Making sure you can be heard

> *One voice can change a room, and if one voice can change a room, then it can change a city, and if it can change a city, it can change a state, and if it can change a state, it can change a nation, and if it can change a nation, it can change the world. Your voice can change the world.*
>
> BARACK OBAMA[7]

To tell a story well, we must find our voice – in the sense of both claiming the space to speak and speaking audibly and clearly enough for our audience to hear us. In this section, I'm going to assume that you feel entitled to speak in your particular context; you've decided that telling a story is helpful and appropriate; and you've got a story to tell. What can you do to make sure that your voice conveys the story to your audience as you want it to?

There are technical aspects of voice production and voice projection that help to make the voice more expressive and more audible. The tips on breath, body, and gaze in the previous section will all help and for those who want to go much deeper, I recommend using a professional voice coach. You'll get an idea of the coaching techniques from Patsy Rodenburg's classic *The Actor Speaks*[8] or Barbara Houseman's excellent *Finding Your Voice*.[9] I'm going to focus on a few key practical issues that I've found enormously helpful and which my clients have successfully applied to their storytelling and other forms of presentation. What I have to say here isn't novel – it'll be familiar to many of you. As ever, though, the benefit comes not just from knowing about it, but doing it!

First, check the acoustics of the room in which you will be speaking. Even if you know the venue it is good to acclimatize yourself to the space before you get up on your feet. Get used to the sound of your voice in the room before it fills up with people and remember that it will sound different when it is full: sound carries further in an empty room than it does in a full one. Fumbling with the microphone or being drowned out by the screech of electronic feedback will distract you and your audience. So, if your voice is going to be amplified, get the technician to give you a live sound check with the same microphone that you will be using, and familiarize yourself with the on/off/mute buttons.

Second, if your voice is not going to be amplified, then it helps to know how to project your voice to all parts of the room. Do not confuse projecting your voice with speaking loudly: a trained actor can project a whisper as far as a shout. The secret is to direct your voice to where you want it to be heard; your voice will follow your intention and your attention. Left to its own devices, your voice will tend to go where you are looking (including at your own feet), which is why extending your gaze to cover the whole room is important for being heard.

Third, be whole-hearted: tell your story confidently and freely. We will not be heard either by mumbling our words or by gabbling our way through them to get to the end. We want the audience to catch our words, so we need to make sure they can be caught. We should be agile and unhurried, follow through on our delivery, see where our words land, how they are received, and adjust tone, pitch, and projection accordingly. Give your story generously to the audience and you will be heard.

9. Projection: Learn to project your voice by directing it to different places in the room; experiment by "placing" particular words and phrases; imagine that your words are pulled out of you rather than you pushing them out; use your storytelling coach to give you feedback on the difference this makes to the sound of your voice and how well you can be heard.

Finding the right language

> *She discarded harsh, cold words, words that were too*
> *flowery, words worn from abuse, words that offered*
> *improbable promises, untruthful and confusing words,*
> *until all she had left were words to touch the minds of*
> *men and women's intuition.*
>
> ISABELLE ALLENDE[10]

The way Allende describes her character Belisia Crepusculario searching for inspiring words to put into the mouth of the rough-mannered presidential candidate El Colonel teaches us something about the kind of language that works best for oral storytelling, although I disagree with her artificial and fanciful distinction between the minds of men and women's intuition. What we need are stories that touch the hearts and minds, imagination and intuition, of both men and women – and language that does not turn people off or get in the way of those stories.

When we read a story – a novel perhaps – we can appreciate fine writing: subtle language and complex sentences; unusual words and extensive vocabulary. But the ear generally prefers simple language and plain words; if we do not have to make an effort to understand what is being said then we can give our imagination free rein.

Finding the right language for our stories is less a matter of reaching for clever words than of stripping away pretensions and avoiding the clichés and jargon that pervade organizational life. Stories work best when we use our own words: plain language coupled with lively descriptions and evocative metaphors. Here is a wonderful example of the type of language to avoid. It is from a press release issued by an international bank in December 2012, announcing that it is about to cut its workforce. I have anonymized it to spare the bank's blushes:

> *HugeBank today announced a series of repositioning*
> *actions that will further reduce expenses and improve*
> *efficiency across the company while maintaining*
> *HugeBank's unique capabilities to serve clients, especially*
> *in the emerging markets. These actions will result in*
> *increased business efficiency, streamlined operations and*
> *an optimized consumer footprint across geographies.*

This kind of mealy mouthed corporate-speak fudges the truth and obscures reality rather than illuminates it. If we wanted to say the same thing in plain English (language suitable for a story) how would we put it? Something like this perhaps:

> *HugeBank today announced that it will lay off 11,000 people. This will save it $1.1 billion a year.*

Our choice of language is a more serious matter than this rather trivial example might suggest. Australian author Don Watson pointed out in *Death Sentence: The Decay of Public Language*[11] that public language that defies normal understanding is a conscious (and sometimes unconscious) repressive device that leaves us almost literally speechless in response because there is nothing to get hold of: how can one either agree or disagree with something that is essentially meaningless? Such weasel words should have no place in a storyteller's vocabulary except to ridicule them.

Lastly, once you have introduced your story, got your audience's attention, made sure that you can be heard, and found the right language, remember to let the story do the work. Stories tell us who was involved, what happened, where and when it happened. But, as described in Chapter 5, they *show* us how and why things happen. Although, as leaders, we tell stories to make a point, we must not ram the point (the moral or meaning) of the story down our listeners' throats. To do so is both ineffective and unnecessary, because as Roger Schank says:

> *Stories illustrate points better than simply stating the points themselves because, if a story is good enough, you usually don't have to state your point at all; the hearer thinks about what you have said and figures out the point independently. The more work the hearer does, the more he or she will get out of your story.*[12]

10. Language Check: When doing any of the exercises with your storytelling coach, ask him or her to make a note of any clichés or jargon words that have slipped into your telling of the story; go back and find your own words instead for what you wanted to say. Notice how fresh this sounds.

The frameworks, exercises, and tips on repertoire, composition, and performance in Chapters 10, 11, and 12 provide all you need to find the right story and tell it well enough to make an impact. Now all that is required to develop your storytelling prowess, as my old tennis coach used to say, is practice, practice, practice.

Bonus: *The King's Speech*

The Oscar-winning film *The King's Speech* stars Geoffrey Rush as speech therapist Lionel Logue and Colin Firth as newly crowned George VI struggling to overcome his lifelong stammer to speak to the people of the British Empire on the brink of the Second World War. Watch it, not for the speech exercises (interesting as they are), but to relish the sight of someone under enormous pressure finding their authority and their voice. Some versions of the DVD include recordings of the real George VI speaking on radio and newsreel; his courage and the effort it took to control his stammer are quite apparent and very moving.

A recent *Harvard Business Review* article by TED Curator Chris Anderson (about which I will say more in Chapter 15) highlights several different styles of highly effective presentation. It is well worth spending a bit of time trawling through some online talks to watch ordinary people telling extraordinary stories. Notice which ones you especially like or are moved by: What was it about the speaker, the story, and how it was told that caught your fancy? What can you learn from them about repertoire, composition, and performance?

Summary

- Developing performance skills requires practice (like driving a car); ask a friend or colleague to be your storytelling coach; use the activities in this chapter as if you were in the rehearsal room where there are no mistakes.
- Gossiping a story is a great way to bridge the gap between the semi-formed stories in our heads and the words that come out of our mouths.

Once you have cleared this hurdle, all the other performance techniques become available.

- Telling and listening to a story require a different "contract" from conversational mode; use a clear trigger to signal your intention to tell a story and get eye contact to check for your audience's assent.
- Storytelling is an embodied act; the way we use our breath, body, and gaze influences how others experience us and we can learn some simple techniques from the performing arts to enhance our presence.
- As storytellers, we can influence but we cannot control the relationship between the audience and the story; we must focus on our relationship with the story and with the audience to tell our story as well as we can.
- Check the acoustics and amplification at your storytelling venue; direct your voice to where you want it to go; tell your story confidently and generously to make sure you are heard.
- Stories work best when we use our own words: plain language coupled with lively descriptions and evocative metaphors. Avoid complex sentences, jargon words, clichés, and corporate-speak.

Notes and References

1 Couplet 723, from Thirukkural/Tirrukural, also called the Kural – attributed to the Tamil poet Thiruvalluvar, said to have lived sometime between 200 and 10 BCE.
2 Lipman, D. (1995). *The Storytelling Coach* (August House: Little Rock, AR).
3 Hollingsworth, S. and Ramsden, A. (2013). *The Storyteller's Way: Sourcebook for Inspired Storytelling* (Hawthorn Press: Stroud).
4 Attributed to Phyllis Klotz, Artistic Director of the Sibikwa Community Theatre, South Africa, in *Sunday Times* (Johannesburg, South Africa), November 14, 2004.
5 Quoted by Nelson Mandela at his inauguration as President of South Africa, from Williamson, M. (1992). *A Return to Love: Reflections on the Principles of "A Course in Miracles"* (HarperCollins: New York).
6 Lipman, D. (1999). *Improving Your Storytelling* (August House: Little Rock, AR, p17).
7 Obama, B. (2007). Presidential Campaign Speech, South Carolina, December 9.
8 Rodenburg, P. (2005). *The Actor Speaks: The Voice and the Performer* (Methuen: London).

9 Houseman, B. (2002). *Finding Your Voice* (Nick Hern Books: London).
10 Allende, I. (1991). *Stories of Eva Luna* (Hamish Hamilton: London, p9).
11 Watson, D. (2003). *Death Sentence: The Decay of Public Language* (Knopf/ Random House: Sydney).
12 Schank, R. (1995). *Tell Me a Story: Narrative and Intelligence* (Northwestern University Press: Evanston, IL, p12).

Section Five
Time and Change

Chapter 13

Time and Narrative

Time present and time past
Are both perhaps present in time future
And time future contained in time past.

T.S. ELIOT[1]

I have borrowed the title of this chapter from Paul Ricoeur's book of the same name.[2] In a sweeping 750-page analysis, he proposes an underlying circular relationship between the activity of narrating a story and the temporal character of human experience. The relationship between time and narrative is a fascinating and rewarding subject for philosophical study, but for our purposes the essential point is that telling stories is how we make sense of our experience in relation to the passage of time – past, present, and future.

This deceptively simple idea leads directly to the proposition that underpins this book: telling a convincing story that acknowledges where an organization (a group of people, an idea, or movement) has come from, recognizes the realities of the present situation, and offers a worthwhile future is a fundamental task of narrative leadership.

Remembering that a story is an *imagined (or re-imagined) experience narrated with enough detail and feeling to cause your listener's imagination to experience it as real*, it is relatively easy to see how stories can be used to make sense of things that have happened in the past. By selecting particular events and placing them in a certain sequence, we imply motives and causal relationships. Indeed, we commonly tell stories in the past tense to give them plausibility: so and so happened, then this happened, then that happened. I will demonstrate with a random paragraph from Arundhati Roy's novel *The God of Small Things*.[3] Here it is, as written, in the past tense:

> *Since things were not going well financially, the labour was paid less than the minimum rates specified by the trade union. Of course, it was Chacko himself who pointed this out to them and promised that as soon as things picked up, their wages would be revised. He believed that they trusted him and knew that he had their best interests at heart.*

And now, transposed into the present tense:

> *Since things are not going well financially, the labour is paid less than the minimum rates specified by the trade union. Of course, it is Chacko himself who points this out to them and promises that as soon as things pick up, their wages will be revised. He believes that they trust him and know that he has their best interests at heart.*

The first version – in the past tense – gives more credibility and authority to the narrator: she is telling us what has happened. Conversely, reading the second version – in the present tense – one gets the sense that the narrator is merely asserting what might be happening. What else can the narrator do in the midst of an experience; how can she really know what is happening, let alone understand why things are happening, when they have not yet been played out?

It seems that using stories to make sense of the present is not the same as using them to make sense of the past. How can we tell what the story is when we are in the middle of it? And what about stories of events that have not yet occurred: how can we use them to make sense of the future; what weight can we give them?

> *Since things won't go well financially, the labour will be paid less than the minimum rates specified by the trade union. Of course, it will be Chacko himself who will point this out to them and promise that as soon as things pick*

up, their wages will be revised. He will believe that they trust him and know that he has their best interests at heart.

The narrator cannot know that this is what will happen; she is speculating, presenting what she thinks will (or might) happen based on her knowledge of the parties involved and imagining their behavior under supposed circumstances. But this is only one of many possible futures. Events could easily take a different turn and, as readers, we may find it difficult to decide how likely it is that the narrator's prediction will come about. Of course, it is even more difficult to gauge the likelihood of possible futures when dealing with real-life events rather than those depicted in a novel. In real life too, some futures will suit us better than others and we have an interest in shaping the future as well as trying to predict it.

As Søren Kierkegaard once said, "Life can only be understood backwards; but it must be lived forwards."[4] Using stories to make sense of the past is hard enough (place 100 historians end to end and you still won't reach a conclusion) but at least we are used to the process. Using stories to help make sense of the present and of the future presents new challenges and calls for different approaches.

The rest of this chapter will explore the use of story to make sense of all three domains: past (the told story); present (the unfolding story); and future (the imagined story). We will consider some of the issues in each domain and look at some practical tools and techniques. First, though, here are some questions to help you relate what follows to your own circumstances:

1. The Big Picture: Take as much time as you need to answer these questions. Some people find discussing them with a partner helpful. Answer them from the perspective of the organization, group, or movement in which you exercise leadership rather than from your own individual point of view.

   • What images and metaphors speak vividly about your past?
   • What do you want to honor from the past?

   (continued)

- What was unique or distinctive about your origins?
- What is essential from your past for continuity?
- What about your past do you want to distance yourself from?

- What images and metaphors speak vividly about your present?
- What do you want to name about the present?
- What is unique or distinctive about you now?
- What are your core strengths and values?
- What is changing or needs to change?

- What images and metaphors speak vividly about your future?
- What makes the future of your organization etc. worthwhile?
- What is unique or distinctive about your future?
- What represents a small step, a step change, a big stretch?
- What key challenges are you are facing?

Your answers to these questions (and to the others that occurred to you as you were thinking about them and/or discussing them) begin to sketch out the domains of past–present–future within which you exercise leadership. What did you notice about the different gestures of looking back at the past, looking around at the present, and looking ahead to the future? Because our temperaments vary, we are likely to find ourselves drawn more to some domains than others. Which domain did you find most challenging to address? Which did you find easiest? What does this say about the way you lead? To what extent are you rooted in the past; open to the present; and focused on the future?

Learning from the past: The told story

There is only one thing more painful than learning from experience and that is not learning from experience.
ARCHIBALD MACLEISH[5]

When we experience events that either our conscious or subconscious mind judges to be significant we store them as memories. To remember them we shape them into stories that we tell to other people (and sometimes to ourselves). Roger Schank goes so far as to equate story creation with memory:

> *We need to tell someone else a story that describes our experience because the process of creating the story also creates the memory structure that will contain the gist of the story for the rest of our lives.*[6]

It is by retelling such stories and reconsidering their meanings in changing circumstances that we are able to learn from the past, strengthening the influence of stories we deem to have positive effects and loosening our grip on those that no longer serve us. Most schools of coaching, counseling, and psychotherapy are based on this premise and we can apply the same principle to learning from our collective experience in organizations, groups, and movements.

If, as leaders, we want to encourage learning from the past we can tell a story ourselves or we can initiate a collaborative process to enable the production of a *jointly told tale*[7] engaging a range of people and encompassing multiple perspectives. Our primary concern might be to look for what has previously served us well and to build on it, in which case we can use appreciative methods of storytelling. For example, the success of Team GB (British Olympic and Paralympic Associations) in the 2012 London Olympic Games came in part because they learned from appreciative stories about the coaching methods of the world-beating British cycling squad.

If our main concern is to identify what has gone wrong in the past to avoid making the same mistakes again, we are more likely to adopt a critical stance. The US government's investigation into the BP Deepwater Horizon blowout and oil spill in the Gulf of Mexico in 2010 (which caused 12 human deaths and untold damage, and which, as at February 2013, had cost BP over $40 billion) is a good example of focusing on negative stories.

Or, we might hold a more neutral stance as we inquire into something that has happened, wanting to understand a complex experience "warts and all," in which case we will be interested in both the "good" and "bad" nuances of the stories that arise. The Truth and Reconciliation Commissions referred to in Chapter 8 were designed to value all aspects of the stories they unearthed – as sources of learning and to promote inclusion and the healing of religious, racial, and social divisions. The *graphic history* and *learning history* methods described below are good examples of taking this more disinterested approach in pursuit of jointly told tales; in both cases external facilitators/researchers were used to elicit and compile the stories.

In Chapter 2, I spoke about leaders participating in an ongoing social process of sense-making (as opposed to taking charge and making things happen). Collaborative storytelling processes offer powerful and effective ways of engaging creatively in making sense with others, so that is where we will aim the spotlight in this section. I will say something about the rationale for *appreciative storytelling* and then give examples of the graphic history and learning history methodologies.

Appreciative storytelling

I have adapted this term from the process of appreciative inquiry which was first formulated by David Cooperrider and Suresh Srivastra at Case Western University.[8] Appreciative inquiry is based on the premise that the best way of creating the future we want is to learn from the positive aspects of the past (without denying that negative aspects will almost certainly have occurred). Cooperrider and Srivastra point out that taking a critical stance actually enfeebles organizations, groups, and movements by centering the discourse of change around past failures and deficits:

> *As people in organizations inquire into their weaknesses and deficiencies, they gain an expert knowledge of what is "wrong" with their organizations, and they may even become proficient problem-solvers, but they do not strengthen their collective capacity to imagine and to build better futures.*[9]

To overcome the unintended consequences of taking a critical stance, appreciative inquiry takes an asset-based approach to change and development, beginning with the choice of a positive topic (e.g., "building an enthusiastic organization" rather than "overcoming low morale"). Having chosen and framed the topic, the next step is to explore concrete examples of "the best of what is." This is where appreciative storytelling comes in, as the starting point for tapping into our existing capacity for excellence (no matter how small) and developing a shared positive vocabulary for us to consider what good, better, and best would be like.

Appreciative inquiry is a widely practiced and sophisticated approach to organizational development that has achieved much success in "liberating the socially constructive potential of organizations and human communities."[10] But its underlying principle of taking an appreciative stance can also be used – either in the moment or in a planned way – to address a wide range of issues. You might tell an appreciative story yourself to set the tone of a sense-making discussion or as you participate with others in a collective storytelling process.

Here, for example, is a framework I once used in the early stages of working with the chairman and board of a public body to improve their effectiveness. The board was not in tatters but they had asked me to work with them because (for different and opposing reasons) many of them believed that they were not using their time as well as they could to support and oversee the work of the organization's executive team. The most obvious "fault-line" was between those who wanted to focus exclusively on the big-picture strategic issues and those who were adamant that good governance required a sound grasp of detailed operational matters. I put them in pairs (one from each camp), and gave them the following task, designed to elicit appreciative stories:

> *Working in pairs, use the time allotted (40 minutes) to ask each other these questions. The listener's task is to help the speaker articulate the stories themselves and avoid getting into "analysis-paralysis." Help each other be brief and specific.*
>
> 1. *Recall a time when you felt you made a significant individual contribution as a member of the Board. Tell me about that time. What was your contribution and how was it significant?*
> 2. *Recall a time when you felt that the whole Board worked at its best. Tell me about that time. How did you contribute to achieving that collective success? What did others do?*

Afterward, each person told the whole group not their own stories but the stories they had heard from their partner. Their brief was to tell these stories as well and as faithfully as they could. In order to do this, they temporarily had to see the world from their partner's opposing viewpoint, which began to reduce the divisive influence of the fault-line and to soften the edges of the disagreement on both sides of the debate. Suffice to say that, on the basis of these stories, the board found their way to a new way of working that recognized their role in both setting the strategic direction of the organization and monitoring key performance data. Telling someone else's story is a great way of getting under their skin!

Learning history

> *Most organizations are "mythically" deprived. Official documents and presentations are bereft of stories; managers talk in terms of highly rationalized, abstract explanations that do not typically tell how their numbers or policies really evolved.*
>
> ROTH AND KLEINER[11]

George Roth and Art Kleiner developed the learning history method at the Massachusetts Institute of Technology (MIT) in the 1990s because, although many organizations espoused the virtues of corporate learning, in practice they found that leaders and managers were continually pressed to take action and were actively discouraged from taking time to generate and reflect on stories of their individual and collective experience. They created a structured approach for reflection and learning, facilitated by an external researcher, that elicits the human stories underlying a project, initiative, or event (the "mythic" dimension) and balances them with rigorous collection and analysis of relevant data. The polyvocal narrative distilled from this data and from interviews with a wide range of participants and stakeholders is then validated for accuracy and presented back to the organization for further reflection and dissemination.

The creation of a learning history is a planned, systematic intervention resulting in a "jointly told tale" with the explicit purpose of learning from the past. It differs from the more generalized, abstracted description of a conventional case study because of its emphasis on story and its inclusion of vivid details and the personal voices of those involved. Learning histories have been conducted within business corporations, NGOs, local and national government organizations, and across wider systems involving multiple players.

For example, at the Centre for Action Research into Professional Practice (CARPP) PhD student Rupesh Shah used the learning history methodology with Shell Oil and the NGO Living Earth as a tool to explore the environmental effects of oil production in the Niger delta.[12] In another study, Margaret Gearty used multiple histories to contrast the experiences of introducing carbon reduction projects in five different UK local authorities.[13]

In one of the more ambitious learning history projects on record, a team of CARPP researchers with Research Council funding explored the human dimensions of adopting low-carbon technology. Their 2009 report, *Insider Voices*,[14] brought together six learning histories of low-carbon projects in the food, agriculture, engineering, manufacturing, energy, and heating/ refrigeration sectors from which 10 ingredients for successful low-carbon projects were distilled along with a number of key issues for policy-makers and research funders. One of the report's conclusions was that:

> *The potential for change is evoked by stories and narratives, particularly stories of what has worked. Thus one of our messages is to create your own stories and narratives of change because these stories really do matter. We are seeking to amplify small stories, to show examples of what is going on, around which different kinds of stories could be built. We learn to notice the patterns that enable innovation to happen more easily through the stories we tell and the stories we hear.*[15]

Learning histories undoubtedly have the potential to enable individuals, organizations, and systems to learn; the question (as Roth and Kleiner identify) is whether they are willing to invest the necessary time, courage, and honesty.

The image below shows a couple of typical pages from the *Insider Voices* report. Although the words are not legible at low resolution, I wanted to give you an example of how a well-presented learning history attempts to represent graphically a plurality of voices while maintaining a clear narrative thread.

Learning on the hoof

Holsworthy anaerobic digestion

This is the story of a pioneering group of farmers and businessmen in North Devon, who built the first large-scale anaerobic digestion plant in the UK. It is a heroic story of grand ambitions, of crossing boundaries, of building coalitions and of 'learning as you go'. It is also a story of perseverance and struggle. Struggle against a regulatory system where this new technology was not fully understood or appreciated. Struggle to transfer the design and technical knowledge from a continental European context into a UK one, and struggle against a vocal minority of local residents who continue to oppose the plant. This is not a classic success story, but rather a story about what it takes to keep going against a backdrop of constant change and uncertainty.

An exciting idea

The story of the Holsworthy Biogas plant begins in 1993/94 when an enterprising group of local business people from North Devon and Cornwall formed the North Tamar Business Network (NTBN). They had access to EU funding (provided under the EU 'LEADER' community development programme) to pump-prime local projects. The Executive Leader of the group was Joe Talbot, and Charles Clarke was a well-known local farmer and founding member. It was Joe Talbot who first introduced the idea of an agricultural project, based around the production of biogas from farmyard slurry, having heard about the process at a recent conference.

> The Executive, Joe Talbot, came up with four categories of project: agriculture, education, tourism and business. My hat could have gone on any one of those four at that particular time, but I went with agriculture. And one of the things that Joe Talbot mentioned was biogas. Well, having an inquiring mind I said, 'What's biogas?'
> Charles Clarke

Wide vision

Both Joe Talbot and Charles Clarke were acting in a strategic capacity here, with an eye on the bigger picture. Joe Talbot was able to spot a timely opportunity, and Charles Clarke was willing to keep an open mind and to explore how this opportunity might fit within the NTBN's wider plans.

The biogas idea took hold, and in 1996 the network decided to conduct a feasibility study. They had high hopes that this new technology, called anaerobic digestion (AD), could provide a way forward for local farmers suffering from falling incomes and the effects of the BSE livestock epidemic at the time.

> Holsworthy is predominantly a farming community and in common with most rural areas it has suffered in recent years from the effects of the agricultural recession, in particular the BSE crisis. The local economy is dependent on milk production, cattle rearing and tourism... The fragility of the rural economy and the opportunity that the biogas plant offered to stabilise the economy was one of the key factors behind the development of the project.
> Energy Management Feb 2000

Sociotechnical transition framework

The momentum for this project did not come out of nowhere. It emerged out of a context of growing economic instability in the farming regime which could be linked to wider systemic issues around farming practice in the UK at the time. This instability may have provided the impetus for the farmers in Devon to be actively looking for ways to diversify, thus providing a 'window of opportunity' for a niche energy technology such as AD to break through.

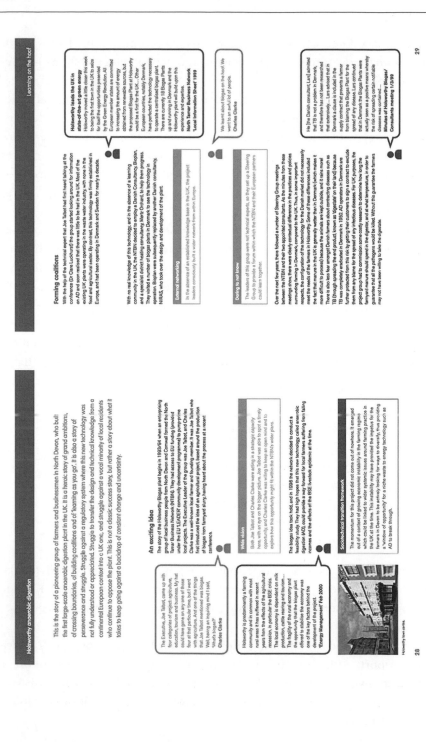

Holsworthy farm centre.

28

Forming coalitions

With the help of the technical expert that Joe Talbot had first heard talking at the conference (Dr Clare Lukehurst) the group started looking around for information on AD and soon realised that there was little to be had in the UK. Most of the existing UK plants were operating in the waste water industry, with none in the food and agricultural sector. By contrast, this technology was firmly established in Europe, and had been operating in Denmark and Sweden for nearly a decade.

With no real knowledge of this technology, and in the absence of a learning community in the UK, the NTBN decided to employ a Danish Consultancy, Bioplan, and a specialist district heating consultancy, Martz Orchard, to help them progress. They visited a number of biogas plants in Denmark to see the technology in operation. Bioplan were subsequently replaced by another Danish consultancy, NIRAS, who took over the design and development of the plant.

External networking

In the absence of an established knowledge base in the UK, the project leaders consciously built a wider network from within Europe.

> **Holsworthy leads the UK in state-of-the-art green energy**
> Holsworthy moved a little closer this week to being the first town in the UK to seize for itself the opportunities presented by the Green Energy Revolution. All European member states are committed to increasing the amount of energy obtained from renewable sources, but the proposed Biogas Plant at Holsworthy would be a first for the UK... Other European countries, notably Denmark, have perfected the technology necessary to operate a centralised biogas plant. There are currently 18 Biogas Plants up and running in Denmark and the Holsworthy plant will build upon this experience and expertise.
> North Tamar Business Network
> 'Local Information Sheet 1999'

> We learnt about biogas on the hoof. We went to an awful lot of people.
> Charles Clarke

Daring to not know

The leaders of this group were not technical experts, so they set up a Steering Group to provide a forum within which the NTBN and their European partners could learn together.

Over the next few years, there followed a number of Steering Group meetings between the NTBN and their two appointed consultants. As the minutes from these meetings show, there were clearly contextual differences in the practices and policies surrounding farming in Denmark, compared to the UK. Thus, in some important respects, the configuration of the technology for the Danish market did not necessarily meet the needs of the farmers in Holsworthy. Some of these differences included the fact that manure in the UK is generally wetter than in Denmark (which makes it more difficult to process) because the animals are kept outside, and it rains more! There is also less fear amongst Danish farmers about contracting diseases such as TB (through spreading the end product, known as 'digestate' on the land) because TB is completely eradicated in Denmark. In 1952 AD operations in Denmark are further protected from this risk by getting their customers to sign a contract to exclude them from any blame for the spread of any infectious diseases. For UK purposes, the project group had to commission some costly research to determine how long the farmyard manure should spend in the digestor, and at what temperature, in order to guarantee that all the pathogens would be killed. Without this guarantee the farmers may not have been willing to take the digestate.

> He [the Danish consultant, Lars] admitted that TB is not a problem in Denmark, and therefore has not been researched that extensively... Lars advised that in Denmark a clause is included in the supply contract that prevents a farmer from blaming the Biogas Plant for the spread of any disease. Lars continued that in Denmark the Biogas Plants were actually seen as a positive means whereby the risk of spreading certain notifiable diseases was contained....
> Minutes of Holsworthy Biogas/AD Consultants meeting 1/3/99

29

The *Insider Voices* report can be viewed in its entirety and download-ed at www.bath.ac.uk/management/news_events/pdf/lowcarbon_insider _voices.pdf.

Graphic history

When the need to make sense of the past is more contained and immedi-ate, we can use a graphic recorder to help us make a graphic history.[16] The graphic recorder (sometimes with a second facilitator) works in real time to elicit and map the individual and collective memory of a group about a particular set of experiences. By representing the group's knowl-edge, recollections, and reflections graphically, the whole is made visible to the group and can be used as a rich source of learning. As with learn-ing histories, the process brings together multiple perspectives on the whole story before seeking common understanding: divergence before convergence. The product is a permanent visual record of the group's deliberations, using its own wording and imagery rather than those of the facilitator.

Let's take a real-life example to show how this works in practice. The image below[17] shows a graphic history created by my colleague Chris Seeley during a one-day project review that she and I recently facilitated. You will not be able to read the words (the content is confidential to the client) but you will be able to see the overall pattern that built up during the day. The original "document" was about 1.25 meters high and 4.0 meters long; it was produced on a single unrolled sheet of paper, stuck to the wall.

Chris (a trained graphic reporter and facilitator) and I had been asked to work with a project team whose task had been to close a residential school for children and young people with learning disabilities. The charitable organization running the school had explored every possible avenue to keep the school open, but although it had an excellent reputation, declining numbers of pupils and referrals meant that it was no longer viable.

Closing the school had been a sensitive, complex, and – at times – painful project. The team believed that they had done a good job under difficult circumstances and wanted to pool their learning so it could be presented back to the organization as part of the final project report. Additionally, several members of the team were about to retire or move out of the organization and this project review would be the last time they would all meet together. Representing their emotional journey through the project would be every bit as important as recording the external events.

At the beginning of the day, the paper was blank apart from the imaginary landscape drawn along the bottom of the sheet. The first thing to be added was the timeline along which the project had occurred – in this case from August 2010 to May 2013. Each team member then marked on the timeline the various dates when they had first become involved in the project. Our "canvas" was now ready to receive the different layers or elements of the graphic history.

For the first round of reflection, individuals were invited to choose two or three images (from a collection of postcards) that represented something about the qualities they had experienced in the project team. As they spoke about these images to the other team members, their words were captured in the two columns on the left hand side of the sheet.

Next, each member of the team wrote down key moments in the project on Post-it notes, and then used them to build up a shared chronology of what had happened. As they placed their Post-it notes across the center of the sheet they spoke about their different perspectives and experiences. Telling their stories to each other and drawing them together in this way was both informative and cathartic.

In the following round we asked them to reflect on their own emotional highs and lows during the project and to write a few words about each one on an arrow-shaped Post-it. As they took it in turns to speak about their emotional experiences and place their arrows along the timeline, they expressed a wide range of feelings: anger, sadness, satisfaction, relief, frustration, liberation, compassion, love.

We then facilitated a whole-group conversation about the hurdles they had faced and overcome (or stumbled at) during the project and what they had learned from each one. These insights were recorded along the top of the sheet and proved to be a rich source for the final stage of deciding what messages they wanted to give the organization to inform future projects. Working first in pairs, then fours, then as a whole group, they distilled their learning into eight clear recommendations to be included in the project report.

Finally, to close the day – and to acknowledge the ending of both the project and the team – each person walked slowly along the timeline until they stepped over from "now" into the "future," wrote a few words about how they saw their own future on the right hand end of the sheet, and signed their name as one of the makers of this graphic history.

This way of producing a jointly told tale is very immediate and, because it is co-created in real time, its makers generally have a strong sense of shared ownership. It is a very good way for a group to interrogate its experience and learn from the past: the graphic document itself is a means to this end, a transitional object that probably will not make much sense beyond the group that produced it. In contrast, the process of producing a learning history is asynchronous and its impact therefore less immediate, but its more analytical and literary form makes effective dissemination beyond those involved in its production more likely.

> 2. Jointly Told Tales: As a leader, when could you use the techniques of appreciative storytelling, learning history, or graphic history to learn important lessons from your experience? What subject or theme would you choose and who would you ask to participate?

Standing in the present: The unfolding story

[We] make our existence into a whole by understanding it
as an expression of a single and unfolding story. We are

in the middle of our stories and cannot be sure how they
will end; we are constantly having to revise the plot as new
events are added to our lives.

DONALD POLKINGHORNE[18]

How can we come to know – let alone make sense of – the constantly moving present moment that is *now*? In the very act of seeking to incorporate the present into our story, it becomes the past. "At this point in time," we say – but the very definition of a point is something that, although it has a location, has no size and a point in time therefore has no duration. For practical purposes, most of us get round this awkward fact by stretching our notion of the present to include the immediate past and the near future; we think of it as a zone within which things can happen (and therefore about which stories can be told, albeit unfolding stories whose ends are unknown).

In the zone of the present, we seek to make sense of our life as we encounter new information and events. Our difficulty is that attachment to the accumulated stories we have told over the years to make sense of our experience can blind us to disconfirming data: we have a tendency to ignore, disbelieve, or distort the data to maintain our self-identity, sense of belonging, and view of the world. If this level of selective attention sounds unlikely to you, then watch Dan Simons and Christopher Chabris's highly convincing experiment. Since knowing what it contains would spoil the effect, I will not say anything else about it here. It is well worth trying and you can access it on YouTube at http://www.youtube.com/watch?v=vJG698U2Mvo.[19]

Knowing in the present moment requires us to pay attention to how we respond to the flow and flux of events, maintaining as much openness as we can to both confirming and disconfirming data. We need not abandon our stories (indeed we may continue to believe in them) but we do need to be aware that they *are* stories – stories that we have constructed to make sense of past events – and hold them lightly enough to allow the possibility of change.

In his best-selling book *Theory U*,[20] Otto Scharmer suggests that the creative journey involves letting go of our stories and preconceptions from the past, and standing in the present with open mind, heart, and will, in order to let come the future that is seeking to emerge. Stepping outside our stories (whether they are stories of who we are, or of where we belong, or of how we see the world) is difficult. We can practice through meditation, yoga, running, walking, etc., to slip the leash of our conscious sense-making minds long enough to become present to our experience. Those who learn how to become fully present to their experience more than momentarily are fortunate; those who can do so for extended periods are called enlightened in many wisdom traditions. I make no claim to enlightenment but I will share a personal story that might give you a flavor of what I mean:

> *In 2002, a few months before I left the police service, I decided that I wanted to do something that would help me make the imminent step change into a different life. Although I did not meditate regularly, I fancied that meditation might be what I needed. Accordingly, I booked my place on a 6-day Zen Retreat and drove to a large country house where I imagined we would sit around on cushions for a few hours each day, chat with fellow retreatants and be served good food.*
>
> *I've never been one to read the small print, so being woken before dawn and spending 8 to 10 hours each day on a cushion whilst staring at a blank wall came as something of a surprise – as did a regime of complete silence and a mountain of washing up each mealtime. Nevertheless, I decided to stay and give it a go. For three and a half days, I found the meditation sessions agony: I dutifully sat on my cushion and stared but my mind was constantly busy, thinking about past experiences and longing for the bell that signaled the end of the session. But during the afternoon of the fourth day, something changed. A thought arose unbidden; an inner voice spoke with complete clarity: "Wherever I am, it's just me. I might as well be here."*
>
> *For the last two days of the retreat I was quite untroubled. I sat on my cushion, I looked at the wall, and I did*

the washing up with equanimity and enjoyment. When my mind wandered – as it inevitably did – I gently brought myself back to the present moment, to my breath and to my being. I won't say that the experience transformed me (and I've never gone back to repeat it) but it has stayed vividly in my memory for more than a decade. In hindsight it was a pivotal moment, a turning point after which my life began to take a new direction.

Looking beyond our own stories to those of the groups, movements, and organizations in which we exercise leadership, how do we release our grip on the dominant stories of the past to allow the emergence of the new? Letting go of our collective stories is not easy but we can use group-based conversational techniques such as Dialogue[21] or Peer Council[22] to disrupt our usual arguments, suspend our normal assumptions, and listen in ways that allow fresh stories to emerge. Or we may attempt to unlock ourselves from our current stories by exposure to radically different surroundings (a wilderness retreat, for example, or visiting an unfamiliar country or culture). I have seen the benefit of this approach first hand, accompanying Lindsay Levin of Leaders' Quest[23] and a group of senior public service leaders to India, where our meetings with NGOs, social activists, villagers, street children, women's groups, and slum-dwellers gave us all new perspectives on the meaning and purpose of our lives.

Another strategy is to encourage a multiplicity of stories by using techniques like the story circles described in Chapter 8. But organizations, religions, sciences, and political and social movements are notoriously prone to establishing orthodoxies that set the limits for disagreement (i.e., the stories that can or cannot be told; will or will not be heard). As leaders, therefore, our task may be to make room for the countervailing stories that challenge our own beliefs or to speak out against official stories when we believe them to be outdated or wrong.

The stories told by radicals and whistleblowers are rarely welcomed in their own time though they may be praised by later generations as necessary interventions. Those who transgress the prevailing "regimes of truth" either by telling or listening to such stories are liable to be considered deficient, delinquent, or dangerous by those with a vested interest in maintaining them, which is why narrative leadership sometimes requires courage as well as skill and awareness. The last State President of apartheid-era South Africa, F.W. de Klerk, for example, had the courage to listen to the countervailing stories of Nelson Mandela and the African National Congress. Rightly, Mandela (teller) and de Klerk (listener) were both awarded the Nobel Peace Prize in 1993.

3. Reflection: Whose stories do not get heard in your organization, group, movement, etc.? As a leader, what can you do to welcome a multiplicity of different stories? What dominant stories do you most want to challenge?

Shaping the future: The imagined story

We look at the present through a rear-view mirror. We march backwards into the future.

MARSHALL McLUHAN[24]

When Marshall McLuhan – 1960s' guru and media analyst – made this statement, he was reiterating a much older view of time. The ancient Greeks thought of themselves standing in the present moment with the past receding in front of them and the invisible future behind them. For them, the mythical Golden Age of the past was the primary point of reference. In the modern era, the primary point of reference switched from the past to the future. The ideology of progress promised better things to come and 150 years of increasing material prosperity for industrialized societies served to reinforce this belief. It was as though the magnetic poles of our psyches flipped.

In periods of relative stability, we still imagine that the past is a good guide to the future, but this illusion has been shattered by the complexity and turbulence of the post-modern era in which the only constant is change itself. However, the modernist conceit that we can put our past behind us and walk forward into the future, as if we could see it coming, is hard to shake off. Benjamin Franklin told us that death and taxes are the only certainties in life but many of us still look to religious and political institutions to safeguard our traditions and to tell us what the future holds or could hold for us; we reward our bankers for guessing which way financial markets will move; we estimate and insure against future risks; we invest on the basis of expected future performance; we appoint people to leadership roles to bring about "transformation"; we discard old technologies and look forward to the next upgrade. For good or ill, the future has been the main locus of our attention.

Unlike the present, the future is not a point in time. Like the past, the future has duration and therefore we can tell stories about it. The way we construct those stories (as opposed to their content) will depend on how we conceive our relationship to the future. Jack Petranker of the Center for Creative Inquiry suggests that we consider the future in terms of three complementary aspects: the *objective future* (logico-scientific calendar time in which Wednesday follows Tuesday); the *subjective future* (the story of what-will-have-happened); the *dynamic future* (the ever-emerging boundary between present and future).[25]

All three aspects are potentially useful and each one demands a different approach. Working with the objective future, we might use project management techniques or statistical analyses to plan activities and predict events. This is familiar territory for anyone concerned with process control, logistics, or manufacturing. At the other end of the spectrum, the dynamic future calls for responsiveness and improvisation as we seek to manifest our intentions moment by moment. Patricia Shaw gives an excellent account of this approach in *Changing Conversations in Organizations: A Complexity Approach to Change.*[26]

It is in the imaginative realm of the subjective future that storytelling comes into its own. I fully accept Petranker's view that our lived story (what we actually do) is governed by our values and intentions and that we improvise our actions moment by moment, but I assert that our values and intentions are shaped in turn by stories from our past and imagined stories of the future. It is through such stories that we imagine what might be possible, desirable, and worthwhile; it is through such stories that we seek to give substance to the future we wish to make manifest.

Let me show you what I mean, using a metaphor from Robert Fritz's *The Path of Least Resistance*.[27] He says that there is always a dynamic tension (like stretched elastic bands) between our present situation and any preferred future that we might imagine. We want the attraction of the preferred future to move the present state toward it, but if the pull of the present is too strong the preferred future will collapse back toward the status quo.

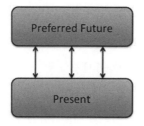

Changing requires us to break our familiar patterns of thought and behavior in order to adopt new ones. That is often difficult: how many New Year's resolutions do we actually keep? We make them in good faith, we may even change for a while (give up smoking, go on a diet, read the classics, learn French), but all too often we give up. Why? Because we are too attached to our old patterns – and this is every bit as true for organizations, groups, and movements.

The odds are stacked against the preferred future because the present is anchored to the past by a myriad of stories. Unless we create them, the future has no stories with which to counteract these story anchors. I have worked with several NHS Boards who could not understand the level of public protests about the closure of small, outdated, local hospitals despite their projections of improved patient care, lower waiting times, and more sophisticated care pathways offered by the prospective new, centralized hospital facilities. The problem they faced was not that their data was inadequate or their argument faulty, but that both were trumped by the stories the public told about their experiences at the cottage hospitals: the birth of a child; the care of an elderly mother; the mended limb; the extracted appendix. In fact, the relationship between the present and the preferred future looks rather more like this:

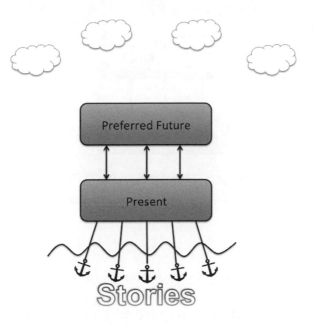

In these circumstances, two things will help: reducing the influence of the stories that are anchoring the present to the status quo; and imagining future stories (not just information and arguments) to give the preferred future some substance and pull. In the case of the NHS hospital reconfiguration referred to above, there may be some true countervailing stories about particular problems at the cottage hospitals, though it would probably be impolitic to focus on past failures. In other circumstances (say, if the doubts and objections were primarily from managers and staff) then it might be appropriate to use techniques like Dialogue and Peer Council to loosen the grip of the prevailing stories. In any event, the Boards certainly need to imagine and tell stories about the better experiences patients and relatives will have in the planned new hospitals, to make it real for the public. If they can do that, the situation becomes more like that shown in the following diagram and we can feel rather more optimistic about moving toward the preferred future.

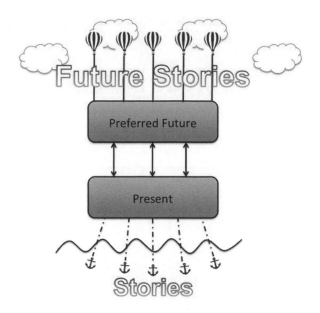

I am aware of the irony of using balloons to represent Future Stories because such stories can be accused of being just a lot of hot air; they can be shot down or deflated if they are mere whimsy. But if we get them right, they can exert tremendous pull. In using imagined experiences to make the preferred future seem real to listeners, we need to draw on everything we know about how stories work: detail and feeling are every bit as important in fictional stories as they are in factual stories. We have to work that much harder to find authentic detail and to connect with our real feelings – but that is what storytellers do.

In the next chapter, we will look at a range of storytelling techniques we can use when we want to bring about change. Most of them involve creating or co-creating stories of a preferred future although, as we saw in the film *An Inconvenient Truth* (DVD Bonus in Chapter 5), sometimes we might want to warn against future threats, or to preserve something that is threatened with damaging change, by telling stories that give more weight and substance to the status quo. It is also important to remember that narrative leadership is not the exclusive preserve of "men in high places"; it is available to all kinds of leaders in every field of endeavor.

Bonus: *The Insider*

The difficulties and dangers of speaking out against a "regime of truth" are dramatically revealed in Michael Mann's (1999) film *The Insider*, based on the real-life story of Jeffrey Wigand, former Vice President for Research at Brown and Williamson, a big US tobacco company. In 1995, Wigand testified before a Grand Jury and appeared on the CBS news program *60 Minutes* to confirm that – despite their previous sworn testimony to the contrary at a Congressional hearing – senior executives in the tobacco industry were perfectly well aware of the addictive properties of nicotine.

The short scene, in which the CEOs of the seven largest US tobacco companies were interrogated under oath about the addictive properties of nicotine by Congressman Harry Waxman in 1994, is one of the most damning in the film. You can see the real thing at http://www.youtube.com/watch?v=e_ZDQKq2F08. It is a wonderful example of something novelist Upton Sinclair said nearly a century before: "It is difficult to get a man [*sic*] to understand something, when his salary depends on his not understanding it."[28]

In the end, Wigand's story carried the day; the tobacco industry lost its case – first in the court of public opinion and then in the law courts – settling the lawsuits filed against it by Mississippi and 49 other states for a total of $246 billion in 1999. In speaking out, Wigand breached the terms of a legal non-disclosure agreement that he had been obliged to sign to secure financial and health benefits for himself and his family as part of his severance package. Obliging people to make such agreements is one way regimes of truth seek to protect their story and prevent "whistleblowing."

The film shows that Wigand was placed under enormous pressure not to testify and that CBS initially did not broadcast his interview because of the possibility of legal action from Brown and Williamson. The Kafkaesque logic of the threatened suit for "tortious interference" was that the truer Wigand's testimony and interview, the more he had breached the non-disclosure agreement and the more liable he and CBS would be for damages.

The events in the film occurred nearly 20 years ago but we should not think that such things no longer happen – or that they only happen in the private sector, or only in the United States. For example, despite protective legislation for whistleblowers in the United Kingdom, there have been several high-profile cases recently of gagging clauses being imposed on outgoing senior NHS executives. The government has issued new guidelines for the NHS forbidding the practice but the propensity for the system-world to protect its own interests is extremely high. Telling insider (or outsider) stories that challenge the dominant story will always take courage.

Summary

- Telling a convincing story that acknowledges where an organization, group, or movement has come from, recognizes the realities of the present situation, and offers a worthwhile future is a fundamental task of narrative leadership.
- Through individual and jointly told tales, we are able to learn from the past, strengthen the influence of stories we deem to have positive effects, and loosen our grip on those that no longer serve us.
- Methodologies such as appreciative storytelling, learning history, and graphic history provide opportunities to explore complex polyvocal stories, combining rigorous research with the richness of narrative.
- In the zone of the present, our task is to loosen the grip of dominant narratives and allow a multiplicity of stories to be heard. Techniques such as Dialogue and Peer Council can help groups become open to new stories.
- Speaking out against the dominant stories of "regimes of truth" – and being willing to listen to them – requires courage. The stories told by radicals and whistleblowers are rarely welcomed by those in power.
- It is in the imaginative realm of the subjective future that storytelling comes into its own. The values and intentions that govern our lives are shaped by stories from our past and imagined stories of the future.
- We need robust and evocative future stories to counteract the stories that anchor us to the status quo. Conversely, we might want to defend the way things are, or warn against the prospect of damaging change.

Notes and References

1 Eliot, T.S. (1944). *Four Quartets* (Faber & Faber: London). Reproduced with permission.
2 Ricouer, P. (1984). *Time and Narrative*, 3 vols. (University of Chicago Press: Chicago).
3 Roy, A. (1997). *The God of Small Things* (Flamingo: London, p120).
4 Søren Kierkegaard, *Journals*, IV A (1843). "It is quite true what philosophy says; that life must be understood backwards. But then one forgets the other principle: that it must be lived forwards."
5 Attributed to Archibald MacLeish (1892–1982), Librarian of US Congress.
6 Schank, R. (1995). *Tell Me a Story: Narrative and Intelligence* (Northwestern University Press: Evanston, IL, p115).
7 A term borrowed from ethnographer John Van Maanen.
8 Cooperrider, D.L. and Srivastra, S. (1987). "Appreciative Inquiry in Organizational Life," in W.A. Passmore and R.W. Woodman (eds.), *Research in Organizational Change and Development*, Vol. 1 (JAI Press: Greenwich, CT).
9 Ludema, J.D., Cooperrider, D.L., and Barrett, F.J. (2001). *Appreciative Inquiry: The Power of the Unconditional Positive Question: Handbook of Action Research*, 1st ed. (Sage: London, p191).
10 Ibid., p196.
11 Roth, G. and Kleiner, A. (1998). "Developing Organizational Memory Through Learning Histories," *Organizational Dynamics*, Autumn: 43–60.
12 Shah, R. (2001). "Relational Praxis in Transition Towards Sustainability: Business-NGO Collaboration and Participatory Action Research," PhD Thesis, University of Bath, http://people.bath.ac.uk/mnspwr/doc_theses_links/r_shah .html.
13 Gearty, M. (2009). "Exploring Carbon Reduction through Tales of Vision, Chance and Determination: Developing Learning Histories in an Interorganisational Context," PhD Thesis, University of Bath, http://people.bath.ac.uk/ mnspwr/doc_theses_links/m_gearty.html.
14 Reason, P., Coleman, G., Ballard, D. *et al.* (2009). "Insider Voices: Human Dimensions of Low Carbon Technology," www.bath.ac.uk/management/news _events/pdf/lowcarbon_insider_voices.pdf. The authors have waived copyright to enable widespread dissemination of the contents.
15 Ibid., p104.
16 One of several methods of graphic recording and facilitation originating at The Grove, San Francisco, http://www.grove.com/site/index.html.
17 Image reproduced with the kind permission of the client and those involved in its production.
18 Polkinghorne, D. (1988). *Narrative Knowing and the Social Sciences* (SUNY Press: Albany, NY, p150).
19 I was first shown this film at a conference as one of a 300-strong audience. Only nine members of the audience (not including me) saw the gorilla!

20 Scharmer, O.C. (2007). *Theory U: Leading from the Future as It Emerges* (Society for Organizational Learning: Cambridge, MA, p163).

21 Isaacs, W. (1999). *Dialogue and the Art of Thinking Together* (Currency Doubleday: New York).

22 Baldwin, C. (1998). *Calling the Circle: The First and Future Culture* (Bantam Books: New York).

23 To learn more about Leaders' Quest visit http://www.leadersquest.org/.

24 McLuhan, M. and Fiore, Q. (1967).*The Medium is the Massage: An Inventory of Effects* (Bantam Books: New York, p74).

25 Petranker, J. (2004). "The When of Knowing," *Journal of Applied Behavioral Science*, 41(2): 241–249. I thoroughly recommend this fascinating and challenging article, which has greatly informed my understanding of the relationship between time and narrative.

26 Shaw, P. (2002). *Changing Conversations in Organizations: A Complexity Approach to Change* (Routledge: London).

27 Fritz, R. (1989). *The Path of Least Resistance* (Fawcett Columbine: New York).

28 Sinclair, U. (1994 [1935]). *I, Candidate for Governor: And How I Got Licked* (University of California Press: Berkeley, CA, p109).

Chapter 14

Storytelling for a Change

The way we imagine our lives is the way we are going to go on living our lives. For the manner in which we tell ourselves about what is going on is the genre through which events become experiences.

JAMES HILLMAN[1]

The stories we tell are fateful: our ability to change ourselves, our organizations, and our world depends on our capacity to re-imagine them; nothing changes unless the stories change. The snag is that changing our stories is not easy. The stories we currently tell ourselves and others about who we are and how the world works have come from our attempts to make sense of our experience; they are hard won and we are generally quite attached to them. We know that changing the way we live and work will probably require considerable effort and, as long as things seem good enough, we will stick to the stories we know: the "story anchors" will stay firmly embedded in the status quo.

The desire to change our stories may begin because we are dissatisfied with how things are, but it is our ability to imagine a significantly better state of affairs that is worth striving for, that enables us to move toward something different. As James Hillman implies in the quotation above, it takes imagination to unlatch the gate to change. We then have to decide whether to push open the unlatched gate and step through into the new world. Imagination, will, and action are all required for change to occur, but a failure of imagination means that we will not even get started: we need the lift of new stories to get change off the ground.

My last book, *Coming Home to Story: Storytelling After Happily Ever After*, looked in depth at how we can change our self-stories when they become stuck or dysfunctional. Here, in the context of narrative leadership, we will focus on how we can use stories and storytelling to unlatch the gate for collective change. To achieve this, it is essential for leaders to understand and apply the power of positive framing that was touched upon in Chapter 13 in connection with appreciative storytelling. We will begin by taking a look at the ground-breaking linguistic work of cognitive scientist George Lakoff and go on to explore some practical techniques for generating and telling positive stories of the future.

Don't think of an elephant

> *Frames are mental structures that shape the way we see the world. As a result, they shape the goals we seek, the plans we make, the way we act, and what counts as a good or bad outcome of our actions.*
>
> GEORGE LAKOFF[2]

In his early work on semantics, Lakoff explored the intrinsically metaphorical nature of language, showing how our understanding of ideas and concepts rests on implicit mental constructs through which we filter our perceptions. For example, if I say "My sister's recent back operation was a clinical success," then in order to make sense of my statement your mind will automatically invoke your framing of a clinic: surgeons, nurses, operating theaters, instruments, anesthetics, consciousness, pain, mobility, etc.

But even an apparently neutral word like "clinical" carries an emotional and value-based charge; the cluster of thoughts it evokes will be subtly (perhaps even substantially) different for each of us. For the sake of argument, let's say that the following arise in your mind: precision, control, sterility, objectivity, and detachment. If I then use the word "clinical" in a different context to describe, say, an air strike or a kiss it will trigger the same frame, though its implications are quite different. Whereas "clinical" is probably a desirable attribute for an air strike, it is not at the top of my list for kisses.

Lakoff's great contribution to my love life is his insight that "When we negate a frame, we evoke the frame."[3] He reminds me that I'm not likely to put my partner in the mood for a passionate kiss by saying "Let's not kiss clinically," because I'm still entangled in the "clinical" frame and I've just invited her to join me in that entanglement.

How are you getting on with that elephant, by the way? Still not thinking about one? The serious point of Lakoff's paradoxical injunction – not to think of an elephant – is that the very act of asking you not to think of it will make you think of it. If I really don't want you to think of an elephant, I'm much more likely to succeed if I invite you to think of a lion, or a tiger, or an earwig, or whatever it is that I *do* want you to think about.

This is a much more serious matter than it might at first appear. Elections are won or lost depending on the way in which political arguments are framed; issues such as social justice, the way we do business, and international relations are determined by the nature of the discourses we engage in; religious conflicts revolve around the framing of our relationship with the divine.

Republicans and conservative institutions in the United States have spent billions of dollars since the 1970s on think tanks and academic posts with the express intention of claiming (they might say reclaiming) the language of political debate. Thus, for example, anti-abortion became pro-life, tax cuts became tax relief, and benefit reductions became welfare reform. It took a while for Democrats and progressive institutions to wake up to the power of this kind of framing and to understand that it was not enough to rail against their opponents. To win back political power, they had to present their own arguments and policies in their own language. They had to reframe the issues in the minds of voters – they had to tell new stories using new language:

> *Reframing is changing what counts as common sense.*
> *Because language activates frames, new language is*
> *required for new frames. Thinking differently requires*
> *speaking differently.*[4]

Used cynically, the language of reframing takes on an Orwellian quality; the worst examples are reminiscent of the oxymoronic "Newspeak" in the dystopian novel *1984*.[5] In the United States, we might question the naming of the "Healthy Forests" program which allows logging of protected wilderness areas and the "Clear Skies" initiative which removes the restrictions on businesses which pollute the air. In the United Kingdom, the idea of the "Big Society" is proffered as a substitute for adequately funded welfare benefits and the term "Public School" has always been reserved for fee-paying schools largely used for the education of middle- and upper-class children.

Used with genuine intent to signal a substantive difference, the language of reframing – though it may be aspirational – can help to bring about real change. One example from my experience was the shift from "Police Force" to "Police Service" that occurred during my time as a UK police officer. It is an interesting case because policing involves both enforcing the law and providing assistance, relief, and comfort to people when they are frightened or vulnerable. Both functions are necessary, but reframing "Police Force" to "Police Service" emphasized the importance of community involvement; it reframed policing from something that you do to people to something that you do with people. My generation of UK police officers experienced a deep-seated change in attitude toward the public and the nature of their own profession.

Such changes in mental frames are more than passing thoughts. Neuroscientists claim that they cause physical changes in our brains, strengthening new neural pathways and weakening old ones. Paying repeated attention to new stories and new language actually rewires our brains. The brainwashing techniques[6] used in Maoist China for the "re-education" of dissidents and in North Korea on captured US troops starkly revealed the abuse of this phenomenon. Consumerist marketing and advertising also rely on repeated exposure to certain images, language, and stories to influence our behavior.

Two recent books by American authors illustrate my point: *Whoever Tells the Best Story Wins*[7] and *Winning the Story Wars*[8] both frame storytelling as a competition, and – in a sense – they are right. The stories and language that frame and reframe our understanding of the world are indeed powerful,[9] which is why, as leaders, we must reflect carefully on the purpose and scope of our leadership and our stories. The sea of stories in which we swim does contain some stories that exclude and compete with each other, but it also contains stories that are inclusive and welcoming of difference.

Narrative leadership invites us to question the stories and frames by which we live and to make conscious choices about those to which we lend our weight. The tragedy of Boxer the carthorse (representing the proletariat) in George Orwell's allegorical novel *Animal Farm*[10] was that his only solution to any difficulty was to pull harder; not once did he stop to consider whether he was pulling in the right direction. This book is not a polemic, it is for each of us to make the decision as to which we think is the right direction, but I do advocate that we reflect carefully on the world that our frames and our stories help to bring into being.

The example of working with Lakoff's notion of reframing that I am about to give, does exactly that. It takes a number of conventional (often implicit) frames about our relationship with the planet, calls them into question, and explores some alternatives. My partner Chris Seeley and I used this material (published by Joe Brewer of the Rockridge Institute)[11] with a UK-based environmental consultancy to help it reflect on the implicit framing it used when working with clients on sustainability issues.

We asked the group of consultants to consider six statements – reflecting commonly held assumptions within the frame of the industrial growth society – and devise different language that better expressed their assumptions and understanding. I cannot report their responses, which were given confidentially, but you can try for yourself. The reframings that Joe Brewer originally came up with are in the following box.

I.   Nature is a resource to be exploited.

> *Nature is the basis of our survival. We depend upon breath-
> able air, drinkable water, and other "environmental services"
> in order to live.*

II. Wealth is measured simply by money.

> *Wealth is well-being. This includes the empowerment that
> comes with monetary wealth, but it is significantly broader:*

emotional and physical health, having good friends, living in a flourishing community, etc.

III. The economy and environment are distinct and inevitably in conflict with one another.

   A healthy economy depends upon a healthy environment. Our wealth and prosperity are intimately bound to our survival capacity and all that makes flourishing possible.

IV. Polluting is a right, so companies should be compensated for the cost of clean-up.

   We all own the air. It is our right to have it clean. Companies have been damaging our air without paying the full cost of doing business. Companies should pay for damage to this collective wealth. This is the fair thing to do.

V. Markets are natural and naturally good.

   Markets are tools for achieving societal goals. Markets must serve our purposes. We construct them to do so. Solving the climate crisis is a matter of shaping markets so that they generate wealth in the broad sense.

VI. Government is distinct from markets and intrudes upon them.

   Government makes markets possible. Markets cannot function without rules of operation, courts to enforce those rules, banks to secure financial transactions, stock markets to manage the exchanges, and more. All of these features come from government.

The six numbered statements characterize one viewpoint and the italicized statements characterize another. Frames and stories are not neutral; the values embedded in them guide our actions and they have real consequences – in this case for how we treat the planet. Lakoff points out that whether the frames we use reflect or challenge the dominant story, they are equally political.

Notice that the italicized statements are framed not in opposition to the numbered ones but in their own terms. This is a key lesson for the way we use stories to shape the future: there are times when we want to speak out against the dominant story or to deflate an opposing story, but the most powerful storytelling for change offers positive images of the future. Effective future stories show what might happen if we follow a particular course of action, rather than tell us not to follow an alternative course. Using the analogy of a positive photographic print, they illustrate what is present in our vision of the future rather than highlight what is absent.

Empires of the mind

> *The empires of the future are empires of the mind.*
> WINSTON CHURCHILL

I hope that Winston Churchill, were he alive, would not mind me borrowing these words from a speech he made in September 1943 when receiving an honorary degree from Harvard University. The world was at war and the outcome by no means decided, yet Churchill was already looking ahead to the world to come. A mighty weaver of words, he knew the importance of language and the power of a good story.

We may not have Churchill's instinctive grasp of rhetoric or his talent for finding the *bon mot* but we can still use the imaginative power of stories to encourage and support movement toward our "preferred future." In the sections below, I am going to describe four tried-and-tested techniques for doing just that.

Green shoots

In the 1990s, Stephen Denning, then an executive at the World Bank, was tasked with recommending how the organization could strengthen its capacity to transfer information and know-how between people and countries. Finding that his comprehensive analyses, flow charts, and technical presentations received general assent but did not result in action, he "stumbled upon" storytelling. In particular, he discovered that telling a brief anecdote to exemplify the beneficial effects of knowledge transfer enabled his audience to imagine the possibility for themselves. This is the spare – almost skeletal – story he used:

> *In June 1995, a health worker in Kamana, Zambia,*
> *logged on to the Center for Disease Control website*

and got the answer to a question on how to treat malaria.[12]

In his book *The Springboard* Denning tells us how he used the story as a catalyst to extrapolate the consequences of spreading this kind of knowledge transfer throughout the World Bank. The book has the pleasing quality of someone sharing their hard-won learning about the power of stories and storytelling and I recommend it unreservedly.

Denning is adamant that a "springboard" story should be relatively low profile and unobtrusive because he does not want listeners to get so lost in the details that they cannot translate the change idea to their own context. It is a valid point but I think he carries the principle of simplicity too far: his story is so devoid of detail and feeling that it fails to make the events real in my imagination. With that caveat, I broadly agree with his definition of the basic elements of a good "springboard" story. I have selected and adapted what I think are the main points from his list:[13]

- *The explicit story should be relatively brief (and textureless)*
- *The story must be intelligible to the specific audience*
- *The story should be inherently interesting*
- *The story should have a "happy ending"*
- *The story should embody the change message*
- *The listeners should be encouraged to identify with the protagonist*
- *The story should deal with a specific individual or organization*
- *Other things being equal, true is better than invented.*

What Denning calls "springboard" stories I think of as "green shoot" stories. To evoke images of a particular preferred future, we look for small signs of it already coming into being. "Look at this green shoot," we say. "Imagine what the future would be like if shoots like this were to take root and grow." Let me give you an example of what I mean.

A few years ago, I advised the executive team of a government department that was attempting to develop a more customer-friendly approach to the service it provided, which included the payment of certain benefits over the counter in high street branches. The HR Director (we will call her Mary) complained to me that although she had frequently told members of staff at briefings and "town hall" meetings about the importance of improving customer service, no one ever asked any questions and nothing seemed to be happening.

"Let's assume that they are not being perverse," I said. "It sounds to me as though they don't understand what improving customer service would look like in practice. It's a fairly abstract phrase. What do you mean by it?"

"Treating claimants with respect; trying to see things from their point of view; being professional but not stand-offish; that sort of thing," said Mary.

She was still talking in rather general terms so I decided to fish for a story: "I know you get out and visit branches regularly. Have you ever witnessed a member of staff actually doing these things; caught someone doing it right, so to speak? A specific occasion that stands out in your mind?"

Mary thought for a moment and then began:

> *I visited Nottingham last month. It was raining quite hard but the branch wasn't far from the station and I had my coat and umbrella so I walked. I remember thinking how horrible it must be for the claimants – mostly young single mums – struggling through the rain to stand in line with miserable wet kids shivering and crying. But it wasn't like that at all. Inside, most of the kids were in one corner of the room playing with some second-hand toys; there were a couple of ancient hatstands for wet coats; and the mums were sitting down on an odd assortment of chairs, chatting and keeping an eye on the kids until their turn came to be called to the counter.*
>
> *When I spoke to Julie the branch manager, she told me that she had got together with her staff to think about how they could make things a bit more comfortable for people. They'd brought in the toys, got the hatstands and chairs from a charity shop and printed the queueing slips themselves. They didn't ask for permission, they just did it.*

That became Mary's "green shoot" story. You will not be surprised that her audience responded with a great deal more curiosity and enthusiasm than previously when she had lectured them on the importance of improving customer service. The purpose of "green shoot" stories and "springboard" stories is not to paint a comprehensive picture of the future, but to open up a realm of possibility for an audience so they can translate one small example of a nascent change into their own potential roles in bringing about a much bigger one.

1. Green Shoots: Identify a change that you are working to bring about. Where and when have you seen a particular example of this change beginning to happen? What "green shoot" or "springboard" story could you tell?

Over the rainbow

What seems far off and unattainable for some people is sometimes the stock in trade of others. If you already know how to do something that I want to do, if you are already living and behaving in ways to which I aspire, then – in a relativistic sense – my preferred future is your present. I do not have to imagine what my preferred future might be like, I can visit you and find out. Instead of telling a fictional story of the future I can tell a factual story based on *your* experiences of how things are for you and how you got there.

The benefit of this kind of virtual time travel was the key discovery in the classic 1980s' organizational case study: The Medic Inn.[14] It is still a good story and it perfectly illustrates another method of imagining the future. It began when Frank Barrett and colleague David Cooperrider from Case Western Reserve University were retained as consultants by the Midwest Clinic Foundation (MCF) to help raise the standards of hospitality and customer care at The Medic Inn – a hotel recently purchased by MCF to provide accommodation (rooms and restaurant) for patients, and the friends and families of patients, attending the adjoining world-class MCF Hospital.

Standards at The Medic Inn were woefully below those demanded by clients and hospital management and months of conventional problem-based consulting interventions had merely heightened tensions among the 260 hotel staff. Barrett and Cooperrider designed a new process in which a representative group of 30 staff prepared for and then went on a five-day field research trip to The Tremont, an outstanding four-star hotel. Their task was to:

> discover those [features] that exhibited fundamental strength and value in terms of the system's people, its management process, its culture and methods of organization.[15]

This was to be an appreciative inquiry into The Tremont and the experiences of the people who worked there. The group of 30 gathered stories, analyzed the data, shared their impressions, and – from the best of what they had found – constructed a visionary portrait, an imaginary blueprint of the ideal four-star hotel. At The Tremont, they had expanded their horizons; they had seen the future (relative to what they had known before) and, in a new mood of optimism, returned to The Medic Inn not merely to copy what they had seen, but ready to develop their own unique forms of excellence.

The case study is full of fascinating detail about the intervention, but there are three crucial points to which I want to draw your attention: (1) The Tremont offered an example of what was already happening elsewhere; (2) the task given to the group of 30 was to inquire into what they found, not merely to report back what they had seen; (3) using this experience as the basis upon which to imagine their own future freed them from many of the limitations arising from their previous stories about themselves. Overall, the intervention enabled the staff of The Medic Inn to "subjunctivize" their reality: to shift their cognitive register from what *is* to what *could be*.[16]

1. Over the Rainbow: Identify a change that you are working to bring about. Does your "preferred future" already exist in some form elsewhere? If so, how could you initiate an appreciative inquiry to help your organization, group, movement, etc., to create new possibilities for itself?

Future perfect

A common approach to leading change involves creating a range of likely future scenarios (extrapolated from current data and trends), then deciding what steps are needed to move toward the most desirable scenario or to avoid particularly undesirable options. It is a powerful method for identifying and managing potential risks and for choosing a strategic direction. But because it is essentially an act of forecasting – grounded in the present – it is unlikely to produce a vision that is radically new. On the other hand, the idealized visions arising from unconstrained blue-sky thinking may be so ungrounded and impractical that they can never be realized.

Somewhere between these two poles, the process of storymaking provides the possibility of a robust vision that is both aspirational and grounded. Taking an imaginative leap into a desired future allows us to test that vision by creating stories of what life might be like for particular characters. Such stories join up the dots of our imagined world to explore the systemic nature of the changes we have envisaged.

Once satisfied, we can then look back from the future to the present – backcasting – to identify what choices and actions we will have taken to get there. Such "future perfect" stories reveal the imagined traces of a journey we have yet to undertake; they not only paint a detailed and realistic picture of where we want to go, but also show us the route we must take to get there. They work best when we imagine particular characters and what they would be experiencing day to day as they go about their lives at a certain time and place in the future.

The process of creating future stories has three phases. I will show them first in the generic form devised by Charlene Collison (a colleague at Narrative Leadership Associates)[17] and then give an example of how she has successfully used a collaborative storymaking process to help the East Sussex town of Forest Row explore possibilities for a more sustainable future.

Good preparation is essential to focus attention on a shared vision. If the parameters are too loose, the exercise is likely to result in generalizations; if they are too tight, then the results will lack significance. Choose an area that has meaning for those involved: a future in which they have a real investment.

Phase One: Preparation	
Step 1	Set up a steering group to drive the process – organizationally, creatively, and editorially
Step 2	Define the boundaries of the area and desired future state you are exploring
Step 3	Map out the main sectors (streams of activity) in the defined area
Step 4	Engage key stakeholders in each of the main sectors to include multiple perspectives
Step 5	Research and identify viable changes in each main sector – prioritized for effectiveness and feasibility

We would probably use all the steps in Phase One for conventional scenario planning but we can also use the unique power of stories to make the imagined future more real and tangible. Phase Two offers a step-by-step approach to collaborative storymaking as an exploration of the future. Because stories involve particular characters experiencing particular events, the process of storymaking challenges abstract ideas and broad assumptions by requiring them to be made concrete.

Phase Two: Story Building	
Step 6	Hold a series of story-building events including as many stakeholders as possible
Step 6(i)	Create some realistic characters who might live in the future you are exploring
Step 6(ii)	Ask questions and let the characters "answer" them: What does this world look like? What are their challenges and concerns?
Step 6(iii)	Mess around in the future. Play with possibilities; try out different situations
Step 6(iv)	Explore the meeting points between different activities and sectors; how do they affect each other? Challenge assumptions
Step 7	Steering group decides on a final set of characters and flow of events. Write/tell/construct the stories
Step 8	Test draft versions with stakeholders and contributors. Get feedback and revise/refine

The conversations, relationships, and impetus for action that the stories create are what really matters. Phase Three is concerned with publishing and sharing the stories in lively ways that engage the organization or community and enable it to take action.

Phase Three: Taking Action	
Step 9	Publish and share the final stories throughout the organization/community (leaflets, talks, online, etc.)
Step 10	Follow up with forums for discussion, decision-making, and action

The main weakness of most attempts at creating an inspiring vision is that they jump straight from analysis to advocacy, from Phase One to Phase Three, missing out the creative exploration, testing, and elaboration of the vision in Phase Two. I am frequently asked to find or create an inspiring story to enliven somebody's vision statement (see for example the anecdote in the introduction to this book about the professional services firm) and, sometimes, I can. But if story and storytelling are an integral part of the process of creating the vision it is much more likely to stir the imaginations and emotions of an audience and inspire them to take action.

In 2007, a group of people in Forest Row – including Charlene – came together to consider one of the most important and difficult-to-ask questions of our time: what can we do to create a better and more sustainable low-carbon future for our community, a future fit for our children and grandchildren? Inspired by the Transition Town movement, they engaged hundreds of residents in a wide variety of events, including the 3 phases and 10 steps of the storymaking process. They wanted a vision that lived, one that:

> *would be talked about in the street, argued over at dinner parties, would give people a glimpse of something that was possible so they would go out and start doing it.*[18]

One of the fruits of this work – a tangible expression of the vision they created – was a booklet published in 2009, *Forest Row in Transition: A Community Work in Progress.*[19] At the heart of the vision are stories of the Foresters, a "typical" family living in Forest Row in 2025, going about their daily lives in a world in which the practical consequences of resource depletion and climate change are very apparent. The stories are not particularly dramatic or compelling (nor were they intended to be) but they do allow us to identify with the characters and their situation so that we can imagine ourselves in their place:

> *It is a tough task to imagine what the future could be like.*
> *The more we can imagine, the more questions arise.*
> *But if we can imagine it, we have the power to create it.*
> *And if we can do it, so can others.*[20]

The proof of the pudding, it is said, is in the eating. Now, several years after the booklet was published, some of the things envisaged in the stories have already happened (a crafts co-operative and a car share scheme, for example) and others – such as a renewable energy project – are beginning to take shape.

2. Future Perfect: What is the future for which you need to create a vibrant, engaging vision? Who needs to be involved in its creation; how could you enlist them in a collective storymaking process such as that described above?

Self, us, now

The fact that Charlene had lived and been active in Forest Row for some years established her credentials as a member of the community, with a personal investment for herself and her family in its future. It seems obvious that the moral authority to claim leadership in any field rests on an authentic connection between leaders and those whom they would lead.

Marshall Ganz of the Kennedy School of Government at Harvard University teaches a program in Public Narrative in which he stresses the importance of public leaders finding and making explicit the connection between who they are, the communities and constituencies of which they claim membership, and the changes for which they call:

> *Public narrative is woven from three elements: a story of*
> *why I have been called, a story of self; a story of why we*

have been called, a story of us; and a story of the urgent
challenge on which we are called to act now, a story
of now.[21]

His formulation – self, us, now – echoes the three practices of narrative leadership: Know Thyself, Only Connect, and Stand for Something. When we have established our moral authority to exercise leadership within a particular community (an authority bestowed by the community, arising from the stories we tell of self and us) then – and only then, says Ganz – are we legitimately in a position to call for what he calls "hopeful action," that is to say, action that has some chance of success.

Barack Obama, who came to politics from a background of community organizing, understood this well. Indeed, Ganz's work is widely credited as one of the guiding inspirations behind Obama's two successful presidential campaigns. Ganz himself, so far as I am aware, claims no personal credit for the influence of his ideas, but in a 2008 Kennedy School paper, he cites Obama's keynote speech to the 2004 Democratic Party Congress as a brilliant example of their application. Obama, then an Illinois State Senator, told the story of his origins – where he came from and who made him what he was; he declared that his story was part of the American story (by virtue of his history and shared values); he called upon the American people to build upon the achievements of their forbears and to vote for John Kerry, the Democratic Party's chosen presidential candidate.

As we know, Kerry's campaign did not succeed but Obama's speech that night established himself in the public consciousness as a potential future presidential candidate. Four years later, he told his stories of self, us, and now on his own behalf to enter the White House not just as the first black US president, but as someone who had inspired hope in men and women of all colors and creeds. We believe we know who Obama is and the values he stands for because his public narrative is so convincing. As Ganz says:

> *Narrative allows us to communicate the values that moti-*
> *vate the choices that we make. Narrative is not talking*
> *"about" values; rather narrative embodies and communi-*
> *cates values. And it is through the shared experience of*

our values that we can engage with others, motivate one
another to act, and find the courage to take risks, explore
possibility and face the challenges we must face.[22]

3. Self, Us, Now: How well can you tell the three elements of your "public narrative?" (1) A story of self: why you have been called to lead; (2) a story of us: what your constituency/community/movement has been called to do; (3) a story of now: the urgent challenge on which you and your community etc. are called to act.

For inspiration as you wrestle with these questions, watch Obama's 16-minute speech on YouTube at http://www.youtube.com/watch?v =_fMNIofUw2I or a shorter edited version at http://www.youtube.com/ watch?v=OFPwDe22CoY with a commentary. Watch it as a historical artifact and as an example of narrative leadership from which we can all learn.

Having looked closely at the relationship between time and narrative, and storytelling for change, the next chapter considers the role of the timeless art of storytelling in the high-pressured, time-bound world of the twenty-first century.

Bonus: The Foresters

If the process of collective visioning and storymaking described in Future Perfect caught your imagination, then you might like to read the *Forest Row in Transition* booklet. It is available to download free as a pdf file under Creative Commons License from the Forest Row Transition website at http://transitionforestrow.org/notes/EDAP.

To whet your appetite, here is a slightly adapted version of one of the Forester stories:

Getting Around in 2025.

Most days Peter goes to his study to work. He's an
IT consultant, helping people set up systems for virtual

meetings and communication with people around the globe. Sometimes he cycles or takes the light rail service to the virtual teleconferencing facilities and hot-desk work centre in East Grinstead.

Today is unusual: he is driving with a colleague to a face-to-face meeting outside Swindon. These are relatively rare because travel is expensive and technology makes day-to-day communication easy. He meets his colleague at one of Forest Row's charging stations where he recharges the car – a fuel cell hybrid. Peter sinks into the seat, appreciating the luxury of going in a private car: his family, when they need one, uses the local car-share scheme. Mostly they manage without, and rely on walking, cycling and the efficient public transport system.

Kate (Peter's wife) walks with the children to school before catching the light rail to East Grinstead. From there she walks to Sackville College where she is teaching preventative healthcare.

Peter's teenage nephew Tom (who also lives with Peter and Kate) sets off on his bike to his carpentry module on Priory Road, a bicycle boulevard as far as Kidbrooke Park. This is just one of the dedicated cycle boulevards that now link Forest Row with East Grinstead, Ashurst Wood and other nearby villages.

Summary

- Imagination, will, and action are all required for change to occur, but a failure of imagination means that we will not even get started: we need the lift of new stories to get change off the ground.
- The stories we tell and the language we use to frame issues are critical. Paying repeated attention to new stories and new language metaphorically rewires our brains, strengthening new neural pathways and weakening old ones.

- Telling leadership stories invites others to join the "story wars." Whether the frames we use and the stories we tell reflect or challenge the dominant story, they are equally political; there is no neutral ground to stand on.
- Green shoot stories open up a realm of possibility for an audience so they can translate one small example of a nascent change into their own potential roles in bringing about a much bigger one.
- Telling stories of a desired future that is already happening somewhere else provides a kind of virtual time travel enabling us to tell real rather than imagined stories of what the future could be.
- Collaborative storymaking about the future is a powerful tool for creating a vision that is both aspirational and grounded. Many attempts to create an inspiring vision fail because they jump straight from analysis to advocacy.
- Marshall Ganz's notion of Public Narrative provides a powerful model for leaders to call people to action by telling stories of self, us, and now. Barack Obama is a skillful – and authentic – exponent of this form.

Notes and References

1 Hillman, J. (1983). *Healing Fiction* (Spring: Woodstock, CT, p23).
2 Lakoff, G. (2004). *Don't Think of an Elephant: Know Your Values and Frame Them* (Chelsea Green: White River Junction, VT, pxv).
3 Ibid., p3.
4 Ibid., pxv.
5 In George Orwell's novel *1984*, the main departments of government were ironically named "Ministry of Love" (secret police, interrogation and torture), "Ministry of Peace" (armed forces and warfare), "Ministry of Truth" (propaganda and alteration of history) and "Ministry of Plenty" (keeping the population in a state of constant economic hardship).
6 Schein, E.H. (1956). "The Chinese Indoctrination Program for Prisoners of War: A Study of Attempted Brainwashing," *Psychiatry*, **19**(2): 149–172. See also Schein, E.H. (1971). *Coercive Persuasion: A Socio-Psychological Analysis of the "Brainwashing" of American Civilian Prisoners by the Chinese Communists* (WW Norton: New York).
7 Simmons, A. (2007). *Whoever Tells the Best Story Wins* (AMACOM: New York).
8 Sachs, J. (2012). *Winning the Story Wars* (Harvard Business Review Press: Boston, MA).

9   I should point out here that Lakoff's insight into the nature of language-as-framing was by no means unique. Among others, Gregory Bateson (*Steps to an Ecology of Mind*, 1972), Milton Erickson (*My Voice Will Go With You: The Teaching Tales of Milton H Erickson*, 1991), and the pioneering work in neurolinguistic programming (NLP) by Richard Bandler and John Grinder all drew upon the power of language to frame and reframe perceived reality.

10   Orwell, G. (1945). *Animal Farm: A Fairy Story* (Secker & Warburg: London).

11   From Cognitive Policy Works' "Why We Are Losing the Global Warming Battle,"   http://www.cognitivepolicyworks.com/resource-center/rockridge-institute/why-we-are-losing-the-global-warming-battle/. Quoted under Creative Commons License. The Rockridge Institute was established by George Lakoff and others to counter the power of the Republican/Conservative think tanks in framing the language of US political discourse.

12   Denning, S. (2001). *The Springboard: How Storytelling Ignites Action in Knowledge-Era Organizations* (Butterworth–Heinemann: Woburn, MA).

13   Ibid., Appendix 1, pp197–199.

14   Ibid.

15   Barrett, F.J. and Cooperrider, D.L. (1990). "Generative Metaphor Intervention: A New Approach for Working with Systems Divided by Conflict and Caught in Defensive Perception," *Journal of Applied Behavioral Science*, **26**(2): 228–229.

16   Bruner, J.M. (1986). *Actual Minds, Possible Worlds* (Harvard University Press: Cambridge, MA, p26).

17   Tables adapted from "Systemic Storymaking: A Collaborative Process for Community Visioning," in Collison, C. *et al.* (2014) *Storytelling for a Greener World: Community, Connection and Change* (Hawthorn Press: Stroud).

18   Charlene Collison, personal communication.

19   *Forest Row In Transition* can be downloaded under Creative Commons License from http://transitionforestrow.org/notes/EDAP.

20   Ibid., p13.

21   Ganz, M. (2008). "What Is Public Narrative?" Unpublished paper, Kennedy School of Government, Harvard, MA, http://wearesole.com/What_is_Public_Narrative.pdf (accessed December 5, 2013).

22   Ibid.

Chapter 15

Life in the Fast Lane

This isn't life in the fast lane, it's life in the oncoming traffic.

TERRY PRATCHETT[1]

It is a constant and ironic complaint that in this age of time-saving electronic and digital devices we have less time than ever. Communication and decision-making spin round in a welter of meetings, conference calls, and emails; the pressure of work increases, deadlines get tighter, and what is important gets lost among what is deemed to be urgent; long-term goals surrender to the exigencies of short-term advantage or immediate survival.

The personal boundaries we once placed around evenings, weekends, and holidays crumble. We are expected and we expect others to be available all the time and everywhere. If we are not careful, we end up chasing our own tails in a frantic effort to keep up with the game; we become like the ancient figure of Ouroboros, the serpent that consumes itself.

Not everyone is caught up in the whirlwind: the elderly, the disabled, the unemployed tend to live in saner – if reduced – circumstances. Some people consciously choose to step out of the rat race and live more simply, but many who work in corporate or public life will recognize the picture I have painted above. As leaders, we might ask if such fragmentation of meaning in our lives is inevitable. Does our self-created demand for immediacy inevitably squeeze out more considered and reflective communication? What is the place of storytelling today in our fast-paced, complex world?

This chapter will explore these questions by considering the practical implications for narrative leadership of some of the most distinctive attributes of contemporary western society: the almost overwhelming pace of life and work; the unprecedented interconnectivity provided by the Internet; the impact of globalization and the intermingling of cultures; and the ease with which the stories we tell can take on a disturbing life of their own.

Modern, post-modern, and hypermodern

Modern man must descend the spiral of his own absurdity
to the lowest point; only then can he look beyond it.
                                             VACLEV HAVEL[2]

We may think that we are modern in our outlook but the notion that we are living in Modern Times is questionable. Charlie Chaplin released his famous film of that name in 1936 and the world has changed greatly since his lovable tramp got caught inside a machine-like factory. If we are no longer modern, then what are we? Are we merely post-modern or something else?

The term "post-modern" was first used in the field of architectural criticism in the 1970s to designate a reaction to the modernist style popularized in the first half of the twentieth century by architects such as Le Corbusier in France and Ludwig Mies van der Rohe and Walter Gropius in Germany. It was soon taken up more widely by philosophers and social theorists as a way of naming the decline of collective historical ideologies and the rampant growth of individualism and pluralism in western societies. Professor Jean-François Lyotard of the University of Paris famously articulated the post-modern phenomenon in 1979: "Simplifying to the extreme, I define postmodern as incredulity towards metanarratives."[3]

The hegemonic stories of modernity – progress, growth, capitalism, socialism, even religion – lost much of their authority and no longer provide universal templates for our lives, at least in western liberal-democratic societies. Although, as philosopher John Gray points out in his essay "Progress, the Moth-eaten Musical Brocade,"[4] despite the bankruptcy of many of the fundamental tenets of modernism, they have proved remarkably hardy. Perhaps this is, as he suggests, because we tend to confuse the tangible and irreversible advance of science and technology with the illusion of ethical and political progress. It may also be the case – as I suggested in Chapter 13 – that our old stories keep us anchored in the past. What business leader or politician has yet found the courage to slaughter the sacred cow of continuous growth, for example?

If pre-modern societies looked to the golden age of the past as their prime point of reference, and modern societies looked to a utopian future as theirs, then post-modern societies focus their attention more and more on the immediate satisfactions of the present. Leaders in all walks of life find that the traditional loyalty of voters, employees, servants, and customers can no longer be depended upon. With new levels of economic and intellectual freedom come greater independence of mind and fickleness: our conditional loyalty can be won but we demand to be wooed.

As if things were not already difficult enough for leaders, the pace of post-modern life continues to grow. Now writers such as Gilles Lipovetsky are heralding the advent of hypermodern times:

> *Hyper-capitalism, hyperclass, hyperpower, hyperterrorism, hyper-individualism, hypermarket, hypertext – is there anything that isn't "hyper"? Is there anything now that does not reveal a modernity raised to the nth power? The climate of [post-modern] epilogue is being followed by the awareness of a headlong rush forwards, of unbridled modernization comprised of galloping commercialization, economic deregulation, and technical and scientific developments being unleashed with effects that are heavy with threats as well as promises.[5]*

Hyper comes from a Greek root meaning over and above what is necessary, excessive. To Lipovetsky's list we can add hyper-consumption, hyper-mobility, hyper-surveillance, hyper-stimulation, and hyper-connection. It remains to be seen if the global financial crash and subsequent recession will calm this perfect storm, though there is little sign of that happening among the western elite or among the newly affluent middle classes in India, China, and Brazil.

No wonder clients say to me that their world is changing so fast that they no longer have any secure foundations. "It's as though," said one, quoting Rilke, "we are standing on fish." "We are operating in so many countries," said another, "that we no longer understand our customers." "I work every weekend and still don't have time to clear all my emails." "I've been in three continents this week; I've almost forgotten what my home is like." "I've got a 30 minute slot in 3 weeks' time; 8.15 Thursday morning." "Our meetings are so full of information we don't have time for stories."

The continual state of agitation and change endemic in the hypermodern world can be exciting, though – like any kind of adrenaline rush – it narrows our focus and we begin to operate on very short time cycles. As we race to meet deadline after deadline, it becomes increasingly difficult to see the big picture; to stay in touch with our sense of purpose; to remember *why* we are doing what we are doing. In our frantic desire to surf the waves of change, life begins to feel like a series of gasps, in-breath after in-breath with no time to breathe out.

Breathing out is every bit as important as breathing in. Taking a few minutes to tell a story is like breathing out. Our logico-rational brains have an immense capacity for rapidly storing and sorting data, but our emotional body and our storied mind follow a slower rhythm. The Bedouin had a poetic way of describing this: they would say that when traveling through the desert by camel they needed to stop frequently at oases not just for physical nourishment, but to allow time for their souls – left behind by the speed of their journey – to catch up with them.

And the intuitive wisdom of that ancient culture is confirmed by recent research in cognitive science. As Guy Claxton demonstrated in his fascinating book *Hare Brain, Tortoise Mind*,[6] we function best when we employ both quick thinking and slower, ruminative mulling. The former locks on to familiar patterns to make sense of new data in terms of what is already known, whereas the latter allows space and time for genuine novelty to emerge.

Beneath the shifting sands of hypermodern life, there lies the bedrock of human nature. It also moves but much more slowly, like tectonic plates inching to and fro. Story is intrinsic to our human nature; we are the storytelling animal and, no matter what medium we are using, the basic elements of a good story have changed little since stories were first told. The adventures of the ancient Sumerian Gilgamesh still intrigue us; the archetypal characters and situations of Greek epic poetry still speak to us; the everyday dramas of ordinary lives fill our screens and newspapers.

So, to the client who told me that there was not time for stories in their meetings, I replied that there was not time *not* to have stories; that a meeting concerned only with exchanging information probably was not worth having; and that a meeting that encouraged people to share specific examples (anecdotes and stories) in support of their arguments would lead to more informed and better decision-making. I also told him about a former client of mine who begins her management meetings by calling for a two-minute story from each team member about a particular high or low from the preceding week. "It's the fastest way I know to feel the pulse of my organization," she would say.

My listener still did not seem convinced. "But we have so much business to get through," he said. "Our agendas are jam-packed and we always run over. I think I understand how powerful stories can be, but we just don't have time." Noticing that I too was in danger of falling into the trap of relying solely on information and argument to make my point, I told him a story:

> *A busy executive once realized that something was lacking in his life. He decided that what he needed was spiritual enlightenment so he instructed his PA to find a slot in his diary to visit a famous Zen master in Japan. Some weeks later, he flew to Tokyo where a limousine whisked him into the mountains. When he arrived at the monastery, a monk ushered him into the master's presence.*
>
> *While the master quietly served tea, the executive talked about his wish to become enlightened. He told the master about his work, his family, his hobbies, what he liked to read, the trials and tribulations of his life, and above all of his desire for the master to teach him. The master*

*smiled, filled the visitor's cup to the brim, and kept on
pouring, spilling tea all over the floor.*

*The executive watched the overflowing cup until he
couldn't restrain himself. "Stop," he blurted out. "It's full.
No more will go in!"*

"Indeed," said the master. "Just like you."

My client sat quietly for some time before speaking: "OK, I get it."

Swept along by the swirling currents of the hypermodern world, it may
seem counter-intuitive to turn and swim upstream: to pause and breathe
out; to stem the flood of information and argument for a few minutes in
order to tell a story. But underneath our frantic hyper-activity, as I have
so often witnessed in my work with leaders, we yearn – as the poet Rumi
said – to bathe in Story Water. A good story, well told, nourishes us and
our audience and gets our point across more effectively than anything
else I know. If telling stories is already part of your leadership practice
then you will also know that to be true; if it is not already part of your
leadership practice then try it and see for yourself what happens.

1. Making Time: Reread the story of the Zen master. When do you feel
    "too busy" to tell or listen to a story? How could you create space for
    a story when you are overloaded with information and argument?

The medium and the message

*The medium is the message. This is merely to say that the
personal and social consequences of any medium—that
is, of any extension of ourselves—result from the new scale
that is introduced into our affairs by each extension of
ourselves, or by any new technology.*

MARSHALL McLUHAN[7]

The hyper-connectivity of the Internet provides both new possibilities and
new challenges for storytelling. Billions of people make public the intimate details of their lives via Facebook, Twitter, and other social media;

knowledge that was once the preserve of the learned is freely available to all; virtually anything can be purchased online and delivered to our door; expensive advertising campaigns languish while YouTube videos of dancing cats go viral. The whole world is just one click away, but how do we get our message across – our story heard – in the midst of this white noise?

Gurus of the digital age like Jonah Sachs and Clay Shirky are experts on contemporary media. Watching them online and reading their books will give you an insider's perspective on using the Internet for social organizing and for marketing ideas and brands.[8] But whatever medium you use for your message, it needs to be a message worth hearing, a story worth listening to. As TED Curator Chris Anderson says, "Presentations rise or fall on the quality of the idea, the narrative, and the passion of the speaker."[9]

Notice how TED talks are recordings of live presentations, not straight-to-camera scripted performances. A really good TED talk can take months of preparation and the best of them give us powerful vicarious experiences of live storytelling; we feel ourselves to be actively witnessing an event rather than passively watching a film; we can identify with the audience as well as the speaker. It is well worth looking at the videos embedded in the online version of Anderson's recent *Harvard Business Review* article,[10] especially the talks given by a 12-year-old Masai boy called Richard Turere about his "lion lights" and neuroscientist Jill Bolte Taylor about what she learned during and after suffering a stroke. According to Anderson, both presenters had to work hard to master their stories; neither of them is a "natural" storyteller, yet both are incredibly affecting and effective. They have good stories to tell and they tell them well enough – above all, they both really "show up" on stage. The resulting presentations are object lessons for would be narrative leaders.

I do not deny the importance of engaging with the digital world (I am a keen blogger, active Facebook user, and occasional tweeter, myself) but this book is primarily concerned with the unique power of oral storytelling to engage the feelings and imaginations of an audience, face to face. Once we know how to tap into the innate human capacity for telling and listening to stories, all the rest follows. Our real challenge is not mastery of a new medium, but making sure we have something worth saying.

> 2. Something Worth Saying: If you had the opportunity to give a TED talk
>   (and the support to do it really well) what subject would you choose?
>   What do you most want to share with the world? What story would you
>   really like to tell?

Storytelling in a global village

*Today, after more than a century of electric technology,
we have extended our central nervous system in a global
embrace, abolishing both space and time as far as our
planet is concerned.*

MARSHALL McLUHAN[11]

So wrote Marshall McLuhan over 50 years ago. What would he have made
of the burgeoning globalization of our hypermodern world today? Cultures and stories have always met and mingled but never as much or as
fast as now. We are experiencing an unprecedented need to communicate
our stories effectively across cultures. For example, when I was recently
asked to run a half-day narrative leadership workshop in Paris for a
French-owned multinational company, I was asked: "How well do our
stories travel; do they make sense to people from other cultures? Do we
need to tell different stories in different cultures?"

These were astute questions, from an organization with a strong storytelling ethos, sensitive to cultural diversity and not wanting to impose its
own style unilaterally or inappropriately on others. My clients were aware
of research studies detailing various dimensions against which national
cultures can be described (e.g., equality versus inequality; individualism
versus collectivism; certainty versus uncertainty; masculine versus femi-
nine qualities; short-term versus long-term orientation). Such models are
commonly used to help expatriate employees understand and appreciate
cultural biases and typical behavior patterns in different parts of the
world, but none of them consider what kinds of story are most likely to
be told or well received.

As a performer who has told stories in many countries, I know
that storytelling is both a universally common and a culturally specific

phenomenon. The answers to the questions posed by the French company are paradoxically both very simple and quite complex, depending on which approach you take. Looking first at cultural specificity, Ronnie Lessem and Sudhanshu Palsule proposed in their book *Managing in Four Worlds*[12] a fourfold model of culture and organization loosely based on Jung's four dimensions of personality – sensing, thinking, intuiting, and feeling – equating these to the four cardinal directions. In the west, they said, sensing predominated; in the north, thinking; in the east, intuiting; and in the south, feeling.

Peter Christie, who worked with Lessem in South Africa, looked at how this theory related to different kinds of stories and suggested that some categorization was possible. Based on these ideas – though differing in some respects – the table below sketches out a somewhat simplified version of their combined model.[13]

Anecdote	Account	Allegory	Folktale
Sensing	Thinking	Intuiting	Feeling
Pragmatic	Rational	Spiritual	Relational
Heroes	Concepts	Meaning	People
West	North	East	South

In the pragmatic, sensing west (particularly North America) heroic individualism is valued highly and anecdotes of exceptional hands-on leaders like Jack Welch of GE and Ray Kroc of McDonald's hit the spot. Tom Peters is a great exponent of this kind of storytelling, of which there are many examples in his classic book with Robert Waterman, *In Search of Excellence*.[14]

In the rational, thinking north (Scandinavia, UK, France, Germany, for example) a more considered and conceptual approach is preferred. Stories cast in the form of case studies and learning histories like the LowCarbonWorks report quoted in Chapter 13 are typical of this style of storytelling.

In the spiritual, intuiting east (India, China, Japan, Korea, Taiwan, for example) the search for deeper meaning prevails. Allegory and myth such as *The Cracked Pot* in Chapter 7 provide a more metaphorical approach to storytelling that suits these cultures.

In the relational, feeling south (South America and Africa, for example) folktales – stories that represent the daily lives and fates of ordinary people – hold sway. The story in the Introduction, *Water on the Rock*, is an example of this kind of narrative.

There is considerable value in distinguishing these four kinds of story and thinking about which categories we might want to draw upon, but attempting to ascribe sensing, thinking, intuiting, and feeling to discrete geographical regions results in crude caricatures that take no account either of individual preferences or the richness and complexity of different cultures. There are undoubtedly some grains of truth within these sweeping generalizations but we should use the model only with great caution. It makes much more sense to think of these different types of story as appealing to four co-existing aspects of all types of personalities and cultures. In this model, north, south, east, and west are metaphorical regions of the human imagination rather than geographical locations.

There are collections of traditional stories from all over the world on my bookshelves, too many to count. There are similar stories and different versions of the same stories in many of them as well as some that are unique to a particular tradition. Within this universal treasure trove, there are also differences of sensibility and aesthetics. I found when storytelling in Japan, for example, that my audiences were especially fond of grue-some ghost stories and mawkishly sentimental tales of childhood. Despite such differences in taste, tales of the human condition have much in common whatever their origin.

Looking again at the questions asked by my client – "How well do our stories travel; do they make sense to people from other cultures? Do we need to tell different stories in different cultures?" – I find myself wanting to give some very straightforward answers. Your stories will travel well and make sense to people in other cultures if you tell them with a gener-ous and inclusive spirit that values their stories as much as your own. You should not breach cultural or religious taboos (unless you do so intentionally for some reason and are willing to take responsibility for the consequences). With that caveat, you do not need to tell different stories in different cultures but you do need to listen to their stories. Sharing our stories has always been how we have got to know each other;

how we have influenced and learned from each other; and how we have shaped the multicultural world we live in.

Signs of the times

> *It is the whole traditional world of causality that is in question: the perspectival, determinist mode, the "active," critical mode, the analytic mode—the distinction between cause and effect, between active and passive, between subject and object, between the end and the means.*
>
> JEAN BAUDRILLARD[15]

Including TV/radio/Internet/newsprint, it has been estimated that an adult living in a city in the United States sees an average of somewhere between 500 and 5,000 advertisements each day.[16] The number is somewhat smaller in the United Kingdom but growing. Add to that all the non-advertising content that we digest and the scale of competing signs, signals, and stories to which we are exposed becomes clear. How are we to make sense of this blizzard of conflicting messages? How can we discern the trustworthiness of what we are being told?

The problem is not just the sheer volume of signs, signals, and stories. Perhaps even more insidious is the cynicism and sophistication with which such attempts to manipulate our understanding and behavior are divorced from any underlying reality. One of the features of our hyper-modern age is that many of the stories we are told (perhaps even some that we tell) are simulations: pretences that create their own reality.

Baudrillard suggests that we can look at the increasing distance between images (or stories) and underlying reality as a hierarchy from representation to simulacrum, thus:

- Representation: the reflection of a profound reality
- Trace: diminishes or denatures a profound reality
- Void: masks the absence of a profound reality
- Simulacrum: has no relation to any reality whatsoever.

If representation is an attempt in good faith to signify or reflect an underlying reality, then a simulacrum might best be described as a copy that has no original (think Disney World) or a fiction that believes itself to be real. In between these extremes, "trace" and "void" represent attempts to erase aspects of an underlying reality from a discourse either by using neologisms and abstract language to obscure a subject or by treating it as though it did not exist.

Why does this matter? Because our use of language (as we saw in the discussion about framing in Chapter 14) is an exercise in power as well as communication. A story that reflects a profound underlying reality such as the one told by Martin Luther King in his famous *I Have a Dream* speech can be told with such personal integrity and moral authority that it claims our attention and demands radical action. Not only do such stories not erase their subjects, they seek to un-erase them; to bring them back into consciousness; to re-mind us of what has been missing from public discourse. King demanded that we think of black men, women, and children in the United States as individual living, suffering human beings, not as an abstract "problem" devoid of humanity.

Language and stories that erase their subjects enable us to normalize behavior that would otherwise be unthinkable. Hannah Arendt made the point dramatically in her book *Eichmann in Jerusalem: A Report on the Banality of Evil*[17] that the Holocaust was conducted almost entirely in the impersonal jargon of bureaucracy. My colleague Arran Stibbe in his recent book *Animals Erased*[18] shows the systematic erasure of animals and the natural world from the discourses of factory farming and (more surprisingly) of environmental monitoring. He quotes, for example, from the preamble to the 2005 Millennium Ecosystems Assessment:

> *Although the Millennium Ecosystems Assessment empha-*
> *sizes the linkages between ecosystems and human well-*
> *being, it recognizes that the actions people take that*
> *influence ecosystems result not just from concern about*
> *human well-being but also from consideration of the*
> *intrinsic value of species and ecosystems.*[19]

Notice that even in this well-intentioned report, designed to highlight the impact of human activities on the planet, everything that is not human is reduced to the abstract phrase "species and ecosystems." Such language unwittingly distances us from underlying reality and enables us to exploit the natural world or be bystanders to its exploitation (and of our fellow humans who are not distinct from it) without unduly troubling our consciences. This is the antithesis of the values inherent in narrative leadership: of naming what *is* and re-minding us who and what has been erased; of re-enchanting a disenchanted world. But let us not be seduced by the naive hope that storytelling is the answer to all the challenges of leadership: narrative leadership is not an end in itself, but a powerful means of engaging the feelings and imaginations of others.

When storytelling is employed thoughtfully and responsibly it can be a force for good, but used cynically and irresponsibly it can do great harm as Christian Salmon demonstrates in *Storytelling: Bewitching the Modern Mind*[20] – a provocative counterblast to what he sees as a dangerously uncritical enthusiasm for storytelling in contemporary business and politics. Here, in the worlds of corporate branding, big business, and government he finds many disturbing examples of simulacra: stories that have no relation to any reality, but exercise enormous influence. I will touch on just a few of them as cautions to us all to choose carefully what stories we tell and to be appropriately wary of stories and storytellers making easy and unfounded promises.

Brand storytelling is all the rage and Salmon quotes Barbara Stern (a professor of marketing at Rutgers University) to tell us why:

> *What branding really is, is a story attached to a product.*
> *When you have a product that's just like another product,*
> *there are any number of ways to compete. The stupid way*
> *is to lower prices. The smart way is to change the value of*
> *the product by telling a story about it.*[21]

But, what story? And what connection should it have to underlying realities? We are bored it seems with stories about how great the product and the company are. Now we consume in order to feel part of a bigger story; the cooler and funkier, the better. Make your customers the heroes of your authentic brand story, urges Jonah Sachs in *Winning the Story Wars*; offer them an opportunity to live their higher values; tell the truth about your products and your organization (and make sure you have a truth worth telling). The same principles hold good, says Sachs, whether you are trying to sell an idea, a set of values, or a product.

Winning the Story Wars is a good read and at first sight Sachs's prescription is attractive – who could gainsay living your higher values and telling the truth? My concerns are twofold: first, the implicit framing that we can sell, consume, and grow our way out of the mess we are in (whether we do so ethically or not); second, as Sachs himself points out, there are many companies out there whose visions of themselves seem wildly out of touch with the dubious benefits of their products. I'm certainly not immune from the lure of brand storytelling as my Akubra (*Crocodile Dundee*) hat and Sebago Docksider (I wish I owned a boat) sailing shoes testify, but I'm not "lovin it" at McDonald's, I don't "live for now" with Pepsi, nor am I persuaded that Coke is "the real thing." I've also, after reading Sachs, relinquished my fond but misplaced belief in BP's much vaunted self-promotion as a green energy company.

Can we believe anything we are told by marketers? It seems that even the marketing gurus themselves are in some doubt. Best-selling author Seth Godin changed the cover and title of his disarmingly named *All Marketers Are Liars* to read *All Marketers Tell Stories*. To be fair, it should be acknowledged that he actually urges marketers to tell the truth, but his underlying thesis is both simple and disturbing:

> *Stories let us lie to ourselves. And those lies satisfy our ideas. It's the story, not the good or service you actually sell, that pleases the consumer.*
>
> *We believe what we want to believe, and once we believe something, it becomes a self-fulfilling truth . . . If you think that (more expensive) wine is better, then it is. If you think your new boss is going to be more effective, then she will be. If you love the way a car handles, then you're going to enjoy driving it.*[22]

Believing the stories we want to believe is also an all-too-common feature of corporate storytelling. In a chapter intriguingly called "The

Mutant Companies of New-Age Capitalism," Christian Salmon focuses on the dangers of being swept up in the fictional webs of charismatic corporate leaders. In the spring of 2001, he tells us, the energy trading company Enron was the seventh biggest corporation in the United States with an estimated value of $70 billion. But its balance sheets were based on the hypothetical self-assessed values of potential future sales that had little if any basis in reality. Enron itself and the stories that founder Ken Lay and CEO Jeff Skilling (the "smartest people in the room") told about its prospects were pure simulacra.

In hindsight, it seems obvious that the Enron bubble had to burst, but the extraordinary power of its rags-to-riches story mesmerized its employees, its stockholders, its accountants, and the US government for years. Once the bubble had been pricked by Bethany MacLean's Fortune article "Is Enron Overpriced?"[23] questioning how the company could maintain the value of its stock which was then trading at 55 times the value of its earnings, it took just eight months to collapse. At the time, it was the largest bankruptcy in US history and subsequent criminal trials revealed massive fraud. Both Jeff Skilling and Ken Lay were convicted; Skilling is still incarcerated, but "Kenny Boy," as George W. Bush liked to call him, died before he could be sentenced. The death certificate records that he had a heart attack, but I think that he died, like the company he founded, of a broken story.

Enron was not the first example of our fascination with an intoxicating fiction nor will it be the last: greed and gullibility are frequent bedfellows. From the South Sea Bubble in the 1720s to Bernie Madoff currently serving a crowd-pleasing 150-year sentence for milking an estimated $18 billion from his wealthy clients, we can see our collective capacity to whip up the stories we want to believe. We remain blinded by the miasma created by these simulacra until someone – like the little boy in Hans Christian Andersen's fable – points out in a way that cannot be ignored that the emperor has no clothes. Our complicity in the simulacrum is that we are blinded because it suits us to be blind: we want the story to be true, besides which it may have gained such momentum that we feel we have too much to lose (or have too little influence) to blow the whistle.

I have claimed several times in this book that stories are ubiquitous and that storytelling is unavoidable. We are swimming in a sea of stories; we cannot choose whether or not to tell stories, but we can and should take responsibility for deciding what kind of stories we will tell and what kind of stories we want to live by. Nowhere is this more important than in the realm of politics and government where in both the United Kingdom and United States in recent decades "controlling the narrative" has become as important as implementing policies and dealing with events.

A burgeoning media industry has placed public figures in a 24/7 spotlight, constantly on trial in the court of public opinion: what is in the news has become the news. In this volatile environment, which is so different from the measured decision-making required for good government and promised by the constitutional structures of representative democracy, political leaders are constantly on the back foot unless they can find ways to control the news agenda.

Enter the spin doctors – complete with focus groups, opinion polls, and messaging strategies. Again, I refer you to Salmon's excellent critique, especially Chapters 5 and 7: "Turning Politics into a Story" and "The Propaganda Empire." His examples are drawn from the United States, notably the activities of the White House Office of Communications under successive presidents from Richard Nixon to George W. Bush, but UK prime ministers were not slow to follow in their footsteps. If Reagan had his David Gergen and Bush his Karl Rove then Thatcher had her Bernard Ingham and Blair his Alistair Campbell.

Telling stories that put ideas, events, and leaders in a good light (or opponents in a bad light) is hardly a new phenomenon: from Homer to Churchill, the victors have shaped the way history is written; propaganda has always been an instrument of power, whether in the hands of church or state. Roman emperors stage-managed the proclamation of their victories against the mighty backdrop of the Coliseum; George W. Bush climbed out of a jet fighter in combat gear onto the flight deck of the USS *Abraham Lincoln* after the Iraq Campaign to declare "Mission Accomplished." What is new is the arsenal of digital and televisual effects we can employ to simulate or dissimulate reality. Simulacra have never been more pervasive or more convincing.

Salmon quotes from journalist Ron Suskind to illustrate the nadir of realpolitik in the Bush years. A White House aide (unnamed, but Salmon speculates that it was probably Karl Rove) took Suskind to task in 2002 after he had written a critical article about a former Director of Communications:

> *The aide said that guys like me were "in what we call the reality-based community," which he defined as people who "believe that solutions emerge from your judicious study of discernible reality . . . That's not the way the world really works anymore," he continued. "We're an empire now, and when we act, we create our own reality. And while you're studying that reality we'll act again, creating other new realities, which you can study too, and that's how things will sort out."*[24]

The aide's claim that reality is what the empire [sic] decides it should be, is chilling. It could be an official from Orwell's Ministry of Truth speaking, couldn't it? Like other examples in this chapter it shows that storytelling does indeed have a bewitching shadow: the power to mask, distort, and erase the underlying reality, even to create its own "fictional reality." Only by fully acknowledging this shadow can practitioners of narrative leadership avoid falling under its spell.

3. Re-minding: What stories in the public domain can you think of that erase, distort, or denature the underlying reality? What are the consequences? What stories could you tell to re-mind yourself and others of that reality?

In the shifting sands of our hypermodern age we need stories that reflect the profound underlying realities of our world and boldly speak truth to power more than ever before. In the next chapter, we will consider what this means in practice for each of us as we step into narrative leadership.

Bonus: *Enron: The Smartest Guys in the Room*

Alex Gibney's (2012) Oscar-nominated documentary *Enron: The Smartest Guys in the Room* reveals fraud and corrupt practice on a gargantuan scale in one of the largest US corporations. It also shows how the stories about the company's profits and prospects told by Chairman Kenneth Lay and CEO Jeffrey Skilling sustained a self-fulfilling prophesy that was entirely unjustified by the underlying realities. Dubious financial structures and accounting practices of Byzantine complexity enabled Enron consistently to bamboozle investors by showing huge non-existent profits each quarter. Whatever truth the stories originally contained, they soon lost all touch with reality. But so many people and institutions had a vested interest in maintaining the illusion of the Emperor's New Clothes that it became virtually impossible to declare that he was naked.

The testosterone-fuelled, macho culture of the company (particularly manifest in the dog-eat-dog environment of the trading rooms) was quite unable to question itself. In the end, two women called "time" on Enron: a young journalist at *Fortune* called Bethany MacLean who wrote an article called "Is Enron Overpriced?" and internal whistleblower Sherron Watkins, Vice President for Corporate Development, who warned Lay that Enron was likely to "implode in a wave of accounting scandals." Footage of Lay and Skilling desperately trying to shore up the story of "the world's leading energy company" as fate closed in on them shows just how fragile the simulacrum had become.

It was Abraham Lincoln who said, "You can fool some of the people all of the time, and all of the people some of the time, but you cannot fool all of the people all of the time." I would like to think that he was right and that Enron's downfall was a case in point, but there are days when I wonder if he just said it to make us feel good. There is another saying (sometimes attributed to Joseph Goebbels who knew a thing or two about propaganda): "The bigger the lie, the more it will be believed." For me, the most worrying aspect of the Enron saga is not the deception perpetrated upon us by a handful of crooks, but what enabled it to happen: our almost infinite capacity for self-deception.

Summary

- The hegemonic stories of modernity – progress, growth, capitalism, socialism, even religion – have lost much of their authority and no longer provide universal templates for our lives, at least in western liberal-democratic societies.
- The pace of the hypermodern world leads us to fill up like the Zen master's tea cup. Paradoxically, when we are most pressed for time is actually when we most need to slow down, breathe out, and empty the cup.
- Our real challenge in the digital age is not mastery of a new medium but making sure we have something worth saying. If we know how to tap into the innate human capacity for telling stories, all the rest follows.
- Despite cultural differences in taste and sensibility, tales of the human condition have much in common whatever their origin. Sharing our stories has always been how we have got to know each other.
- Language and stories that "erase" their subjects enable us to normalize behavior toward the natural world and our fellow human beings that would otherwise be unthinkable.
- At its best, the fashionable trend in brand storytelling commands us to tell the truth about our products, but it still implies that we can sell, consume, and grow our way out of the mess we are in (whether we do so ethically or not).
- Storytelling has a bewitching shadow: the power to mask, distort, and erase underlying reality, even to create its own "fictional reality." As in the fable of *The Emperor's New Clothes* we have a huge capacity for willful self-deception.

Notes and References

1 Attributed to Terry Pratchett (writer of science fiction and fantasy novels).
2 Havel, V. (1990). *Disturbing the Peace: A Conversation with Karel Hvizdala* (Faber & Faber: London).
3 Lyotard, J.-F. (1997 [1979]). *The Post-Modern Condition: A Report on Knowledge* (Manchester University Press: Manchester, p14).
4 Gray, J. (2004). *Heresies: Against Progress and Other Illusions* (Granta Books: London).
5 Lipovetsky, G. (2005). *Hypermodern Times* (Polity Press: Cambridge, pp30–31).
6 Claxton, G. (1997). *Hare Brain, Tortoise Mind: Why Intelligence Increases When You Think Less* (Fourth Estate: London).
7 McLuhan, M. (1964). *Understanding Media* (Mentor: New York, p7).
8 See, for example, Sachs, J. (2012). *Winning the Story Wars* (Harvard Business Review Press: Boston, MA); and Shirky, C. (2008). *Here Comes Everybody: The Power of Organizing Without Organizations* (Allen Lane: London).
9 Anderson, C. (2013). "How to Give a Killer Presentation," *Harvard Business Review*, June.
10 The online version of Chris Anderson's article is available at http://hbr.org/2013/06/how-to-give-a-killer-presentation/ar/.
11 McLuhan, M., op. cit., p3.
12 Lessem, R. and Palsule. S. (1997). *Managing in Four Worlds: From Competition to Co-creation* (Blackwell Business Books: Oxford).
13 Christie, P. (1996). *Stories From an Afman(ager)!* (Knowledge Resources: Johannesburg).
14 Peters, T. and Waterman, R.H. (1982). *In Search of Excellence: Lessons from America's Best-Run Companies* (Harper & Row: New York).
15 Baudrillard, J. (1995). *Simulation and Simulacrum* (University of Michigan Press: Ann Arbor, MI, p22).
16 *New York Times*, January 15, 2007.
17 Arendt, H. (1964). *Eichmann in Jerusalem: A Report on the Banality of Evil* (Viking Press: New York).
18 Stibbe, A. (2012). *Animals Erased: Discourse, Ecology, and Reconnection with the Natural World* (Wesleyan University Press: Middletown, CT).
19 Ibid., p88.
20 Salmon, C. (2010). *Storytelling: Bewitching the Modern Mind* (Verso: London).
21 Ibid., p24.
22 Seth Godin, *All Marketers Are Liars*, p2, cited in Salmon, C., op. cit., p25.
23 MacLean, B. (2001). "Is Enron Overpriced?" *Fortune Magazine*, March.
24 Quoted in Salmon, C., op. cit., p125.

Section Six
Between Stories

Chapter 16

Heart and Soul

I think that now we need those fictional old bards and fearless storytellers, those seers. We need their magic, their courage, their love and their fire more than ever before. It is precisely in a fractured, broken age that we need mystery and a reawakened sense of wonder . . . We need to go down to the bottom, to the depths of the heart and start to live all over again as we have never lived before.

BEN OKRI[1]

It is easy to dismiss storytelling unthinkingly as something that belongs to a bygone age – the province of "fictional old bards." But I agree with Ben Okri that storytelling should serve a deeper purpose and that, floundering as we are in a sea of stories stained with cynicism and polluted by propaganda, we need courageous, inspired storytellers more than ever. We need to find our own magic, courage, love, and fire to tell the stories called for by the time we live in.

That is why the title of this book is deliberately provocative: *heart* and *soul* are big words that do not usually appear in the lexicon of leadership, though we may use them in other aspects of our lives. But this is to make a false distinction between the public sphere of work and the private sphere of home and family. We are innately the same storytelling creatures at work as we are at home; to pretend that we are different people, with different values, logics, and motivations in different parts of our lives, is a schizophrenic fantasy. As mindfulness teacher Jon Kabat-Zin says, "Wherever you go, there you are."[2]

Heart and soul; feelings and imagination; passion and vision. Is it not strange that passion has become a commonplace word in leadership and business (my office is above a food shop that declares itself to be passionate about pastry) and a leader without vision is considered a laughing stock in business schools, yet so many writers on leadership are reluctant to acknowledge where passion and vision come from?

So, let us boldly reclaim these big words – *heart* and *soul* – from poetry and pop song lyrics and wishful New Age thinking to take their rightful place in our vocabularies. Metaphorically, the heart is the seat of our emotions while the soul longs for meaning and purpose. They speak a different language from our logico-rational minds: the heart expresses itself through feelings and the soul deals in symbols and images. Our logico-rational minds are swayed by information and argument but our hearts and souls are moved by stories and their unique power to stir the feelings and stimulate the imaginations of storytellers and their listeners. As storytelling creatures, we delight in being moved in this way: it is no accident that in Greek and Roman mythology, the marriage of heart and soul (Eros and Psyche) resulted in the birth of Hedone, meaning pleasure or bliss.

Narrative leadership calls on us to consult the compass of our souls and the barometer of our hearts to set a course and read the weather on our journey. Only then can we lead with genuine passion and vision; only then can we expect to stir the feelings and imaginations of others. But beware: our souls will not let us play small (their wish is for us to find meaning by serving more than our own egos) and our hearts will soon complain if we betray our potential. Conversely, as George Bernard Shaw wrote, striving in the service of a mighty purpose is the real source of joy and the hallmark of a life well lived:

> *This is the true joy in life, being used for a purpose recognized by yourself as a mighty one. Being a force of nature instead of a feverish, selfish little clod of ailments and grievances, complaining that the world will not devote itself to making you happy . . . I want to be thoroughly used up when I die, for the harder I work, the more I live.*[3]

In this final chapter, we will explore what it means to be a leader in these extraordinary times; examine the scope and ambition of our leadership; consider what paradigms inform the way we lead; look at the role of storytelling in the wake of narrative wreckage; and review the contribution that narrative leadership can make to your practice.

Missing the boat

> *What is the use of a house if you haven't got a tolerable*
> *planet to put it on?*
>
> HENRY DAVID THOREAU[4]

In 1997, like millions of others, I went to the cinema to see James Cameron's epic film *Titanic*. I sat unmoved as Leonardo DiCaprio and Kate Winslet went through their romantic shenanigans, but driving home afterward I suddenly found myself weeping for the needless folly of it all. Why hadn't the ship turned sooner? Why had the captain and crew disregarded the warnings? Why had they been so besotted by their own myth that they hadn't seen disaster looming?

I was reminded of this moment recently, reading Thomas Berry's book *The Great Work*, a meditation on the state of our planet and a call for action:

> *Long before the collision those in command had abundant*
> *evidence that icebergs lay ahead. The course had been set,*
> *however, and no-one wished to alter its direction. Confi-*
> *dence in the survival capacities of the ship was unbounded.*
> *Already there were a multitude of concerns in carrying*
> *out the normal routine of a voyage. What happened to*
> *that "unsinkable" ship is a kind of parable for us, since*
> *only in the most dire of situations do we have the psychic*
> *energy needed to examine our way of acting on the scale*
> *that is now required. The daily concerns over the care of*
> *the ship and its passengers needed to be set aside for a*
> *more urgent concern, the well-being of the ship itself.*[5]

Berry's use of the *Titanic* metaphor piqued my interest so I trawled the Internet for some more historical details of the actual event. I read the stories of survivors and of some who had planned to make the voyage but had changed their minds for various reasons: family affairs, illness, urgent business elsewhere, etc. My favorite "missing the boat" story was that of a certain Mr. Frank Carlson who, at 8.10 p.m. on Wednesday, April 10, 1912 as the *Titanic* slipped its moorings to begin its maiden voyage, was standing by the side of the road 50 miles away kicking the tires of his broken down car in frustration, a first-class ticket for New York in his back pocket.

We *cannot* miss the boat or jump ship. For good or ill, we are all on board and there are no lifeboats. There will be no lucky escapes, no survivors, if our ship goes down. I don't know if there's yet time to avoid the iceberg, but there's no doubt that we're still going full steam ahead and it's pretty clear that those on the bridge aren't listening to the warnings from the crow's nest. It seems to me that any contemporary book on leadership that does not acknowledge our predicament and ask what it means for being a leader is merely rearranging the deckchairs. Surely it is time for us to take more interest in where we are headed.

Of course, millions of people *are* concerned about the direction we are taking and many have devoted their lives and their leadership to helping humans exist in a more harmonious relationship with each other and with the planet. Yet in most mainstream businesses and in government, we only pay lip service to the wider social and environmental consequences of our actions. Having a Corporate Social Responsibility Directorate or a Department of Energy and Climate Change might make us feel better (the *Titanic* probably had a Morale Officer) but it will not save the ship. For that you have to change direction and/or slow down or – if this were a Hollywood movie – send a lone hero to blow up the iceberg.

Knowing what we now know, why is it so difficult for us to change course? Is it a failure of will or of imagination? On June 25, 2013, President Barack Obama gave an impassioned speech at Georgetown University on climate change.[6] It was heartening to hear him declare:

> *I don't have much patience for anyone who denies that*
> *this challenge is real. We don't have time for a meeting of*

the Flat Earth Society. Sticking your head in the sand might make you feel safer, but it's not going to protect you from the coming storm.

Later in his speech he uses a powerful storytelling image to enroll his audience in the issue:

And someday, our children, and our children's children, will look at us in the eye and they'll ask us, did we do all that we could when we had the chance to deal with this problem and leave them a cleaner, safer, more stable world? And I want to be able to say, yes, we did. Don't you want that?

Tacitly recognizing that the vested interests of business leaders and politicians are too entrenched for them to take the initiative, he urges his audience to take action to oblige them to change:

What we need in this fight are citizens who will stand up, and speak up, and compel us to do what this moment demands. Understand this is not just a job for politicians. So I'm going to need all of you to educate your classmates, your colleagues, your parents, your friends. Tell them what's at stake. Speak up at town halls, church groups, PTA meetings. Push back on misinformation. Speak up for the facts. Broaden the circle of those who are willing to stand up for our future.

Convince those in power to reduce our carbon pollution. Push your own communities to adopt smarter practices . . . Remind folks there's no contradiction between a sound environment and strong economic growth. And remind everyone who represents you at every level of government that sheltering future generations against the ravages of climate change is a prerequisite for your vote. Make yourself heard on this issue.

Obama's speech is a timely reminder that leadership is required at every level in order to make a difference. No one can divest themselves of their responsibility for influencing and enabling change. Whatever our role or position, we must choose the stance we take (and the stories we tell) about the world. Each of us – including the author of this book – must decide the scope of our concern and the object of our ambition. To embrace narrative leadership is not just to consider how we lead but to think deeply about the purpose of our leadership.

Ambit and ambition

> *I live my life in widening circles that reach out across the world. I may not complete this last one but I give myself to it.*
>
> RAINER MARIA RILKE[7]

The word "ambit," from which ambition is derived, comes from the Latin word *ambio*, to go around. It means several things: a sphere of influence or control; a border or boundary around something; and the span or reach of actions, thought, and words. It is this latter meaning that I have in mind when asking, "What is the ambit of our ambition as leaders?" I do not mean what we desire in terms of power and wealth, I mean what we are ambitious for: what is the contribution that we want to make; what are we seeking to change, preserve, or disrupt; how much of ourselves will we bring to our leadership?

And when we think about what we stand for as leaders, how "big" or "small" are the stories we tell; how widely and how far ahead do we look when making decisions; who and what do we take into account when gauging the impact of our actions? The sense we have of the scope and purpose of our leadership is hugely significant even though the vital issues of our time are beyond any one person or organization to grasp. The temptation is to think that because we cannot do everything we can do nothing, and therefore to make ourselves powerless in the face of such enormity. The challenge is to find a solid place to stand when the ground is so uncertain and the complexity of the systems in which we are entangled defies conventional logic.

Some of the most profound ways of considering the extent of our responsibilities to our fellow humans and to the planet as a whole have come from the field of deep ecology (a contemporary philosophical perspective that advocates the inherent worth of all living beings). Here, as elsewhere in this chapter, I shall draw on the work of Joanna Macy and the late Arne Naess, two "wise elders" who have contributed much to this way of thinking.

Time is one dimension of our ambition: over what period should we consider the consequences of our actions and decisions? Joanna Macy uses a storytelling exercise that she calls The Double Circle[8] to enable an imaginary conversation between present and future generations. The exercise is most powerful in a group setting but I will present it here in a way that lets you consider the answers you would give to the questions asked in the exercise.

Imagine people sitting face to face in two concentric circles. Those on the outside remain in the same positions and speak as themselves from the present generation. Those on the inside speak as if they were our distant descendants, seven generations in the future, and they move one place between each round. The facilitator explains the scenario: that because of the actions we have taken – in what Macy calls The Great Turning – humanity has survived our present predicament, though in greatly reduced numbers and circumstances. Then he or she asks the present generation a series of questions on behalf of their descendants. Those representing future generations listen attentively to the stories told in response to the questions by the "ancestors" in front of them. After the fourth round, the "descendants" remain where they are and have their turn to speak – responding in a heartfelt way to what they have heard – while the "ancestors" listen. The exchanges are conducted in a respectful and ritualized manner.

1. Round One: Ancestor, I have been told about the terrible times in which you lived: wars and preparations for war, hunger and homelessness, the rich getting richer and the poor getting poorer, poisons in the sea and soil and air, the dying of many species . . . Was that really true? Tell me.

2. Round Two: Ancestor, what was it like for you in the midst of that? How did you feel? What was life like for you then?

(continued)

3. Round Three: Ancestor, we have songs and stories that still tell of what you and your friends did back then for The Great Turning. Now what I want to know is this: How did you start? What first steps did you take?

4. Round Four: Ancestor, I know you didn't stop with those first actions. Tell me, where did you find the strength and joy to continue working so hard, despite all the obstacles and discouragements?

If you are thinking that doing this exercise would take you outside your comfort zone, you would be right. It would and it is supposed to. What looks rather flat and stilted on the page becomes intensely emotional when we allow ourselves to feel some of the painful realities of our world and stretch our imaginations to explore how we would have acted if our actions were to make a difference. Here the creation and telling of imagined stories has as much if not more impact on the teller as it does on the audience. By listening to our own stories we can reframe our responsibilities as leaders and create new possibilities for action.

I was fortunate enough to experience this process in a workshop run by Joanna Macy 10 years ago. It confirmed my belief that the stories we tell are immensely important and it strengthened my resolve to develop the notion of narrative leadership and take it out into the world.

Another dimension of our ambition is breadth: how wide should be the range of our concerns? The Leadership Development Framework described in Chapters 6 and 7 shows an increasingly broad range of concerns as we learn to access successive action logics from the Opportunist who is primarily focused on meeting his or her own needs and desires to the Alchemist whose leadership helps to generate social transformations. But even this extensive model is androcentric, placing humans at the crown of an ecological pyramid rather than recognizing our place in a dynamic web of relationships with other species, all having intrinsic value.

We can thank Arne Naess, Emeritus Professor of Philosophy at Oslo University, for his insight that prevailing notions of self-realization are too limited. We cannot express the fullness of our humanity simply by reference to our egos or our social relationships, he said. Naess declared that we are in and of nature from our very beginning and proposed that the mature self is an *ecological self* – living harmoniously as part of nature, not merely as a moral act (because we should) but because the ecological self understands that:

> *We need the immense variety of sources of joy opened through increased sensitivity toward the richness and diversity of life, through the profound cherishing of free natural landscapes.*[9]

This way of thinking about self-realization gives us a framework against which we can map the breadth of our concern as leaders. When considering the purposes and consequences of our actions, how widely do we concern ourselves; what is the relative weighting of our concern; where does our center of gravity lie on the continuum from egocentric to ecological self?

- Our own egocentric desires
- Our individuated (or higher) self
- Our intimate circle of family and friends
- Our wider social or ethnic group
- Our whole society or nation
- Our whole human species
- Our fellow (sentient) beings
- Our fellow (non-sentient) beings
- Our ecosphere: the planet we all share.

Few of us are able to "think like a mountain" as Naess urged us to do, but unless we are able to develop a higher level of identification with the "more-than-human" world than most of us currently manifest, it is unlikely that the leadership we seek to provide will be either relevant to the needs of our era or sufficient to address them.

I recognize that this proposition is hugely challenging and, though I have made my own stance quite clear, I do not presume to tell you what stance you should take. What I do say is that narrative leadership requires us to reflect deeply on the relationship between the leadership stories we tell and our understanding of the big-picture stories within which we live and work. During workshops I often invite people to spend some time exploring the congruity of the stories they tell with their understanding of the big picture by considering these questions:

- What big-picture story are you are facing?
- What types of leadership story do you tell?
- How well do they fit with the big-picture story?
- What types of leadership story are needed?
- What great stories do you already have?
- What stories (and whose) do *not* get heard?

Some people find there is a good fit between the stories they tell and those that they believe are needed. Most conclude that they have work to do to bring them into line. Often they realize that the stories that are needed already exist in their group, organization, movement, etc., but are suppressed or marginalized. If you want to advance the cause of narrative leadership in your sphere of influence, think about these questions yourself and spend some time discussing them with colleagues. My own responses to these questions are evident throughout this book, which is, in part, my attempt to answer them.

The bigger our ambition, the longer the time frame we consider, the wider the scope of our concerns, the more complex the task of leadership becomes, and the more difficult it is to gauge the likely consequences of our actions. Perhaps we need a simpler rubric to guide us day to day; the next section offers a few touchstones to help us stay on track.

Two countries

> *The test of a first-rate intelligence is the ability to hold two opposed ideas in the mind at the same time, and still retain the ability to function. One should, for example, be*

able to see that things are hopeless and yet be determined
to make them otherwise.

F. Scott Fitzgerald[10]

Polarities are pairs of opposites that do not exist well independently of each other. For example, in Chapter 3 I used the ancient Greek notions of logos (reasoned discourse) and mythos (report, tale, or story) to signify opposing ways of understanding and talking about the world, each of which is valuable in its own way. As leaders we need to be proficient with both forms but, as I have argued elsewhere, logos has become valorized in our society (certainly in the public sphere in which leaders operate) and narrative leadership can redress the balance by championing mythos. That is not to abandon information and argument entirely in favor of stories, rather it is to employ the most appropriate and effective form in the circumstances. The polarity of mythos and logos is a useful touchstone to test the composition of our leadership.

There are many potentially useful polarities and it is good to find your own. I will offer just two more that I have found invaluable. The first of these reveals the contrast between the ends-driven logic of the system-world and the everyday human concerns of the life-world.[11] As mentioned in Chapter 8, it is true that we need both the goal-focused instrumental action of the system-world and the mutual understanding that flows from the communicative action of the life-world. However, the system-world has come to dominate our lives in western society and, for our own sanity and self-preservation, it is surely time to reassert the primacy of the communitarian values of the life-world. The constricting power of the system-world relaxes when people come together on equal terms to share what really matters to them as living, loving, struggling human beings who are part of and not separate from the world that sustains them.

A third touchstone that I find especially useful is provided by the polarity of erasure and enchantment. Erasure (as discussed in Chapter 15) uses abstraction, obfuscation, and dissimulation to take us further and further away from the rich, embodied, underlying reality of life. Paradoxically, it is often the language of logos, striving for objectivity and precision, which leads us in this direction. The German sociologist Max Weber, over a century ago, called the effect of this assumed rationality *die Entzauberung der Welt* – the disenchantment of the world. Its contrary pole is enchantment (or re-enchantment) by which I mean, not magical thinking or the naive belief that wishing a thing makes it so, but the "resurgence of the real."[12] And, as we have seen so often in this book, it is the particular, imaginal, and metaphorical language of mythos – stories – that brings the world alive in our minds.

The original touchstones were pieces of jasper or basalt used by goldsmiths to test the quality of gold quickly by comparing the streak left by rubbing it on the stone to existing streaks left by known standard alloys. You can use these polarities in a similar fashion: ask yourself from time to time how they show up in your day-to-day practice as a leader.

Logos	<· — ·— ·— ·— ·— ·— ·—·>	Mythos
System-world	<· — ·— ·— ·— ·— ·— ·—·>	Life-world
Erasure	<· — ·— ·— ·— ·— ·— ·—·>	Enchantment

These polarities look at the world through different lenses that enable us to see two co-existing paradigms. Writer and artist Arlene Goldbard describes them as the conceptual equivalent of two different countries:

> *One is Datastan, a world in which everything that counts can be counted; the other, The Republic of Stories, a world in which everything carries a story and all the stories matter.*[13]

Effective leaders need to be able to operate within both paradigms, but as we saw in Chapter 2 most members of the academic and professional "leadership industry" of the twentieth and twenty-first centuries have sworn allegiance to the flag of Datastan. My advice? If you're not willing to emigrate, at least get dual nationality.

In the next section I want to pick up on the second half of F. Scott Fitzgerald's remark: are things hopeless; can we make them otherwise; what should we do as leaders when the stories by which we have lived our lives are falling apart? I'll begin with one of my favorite jokes.

Narrative wreckage

A man is walking along the highway of his life and one day – without any warning – he falls into an existential abyss. It's dark, precipitous, and terrifying. He can't see the bottom and he's clinging to the vertical sides by his fingernails.

He is utterly alone. After a while he can't bear the loneliness and calls out into the darkness:

"Is there anybody out there?"

"Yes," an enormous voice booms across the void. "I am here with you."

"Who are you?" calls the man.

"I am God," replies the voice.

"What should I do?" says the man, looking down. "Tell me what to do."

"Let go," says God.

There is a long pause before the man calls again:

"Is there anybody else out there?"

There are times in our lives when the stories through which we constitute our identity no longer make sense. Illness, bereavement, divorce, redundancy, relocation, falling in love, marriage, parenthood, and other major life events can cause us to question the familiar stories we tell ourselves (and others) about who we are. In extreme circumstances we may face what Arthur Frank calls *narrative wreckage*. Many of us experience something like this at some point in our lives. At such times our identities are particularly malleable and open to change.

It is not just individuals who are affected in this way. The stories that sustain groups, societies, nations, and whole civilizations also collapse. Thomas Berry (quoted in the Introduction) says:

It's all a question of story. We are in trouble just now because we do not have a good story. We are in between stories. The old story, the account of how we fit into the world, is no longer effective. Yet we have not learned the new story.[14]

I agree that the old story no longer works and that we are between stories. I think that we are already – collectively and individually – groping for new stories (though the problem may be more that we are reluctant to let go of the old ones). I am pretty sure that we cannot go from the old story to the new story without experiencing a dark night of the soul, a place of narrative wreckage, a shifting, confusing time of emptying that will allow something else to emerge.

I also wrestle with the question of whether we should be looking for *the* new story at all. Perhaps the real challenge of our time is to find ways of moving away from an assumption of competing singular stories and toward the exploration and acceptance of mutually inclusive plural stories. In this view, contemporary leadership should be less about striving to create an illusion of certainty and more about helping people live creatively in the midst of uncertainty.

In story terms, the danger is that we will go on yet another heroic quest, hoping that we can put things right with a bit of magic, luck, and courage. It is time to slacken our grip on the Hero's Journey (always a male archetype) and look to other types of story to guide us, such as the post-heroic stories of mid-life mentioned in Chapter 4. It is not magic, luck, and courage that we need to get us through the dark night of the soul (not magic, not luck, and not the kind of courage that fights dragons) but the kind of courage that helps us endure and stay true to the simple human things that come from living with heart and soul: love, grace, compassion, decency.

The way out of narrative wreckage is telling stories, stories that acknowledge our suffering in order that we can transcend it. We are more than our wounds, but the first step in healing is to move beyond denial. Only then will we find new narratives that enable us to reclaim authorship of our lives and make sense of who we are becoming. For the wounded storyteller (and we are all wounded) sharing our stories remoralizes and makes sense of a chaotic world:

> *The moral genius of storytelling is that each, teller and listener, enters the space of the story for the other. Telling stories in post-modern times, and perhaps in all times,*

attempts to change one's own life by affecting the lives of others.[15]

If we survive narrative wreckage, we might be restored to health, we might even be transformed by the experience, but things will never be same as they were before. About 500 years ago, the Japanese invented the art of *Kintsugi*: mending broken porcelain with a special resin mixed with powdered gold so that the repair itself added beauty to the original object. Broken hearts, broken dreams, and broken lives cannot be unbroken but perhaps – through the stories we tell – they can become whole again, and even more beautiful than before. It makes me think of the story of the *Cracked Pot* in Chapter 7 and I find myself asking, "What if, as leaders, we considered our task to be neither destroying nor saving the world but learning to live more beautifully in the world that we have?"

With that thought in mind, I want to end the book by reviewing how narrative leadership helps us in the quest to become the best leaders we can be and to make you an offer, one that you are free to refuse but that, if you accept, might just be the difference that makes a difference.

Welcome to wonderland

> *You take the blue pill, the story ends; you wake up in your bed and believe what you want to believe. You take the red pill, you stay in Wonderland, and I show you how deep the rabbit hole goes.*
>
> THE MATRIX[16]

I often project an image from the science fiction movie *The Matrix* at the beginning of narrative leadership workshops. The seasoned campaigner Morpheus (Laurence Fishburne) is offering Neo (Keanu Reeves) the choice of the red pill or the blue pill; Neo takes the red pill of course or there would be no movie. Whatever the red pill contains, it allows him to see another reality behind the carefully constructed façade of human existence. He sees that he is living in an elaborate story concocted and maintained by machines and artificial intelligences.

The point of showing it is not to imply that we are in the same fantastical situation as Neo, but to suggest that, once we metaphorically take the red pill and start looking at the world through the lens of story and narrative, we see that stories are everywhere. To continue the analogy, if we take the blue pill and decline to look through that particular lens then we will not see behind the façade that masks the social construction of meaning though stories and storytelling. Taking the red pill opens the doors of perception and offers new possibilities for understanding and communicating the underlying realities of our world. But it comes with a price: greater understanding of the use and abuse of stories brings with it an obligation to take responsibility for the stories we tell and the ones to which we pay heed.

This book offers you that choice and I urge you to take the red pill. Narrative leadership is not an easy option, nor will it transform you overnight into a "great" leader. Indeed, its ethos is rather low key and mundane: steady application of the tools and techniques in this book will repay you with the ability to spark the imaginations and touch the hearts of those around you.

Having read this book, you'll understand why stories matter; you'll have challenged conventional assumptions about leadership; and explored both the logos and mythos of storytelling. You'll have played with fact, fiction, and fantasy; got inside stories to see how they work; and delved into the theory and practice of narrative leadership. You may have come to know yourself better; discovered new ways to connect with other people; and thought long and hard about what you stand for. You'll have a better sense of when to tell stories and what kind of stories to tell; mastered the CASTLE method for putting stories together; brushed up on the basics of performance; and picked up a set of peer coaching techniques to improve your storytelling. You'll have understood how stories help us learn from the past, stand in the unfolding present, and imagine the future. You'll have acquired a whole "storytelling for change" toolkit; considered the place of storytelling in our hypermodern age; and poked around in some of storytelling's darker corners. You may even have extended the ambit and ambition of your leadership in response to the narrative wreckage that surrounds us.

It is a lot and some of it is tough stuff. But few things that are worth-while are easy and we each only have one life; the question is what we do with it. There is no real distinction between leading and living. When we ask ourselves how we are leading, we necessarily ask at the same time how we are leading our lives. The practices of Know Thyself, Only Connect, and Stand for Something offer more than a rubric for leadership. I realized as I wrote this book that they stem from three profound exis-tential questions that every thinking person asks themselves at various times in their life:

Who am I?
Where do I belong?
What do I serve?

We ask these questions because we want our lives to have meaning. Exploring them can help us find our way to more useful and fulfilled lives. Whether you are young or old, inside or outside organizations, at the top of the tree or clinging to the lower branches, fighting for change or protesting that something dear should be left as it is, I hope that *Telling the Story* will help you find some profoundly satisfying answers.

Remember that you are a storytelling creature; stories are in your bones, they are your heritage and your birthright. Take what you want from this book and do it your way. Feel free to tell any and all of the stories it contains; share your learning and insights with people you care about. Let me know how you get on: write, call, or send me a message via the Narrative Leadership Associates website, or come and find me somewhere in The Republic of Stories.

A DVD Bonus and a summary will follow, but I want to leave the last words of this chapter and of the book to Ben Okri, whose novels and writing on story and storytelling I deeply admire. I've been pondering and dreaming about these words for a decade; may they inspire you as much as they have inspired me:

> *Maybe there are only three kinds of stories: the stories we live, the stories we tell, and the higher stories that help our souls fly up towards the light.*[17]

Bonus: *Beasts of the Southern Wild*

It's hard to find a film about climate change that isn't either a cautionary documentary such as *An Inconvenient Truth* (2006), *The 11th Hour* (2007), and *Chasing Ice* (2012) or a blockbusting saga of heroic survival such as *The Day After Tomorrow* (2004) and *2012* (2009). Instead, I've chosen *Beasts of the Southern Wild* (2012), which shows the very plausible consequences of melting icecaps, massive storms, and rising sea levels on a group of misfits, outcasts, and exiles living "below the radar" in ramshackle huts and boats on the wrong side of the levee in southern Louisiana in a community they call the Bathtub. We see the action through the eyes and imagination of a semiferal 6-year-old girl called Hushpuppy (Quvenzhané Wallis).

What makes the film different and so worth watching – apart from some wonderful performances – is that it eschews massive CGI effects and focuses instead on the human dimension of catastrophe. The film is a blend of magical realism and gritty drama that – above all – champions the importance of community. People struggle to survive but never forget to celebrate the extraordinary adventure of being alive, finding beauty even in the midst of death and disaster.

It's a bold and uninhibited piece of storytelling that defies the conventions of formulaic scriptwriting. In the midst of fantasy it shows us glimpses of what might actually happen at the geographical and social margins of our societies in the wake of climate change. If you haven't already seen it then do watch it and notice how – as ever – it takes a good story to make something real.

Summary

- Heart and soul are big words that do not usually appear in the lexicon of leadership; let us boldly reclaim this language. The heart is the seat of our emotions while the soul longs for meaning and purpose.
- Any contemporary book on leadership that does not acknowledge our predicament is merely rearranging the deckchairs on the *Titanic*. Leadership today must focus on where we are headed.

- Reframe the scope and ambition of your leadership in terms of its consequences for future generations by using Joanna Macy's powerful and moving Double Circle exercise.
- Explore the breadth of your concerns as a leader through the lens of Arne Naess's model of self-realization: from the egocentric self to the ecological self. How congruent are the leadership stories you tell with the big picture?
- Use the polarities of logos and mythos, system-world and life-world, erasure and enchantment as touchstones to test which paradigm you are operating from at any particular time: Datastan or The Republic of Stories.
- The way out of narrative wreckage is telling stories that acknowledge our suffering in order that we can transcend it. What is broken cannot be unbroken but it can be made beautifully whole: the art of *Kintsugi*.
- Take the red pill and *Telling the Story* will repay you with the ability to spark the imaginations and touch the hearts of those around you. Stories are in your bones, they are your heritage and your birthright. Enjoy!

Notes and References

1 Okri, B. (1997). *A Way of Being Free* (Phoenix: London, p39).
2 Kabat-Zin, J. (2005). *Wherever You Go, There You Are* (Hyperion: New York).
3 George Bernard Shaw, *Man and Superman*, Epistle Dedicatory.
4 Henry David Thoreau, in a letter to his friend Harrison Gray Otis Blake on May 20, 1860. The collected letters can be found at http://www.walden.org/documents/file/Library/Thoreau/writings/correspondence/LettersBlake.pdf.
5 Berry, T. (2000). *The Great Work* (Broadway Books: New York, p100).
6 Watch a five-minute extract at http://www.youtube.com/watch?v=XB9–MF0tx0.
7 From *Rilke's Book of Hours*, translated by Anita Burrows and Joanna Macy (1996) (Riverhead Books: New York, p48).
8 Macy, J. and Brown, M.Y. (1998). *Coming Back to Life: Practices to Reconnect Our Lives, Our Worlds* (New Society Publishers: Gabriola Island, BC, pp146–148).
9 Seed, J., Macy, J., Fleming, P., and Naess, A. (1988). *Thinking Like a Mountain* (Heretic Books: London, p29).
10 F. Scott Fitzgerald (1936). "The Crack Up," *Esquire Magazine*, February.

11 Habermas, J. (1987). *The Theory of Communicative Action*, Vol. 2, *Lifeworld and System: A Critique of Functionalist Reason* (Beacon Press: Uckfield, pp381–383).

12 Spretnak, C. (1999). *The Resurgence of the Real: Body, Nature and Place in a Hypermodern World* (Routledge: New York).

13 Goldbard, A. (2013). *The Culture of Possibility: Art, Artists and the Future* (Waterlight Press: San Francisco, p20).

14 Berry, T. (1978). "The New Story: Comments on the Origin, Identification and Transmission of Values," *Teilhard Studies*, Issue One: 1.

15 Frank, A. (1997). *The Wounded Storyteller: Body, Illness and Ethics* (University of Chicago Press: Chicago, p18).

16 *The Matrix*, a sci-fi adventure directed by the Wachowski Brothers and released by Warner Bros. in 1999.

17 Okri, B., op. cit., p126.

Appendix: Additional Resources

*The art of storytelling lies within the storyteller, to be
searched for, drawn out, made to grow.*

RUTH SAWYER[1]

In writing this book, I have drawn on a wide variety of sources, which
you can follow up in the Notes and References. In this appendix I want
to focus on some practical storytelling resources that will help you deepen
your understanding and practice of the art of narrative leadership. It
includes a handful of key books and a few useful websites, including that
of Narrative Leadership Associates through which you can contact me.

Books

The art of storytelling
The Storyteller's Way: A comprehensive guide and sourcebook for all
aspects of storytelling by Ashley Ramsden and Sue Hollingsworth of the
International School of Storytelling. The book is full of practical tips and
exercises for all storytellers from absolute beginners to professional
performers.[2]

Improving Your Storytelling: An excellent book from Doug Lipman, a
US-based professional storyteller and coach, which is full of savvy ideas

and practical tips. I've found his model of the storytelling triangle (the relationships between teller, audience, and story) particularly useful and quote it in Chapter 12.[3]

The Storytelling Coach: Doug Lipman's first book on storytelling is especially strong on techniques for helping us to improve our storytelling. I've drawn on his guidelines for setting up effective story-coaching pairs. There's a lot of wisdom in this book about the power of appreciative feedback applicable in many situations.[4]

Storytelling and the Art of Imagination: A classic primer from US storyteller and teacher Nancy Mellon, full of exercises to stimulate the storyteller's imagination and improve his or her ability to create rich vibrant images for the listeners. The book is firmly rooted in the world of traditional stories but has much to teach any budding storyteller.[5]

Reflections on storytelling

Coming Home to Story: My previous book, which charts the journey of being and becoming a storyteller. It explores the power of stories and storytelling to engage our imaginations, heal communities, and bring adventure and passion into our lives. Readers say that the book takes them *inside* the experience of telling stories.[6]

Our Secret Territory: A book full of stories and stories about stories and storytelling from well-known US storyteller Laura Simms, who has practiced her art in some of the world's most troubled places and returned to tell the tale. It's a wild ride and a book to linger over and treasure.[7]

Storytelling in organizations

The Springboard: Steve Denning's first and best book on the subject, drawn from his hard-won experience of "discovering" storytelling as a tool for change while working at the World Bank. The tone is personal and engaging; the appendices include detailed guidance on selecting and delivering "springboard stories."[8]

Whoever Tells the Best Story Wins: A hands-on, "how to do it" book by US storyteller and consultant Annette Simmons. I've recommended it to many people because it includes some great examples and takes a very straightforward approach to storytelling. I've used her excellent definition of story throughout this book.[9]

Websites

International School of Storytelling

Based in Forest Row, East Sussex, UK, ISOS offers a wide range of courses from weekends for beginners to its annual flagship program, the three-month-long Craft of the Storyteller. Courses are also regularly offered in South Africa and New Zealand. ISOS was my storytelling alma mater and I recommend it unreservedly.

Check it out at http://www.schoolofstorytelling.com/.

Centre for Narrative Leadership

I co-founded the Centre in 2007 as a not-for-profit virtual network dedicated to developing the practice of organizational storytelling. It offers occasional events, including an annual gathering, for storytellers, leaders, researchers, and consultants. The website includes articles and papers, stories, and other material relating to narrative leadership.

Check it out at http://www.narrativeleadership.org/.

Narrative Leadership Associates

My company Narrative Leadership Associates is a specialized consultancy that focuses on using the power of story and narrative to improve internal and external communication, develop leadership teams and boards, create scenarios for future strategies, coach individual leaders, build engagement among staff and stakeholders, and many other bespoke purposes. The website includes details of our consultants, case studies, and information about our methods and recent work.

Check it out at http://www.narrativeleadership.com/.

Society for Storytelling

The Society for Storytelling was founded in 1993 to support and promote storytelling in England and Wales. It provides a central place to find out about storytelling events, to ask for advice on using storytelling, and to find storytellers. The site includes details of the major UK storytelling festivals and local performances. It also provides links to many other storytelling resources. It is available to members and non-members alike.

Check it out at http://www.sfs.org.uk/.

Scottish Storytelling Centre

North of the border, the Scottish Storytelling Centre has the world's first purpose-built modern center for live storytelling, in the heart of Edinburgh's Royal Mile. It puts on a wide range of events including a spectacular annual Storytelling Festival. On the website, you'll find details of storytellers and storytelling events across Scotland and read about their education and outreach projects. Since its inception in 2006 the Centre has put storytelling at the forefront of Scottish art and culture.

Check it out at http://www.tracscotland.org/scottish-storytelling-centre/.

National Storytelling Network

The premier US National Storytelling Network grew out of the American Storytelling Revival which can trace its roots back to the first National Storytelling Festival at Jonesborough, Tennessee in 1973. The website is an invaluable resource for all things storytelling, including a wide range of papers on specialized topics and links to state storytelling organizations.

Check it out at http://www.storynet.org/.

Notes and References

1 Sawyer, R. (1951). *The Way of the Storyteller* (Viking Press: New York, p26).
2 Hollingsworth, S. and Ramsden, A. (2013). *The Storyteller's Way: Sourcebook for Inspired Storytelling* (Hawthorn Press: Stroud).
3 Lipman, D. (1999). *Improving Your Storytelling* (August House: Little Rock, AR).
4 Lipman, D. (1995). *The Storytelling Coach* (August House: Little Rock, AR).
5 Mellon, N. (1992). *Storytelling and the Art of Imagination* (Element Books: Rockport, MA).
6 Mead, G. (2011). *Coming Home to Story: Storytelling Beyond Happily Ever After* (Vala Publishing: Bristol).
7 Simms, L. (2011). *Our Secret Territory: The Essence of Storytelling* (Sentient Books: Boulder, CO).
8 Denning, S. (2001). *The Springboard: How Storytelling Ignites Action in Knowledge-Era Organisations* (Butterworth–Heinemann: Boston, MA).
9 Simmons, A. (2007). *Whoever Tells the Best Story Wins: How to Find, Develop, and Deliver Stories to Communicate with Power and Impact* (AMACOM: New York).

Index